In th

(Notes to a Poetry Syllabus)

Selected Essays/Reviews & Interviews

2014-2023

Chris Stroffolino

SPUYTEN DUYVIL

New York City

ISBN 978-1-963908-15-2

Library of Congress Control Number: 2024940210

CONTENTS

Para-Academic Introduction   7

PARA-ACADEMIC INTRODUCTION

This collection of 26 introductory engagements with mostly early 21st century American poetry, or poetry-adjacent, books could be read as a sequel to my *Spin Cycle* (Spuyten Duyvil, 2001), which collected reviews/essays on contemporary poetry & poetics written during the 1990s. In the introduction to *Spin Cycle*, I offered a characterization of the review/essay form that could also apply to the pieces in this collection:

Generally, most discussions of contemporary books of poetry fall into one of two categories. First, and more common, there is the short review that primarily serves a publicity function (even if negative). Because such reviews rarely exceed 2000 words, they rarely illuminate the works they discuss, and at best focus on one aspect of the work, often excerpting a poem to make a point that the part of the poem they do not quote complicates or contradicts.

On the other hand, there is the lengthier scholarly essay, in which the critic/scholar is given more room to elaborate a theory by which the work may be understood. At its best, such writing allows ample space to show the intricacies of the poem itself as well as the scholar's involvement with it. At its worse, such a form becomes so thoroughly mediated by an argument with other critics or an attempt by the scholar to show his or her mastery of a certain legitimizing jargon that the poems themselves, usually discussed near the end of the essay, after the necessary clearing of space, get lost in the shuffle.

This Scylla and Charybdis of contemporary poetry criticism is difficult to avoid, and I cannot, in good faith, presume that the review/essays collected here entirely avoid either of these tendencies. It is my hope, however, that by combining the appeal to the general reader the characterizes the review with the analytical depth of closer readings, this collection may open up possibilities for further critical engagement with the works discussed between those who value breadth & those who value depth. (*Spin Cycle,* 6)

In *Spin Cycle's* concluding essay on poetics, "Against Lineage," such an attitude of liminal hybrid betweenness is also evident. I try to take a bird's eye view of the debates about poetic lineages that many young poets in the 90s found ourselves caught up with, whether the contrasting lineages proposed by Marjorie Perloff and Harold Bloom circulating at the time, or the fissures in contemporary poetry going back to the debates over the "raw" and the "cooked" that ensued in the wake of the near simultaneous publication of the Donald Allen *New American Poetry* and the Donald Hall *Contemporary American Poetry* anthologies in the early 1960s.

In that Y2K zeitgeist, *Spin Cycle* found appreciators. Elder critic Charles Altieri liked that it included both "established contemporaries, about whom many of us write, and other, usually younger writers (Jennifer Moxley, Pam Rehm, Carla Harryman, Laura Moriarty, Jane Ransom & Yuri Hospodar)." Lisa Samuels liked that it "engage[d] the world of contemporary avant-garde poetry as well as clear ways that Shakespeare can speak to that world." Juliana Spahr liked its attention to "poets often overlooked in current criticism's obsession with the divide between language & lyric," while Nada Gordon appreciated its "pomp & punk" and *The American Book Review* observed, it "holds out an olive branch between rival factions, but the branch is sometimes on fire!"

Luckily, I was not alone, as many in our generation also felt this need to bridge or transcend (if we couldn't entirely dodge) these contentious divisions between rigid lineages. In 25 years of hindsight, perhaps we were somewhat successful, especially as more women with capacious tastes in contemporary poetry and fiction began to assert and/or insert themselves in the mid-late 90s NYC scene.

Yet, even though I fancied myself eclectic in my reading interests at the time, in retrospect it's easy to see I had a relatively narrow aesthetic bias, a cringeworthy obsession with Harold Bloom (especially in the David Shapiro essay), a preference for male writers (14 essays on male writers compared to only 7 on women), and, aside from John Yau & Erica Hunt, exclusively wrote about writers who were white.

Twenty-five years later, I find much less of an emphasis on jealously guarded sectarian lineages. As such, *In the Here There* doesn't really have such an internecine historical-poetical axe to grind (though individual essays may). Rather, this new collection grew out of a returning, insistent feeling that, despite accelerated negative trends of techno-plutocratic global disaster capitalism that could make one nostalgic for the 90s, the 21st Century poetry book-scape is better than it was in 1999. Perhaps more poets and critics have come to realize that it is indeed wiser to embrace a more porous and fluid unity-in-diversity attitude among diverse poetics with more equanimity against a common crisis that goes by different names.

Perhaps that is my naivete, but to the extent this is true, I try to celebrate this less divisive spirit as I feel it in the books and writers discussed in *In the Here There,* and the permission that gives beginning writers to seek out their own affinities beyond some ready-made reductive high-school common core curriculum or AI sense of the limits of what proper poetry is.

Collecting the essays that make up this book has allowed me to step back from the apparent mandate to constantly keep up with the demands of the reactive mind that renders contemplation an endangered species. Against a backdrop of accelerating data dumps and a scrolling click bait ethos contributing to shortened attention spans and more cultural amnesia, it's easy to forget that a book we read a decade ago may still have something to tell us today. Roland Barthes wrote, "rereading is a habit that goes against the ideological and commercial habits of this society," and all the works discussed in this book are chosen because they not only stand-up on repeated re-readings, but because they become even more alive with each reading, as time gives weight to the white space in the words.

The same poem can be read in many different ways, even by the same person in different moods, or historical epochs. Even one one-page poem can turn out to give the reader more equipment for living than the 100 page-book of which it is apart. A poem may have more shapes than you think it has. Lyn Hejinian writes, "form is not a fixture, but an activity," and I strive to such social dynamism in the living, if clumsy, art of this collection of review/essays as it circulates as a non-required supplemental text to give future students.

CLASSROOM (CON)TEXT

Since I've never been able to find an adequate book to use when facilitating an introductory multi-genre writing class at a community college to students on a limited budget, I decided long ago it is far better to make/ let the students' own writing be the primary text for the semester. I do, however, bring in handouts of individual poems, often prompted by a students' poems, published poems that share affinities with what the student is doing or trying to do, to validate the student and make them feel less alone, but also give them options to explore other possibilities in the art of revision (or multiple remixes, to borrow a term of music) should they wish to continue writing.

Recently, for instance, while discussing a student's poem, I complimented her on the metapoetic aspects of their poem, but no-one in the class was familiar with the term *metapoetic,* so the next week, I brought in Martine Bellen's poem "Confession," (discussed in this collection), as an example of a meta-poem, and a few students were so blown away by it, so curious about it, they decided to meet me an hour before class to discuss it. On another occasion, I brought my essay on Xu Lizhi into my introduction to literature course as an optional non-required reading, and one of my students wrote me a long letter disagreeing, talking back to my essay, and teaching me (since he could read the Chinese original and understood the contexts of the poems). As a teacher and a writer, I don't think I can ask for anything more. These class discussions even inspired me to write my own meta-poem to share with the class at the end of the semester:

How to Write a Non-Poem

At the end of the fall semester,
go through the notebook of fragments
written in the last 3 months.
that seem-like one-page poem-like things.
Type and print them
so you really see them as things
that could inspire your ears & mouth if need be
& when you feel you got enough for a chapbook,
place them together
in that liminal space between chance and choice
and feel the troubles of the book
eclipse the troubles of the poem—

Does it seem premature?
Surely, these September last year words
that still seem interesting in December,
are trying to tell you something.
Maybe the outtakes are better.
"Cheat" and dig up some older work
that keeps surprising you on repeated readings
and been commented on positively by a friend or two.

Maybe just prune, you over-writer you.
Let inefficiency come like ethical minimalism.
Allow yourself the decadent luxury
of less than 10 lines on a page
as if that white space evokes
the black space in Brian Lucas' recent inks
or at least the music in between
ground up pounding paragraphs of prose…

Move a line that feels out of place in one poem
to another poem it might fit in with better
and it's okay to show the stitches. Marinate well(ness).

Worry, I mean wonder, play with
how it looks on the page
in the eyes of a beloved wolf:
the short-lined stutter poem-like thing
you wrote on a receipt
(like A.R. Ammons wrote on ticker tape)

"Intimacy toys with boundary issues
challenged to barefoot in the tundra
wider than the ecological footprint
between hand and mouth
to play piano for a painter
wearing purple pa(i)nts & a green shirt
painting a gold that felt more
yellow when she was wearing red…"

may work better lined as prose after all.

Make two mixes—a prose mix & a lyric mix,
and send to one friend who works in poetry
and another friend who plays in flash-fiction
and see what they feel they think soundlessly.

The pre-publication party can be more fun
than the book the finished product will be
if you ever abandon it enough to send it
to a friend you're grateful rejected your last MS.
If you're lucky, you'll get one poem out of it.

Meta-criticism about meta-poetry
to leave the poem free to be.

Someone asks me, as author of this collection to provide an introduction that maps out thematic threads and a dominant critical orientation in a systemic way to tie together, and provide form to, what may seem like an arbitrary collection of essays. If the book as object is the fixture, perhaps the best I can say about its form is that it's notes to a syllabus, like a script to a play that allows improvisation with friends in a reading discussion group that could be at least as fun as the more monologic form of the poetry reading, but, alas, that probably doesn't sum it up or tie it together.

Another way to tie it together would be to show commonalities between the writers or books discussed. Such commonalities are often defined by what is excluded. In the contemporary glut of literary riches, any definitive coverage feels impossible, especially for the slower re-readings that I favor in this collection, but there are many poems I love to read that have not inspired me to write essays about them. That does not mean these poems are lesser than the ones discussed here; on the contrary, they may be more intimidating (Nathaniel Mackey, for instance) or inspire me to write a poem without the mediation of prose. So, commonalities between writers don't tie this collection together either (though I suspect it wouldn't be too difficult for a reader to acquaint me with my blind-spots in an enlightening way).

Since these essays mostly focus on books of poems,

and since these books often contain a diversity of poems, even a singular summary of each book can become reductive in its attempt to tie together. For instance, Joanna Fuhrman and ko ko thett could be classified very differently from each other, yet that doesn't mean that one poem by Fuhrman can't actually have more in common with a poem by thett than it does with Fuhrman's other poems. I find this often in my reading.

One poet/journalist I admire who's discussed in this collection, Alissa Quart, is a master of pithy soundbite characterizations. A brilliant word-slinger laboring in the trenches of discursive reframing, when she writes about poetry as both a literary and cultural critic, she has a knack for floating terms that I would love to see catch on in poetic /cultural debates. When I read her characterization of "Hysterical Surrealism[1]" and "Civic Poetry,"[2] I can read much of own poetry and what I love about others' poetry into that category. In addition to those terms, perhaps an emphasis on "Meta-Poetry," then, could be what ties together my approach to most of the books of 21st century poetry discussed in this collection, but only if we allow room to let each particular poem (or line from a poem) on its own terms, on a case-by-case level, resist such category if need be.

---

1 **Hysterical surrealism? A pop culture for our age of economic insecurity**

2 **Don't give up on poetry**! Civic poetry is not your precious, otherwordly poetry. It's public, it's political—about the hard stuff of life. https://www.salon.com/2015/05/20/dont_give_up_on_poetry/

But, what can any of this mean to an imagined general reader who is not already familiar with some of the books or writers discussed? In an essay published on January 8, 2024, "The Case for Never Reading the Book Jacket," Tajia Issen writes:

Rarely do I buy a book because I was seduced by the summary on the back or inside flap....

Being spoon-fed a crude distillation of plot and theme dictates, and therefore circumscribes, the terms of my reading. It tells me what to expect and how to feel in a way that strikes me as controlling, even demeaning. Somebody is trying to sell me something, which prompts me into a defensive pose—skeptical, closed off, incurious—that I don't want anywhere near my experience of art. I just want to get a premise and some vibes, a taste of tone, a flicker of the voice the book contains. I don't want to be told what's about to happen, even in the vaguest sense. And I *definitely* don't want to be told what it's "about." [3]

If book jackets are guilty of this, is not a review even more guilty than a blurb? Why write a review then, especially in what Sianne Ngai refers to as a post critical era? In *Animal Joy* (2022), poet and psychoanalyst Nuar Alsadir writes:

Instead of using guts and imagination to keep the erotic power of the *yes* alive inside themselves, many store it in a killing jar, then pin and frame behind glass what would not otherwise have lent itself to becoming a

---

3 https://thewalrus.ca/the-case-for-never-reading-the-book-jacket/

classifiable specimen attached to categorizable meaning. Critics, after all, tend to gravitate toward what they can write about (*What's your central idea?*), use familiar tools to cut into a work, and pull out what they already know— even if, in so doing it, they kill, as poet Marina Tsvetaeva explains, 'To have an opinion of a thing, you must live in that thing and love it. (50)

I don't know if I live up to Tsvetaeva's standard of living and loving, but I'm trying to bring more awareness to the fact that every poem I mention knows way more than what I say, that every review is a kind of erasure, especially when they prescriptively vet. Many before me have written in prose to defend poetry (as an unknowing that needs no defense) against the rational discourse of prose that often attempts to co-opt or colonize it, and certainly, I won't be the last to do so. But, as the poet Gillian Conoley puts it, sometimes "we have to wire prose into talk to get to the poem." The prose-mind that writes these essays comes to the poems discussed in the spirit of a question mark.

Recently, on Facebook, I was blessed to be part of this exchange:

Uche Nduka: It's not so important to interpret a poem as it is to experience it.

Ben Friedlander: I dunno, maybe. I'm probably the outlier, returning to those that help me think much more than the arouses of sensation.

I found myself agreeing with both points of view, and was happy they were in dialogue with each other, so I wrote, "Sometimes I have to try to interpret it to feel more immensely its irreducibility."

I experienced both of them pressing the like button (whatever that means).

In this sense, though I share Issen's skepticism towards the book jacket, my attitude is slightly different. I try to read the book first, and then when I'm finished reading it once, allow myself to read the blurbs and reviews to see what others say, and then go back to my reading, feeling alive in the ensemble of a plurality of exteriorized voices with different readings and emphases of the same book. I thus believe the reader of this book could find it more useful if they read the books discussed before they read my essay about them (and it made me very happy when my proofreader Karlyn Clarence told me she read each book as she read my chapter on it). I aspire to Issen's alternative:

Point to any book on my shelves and I'll tell you exactly why I bought it: because I heard about it from an essay or a list or a trusted friend or bookseller. Maybe I'm obsessed with reading everything available on the subject. Often, I loved something else the author wrote. I like the cover. I like the publisher. I like—controversially—the constellation of blurbs that tells me who the writer's in community with. Perhaps the writer's in community with me. They're my buddy. My hero. My crush. My nemesis. (Issen)

When Issen writes, "I like—controversially—the constellation of blurbs that tells me who the writer's in community with." I suppose she means such social dynamism is controversial because it implies charges of nepotism. My collection could be accused of that as well. I heard about many of these the books from Facebook friends in other cities. I'm also fascinated by the way books come to me through other forms of community. A few years ago, at a broadside signing, Bay Area writer Maw Shein Win showed me a broadside by Tureeda Mikell, who I had never heard of before. Reading her poem, I told Maw that the poem in some ways reminds me of Judy Juanita. When Mikell arrived, she showed me her book, and it turns out it was blurbed by Judy Juanita. I felt mysterious forces at work drawing me to read her book, which was called *Synchronicity*, and contains many poems about such similar synchronicities between a random appearance of an artifact and her own life as a spiritual healer.

Synchronicity also comes as resonances between books that ostensibly have nothing to do with each other. Alsadir writes:

I sometimes recognize a resonance between ideas merely because the books housing them have landed haphazardly beside one another on a table or my shelf. Books can become metonyms for the ideas they contain, which is why sometimes, to engage with a thought I am not ready to think, I find myself placing books charged with unthought elements beside one another. (259)

During my month of reading Alsadir's book, I had

also been reading Tony Bolden's *Groove Theory: The Blues Foundations of Funk* (2020). When I read Alsadir's quote, I become excited because she described what I had been feeling this past month in going back and forth between these two books. In *Animal Joy,* Alsadir reveals resonances between the specialized discourse and performance of psychoanalysis, on one hand, and the specialized discourse and performance of stand-up comedy on the other. This allows sparks to fly in a conversation between specializations usually not put in dialogue with each other. In *Groove Theory*, Bolden makes a brilliant and passionate argument showing how blues and funk music as a philosophy provide a radical alternative to the dominant Euro-centric Cartesian mind/body dualism. This also allows sparks to fly between specializations that are usually not put in dialogue with each other. After reading Bolden, I can see more clearly the ways in which Alsadir's book also challenges the racist, sexist, classist, logocentric, ocularcentric, dimensions of mind-body dualism.

Perhaps one thing that ties together every writer in *In the Here There* is that they all offer tools to move beyond, between, beneath, the binary thinking of this still dominant Cartesian dualism (seen, for instance, in the increased disembodiment of the 21st century technocracy). It is certainly a recurrent theme.

Perhaps most importantly on a personal level, reading and writing about these books helped me find a language for poetry again after struggling with writer's block for almost a decade. In general, the books discussed here seemed to magically arrive at the right time, without me needing to seek them out, to focus a need I didn't even know I had until they got me writing a poem that turned into prose that may yet turn back into a poem or a silent dance step even the disabled can do.

In collecting these essays, I also felt a sense of community building, as when Brenda Hillman turned me onto Fred Moten & Stefano Haney's *The Undercommons*, when Sandra Simonds and Jeff Johnson, unbeknownst to each other, turned me onto the Chris Nealon's *The Shore*, when Krysia Jopek turned me onto John Burroughs and Maw Shein Win turned me onto ko ko thett—to say nothing of the synchronicity I felt between contemporary Tureeda Mikell and 18th century poet Phillis Wheatley and the spiritual kinship I started feeling between Gil Scott-Heron & David Berman, and between Brenda Hillman and Emily Dickinson.

In this collection, the majority of the poems I discuss are shorter-lyric poems (though there are two essays on prose books which could be considered long poems). The majority of the poets I write about are women, just because they are the poets I've felt I needed most in recent years. They range from eco-poets to contemporary avant-garde conceptual writers to anti-corporate journalist muckrakers to veterans of the Black Arts movement, from Civic Poetry to Hysterical Surrealism.

But just as hunting is not those heads on the wall, neither is gathering beholden to any easily fetishized 'school' categorization. Important, too, to note that many of these writers have published books more recent than the ones discussed here that do very different things than these etiolated snapshots.

Although most of this book consists of reviews/essays written about books of American 21st century poetry, the essays on Emily Dickinson and Phillis Wheatley were occasioned by an Early American Literature course I taught. I included them because I feel that trying to understand the dominant 19th century American zeitgeist through these writers' attempts to change it sheds light on these 21st century writers' interventions into the current zeitgeist. The essay on Dickinson was inspired by a Dickinson poem Hillman sent me on my birthday and was written for her birthday.

The third section takes a side trip into discussing poets who have worked at the intersection of politics and music, Gil Scott-Heron and David Berman. The essay on David Berman is the longest piece in the book. Though it includes a couple of close readings of his song lyrics near the end, this hybrid essay begins with an informational screed into the workings of one of the most powerful corporate lobbyists, Berman's father, and a critique of a negative *ad hominem* review of David's swan-song album. It includes lengthy excerpts from my personal correspondence with David, and is the most autobiographically confessional piece in the book, navigating some stages of deep grief (from anger to wonder) after David took his own life, to celebrate parts of David many of his fans prefer to de-emphasize, as well as how he helped me when homeless, and the love we have for each other. I follow it with an essay on a Gillian Conoley book that helped me work through grief in wonderful ways to aerate the pounding feeling.

Maybe just two of the books discussed here could turn some beginning writer (or skeptical curious veterans) on to the plenitude of 21st century poetry in ways no more partial than the canonicity of the blue & yellow Norton Modern or the light blue Poulin Anthology did, as gateway, for me, at 18, in the 80s. As quirky Sparknotes to a reading list in early 21st century poetry, my hope is that, at the very least, this book can live up to being "anecdotal, wide in reference, shaped by interest and desire rather than argument" (as Juliana Spahr called *Spin Cycle*).

Finally, there are dialogues with poet Daniel Nester, Martine Bellen and uncategorizable multi-media writer Adeena Karasick. These dialogues are the most recent pieces in this collection, and it's a genre whose interactive possibilities I'd like to explore further. Perhaps that is the book project for the next decade.

1.

JOANNA FUHRMAN, TO A NEW ERA
(HANGING LOOSE PRESS, 2021)

"If we are fundamentally / timeless," Fuhrman asks early in *To a New Era* "can we still be damaged by time?" (8) Whether this time is seen as biological aging, or an economic and cultural paradigm shift, or the glut of dystopian thinkers and feelers, Fuhrman claims, "the dystopian surface / …is not enough to satiate / the present, or unmake the water buffalo of the past" (42) without having to resort, on the other hand, to utopianism.

Rather, the sentience in this book inhabits the empty core in the circle of history—or discursive prose—to destroy "ghostly bodies and conspiracy tambourines" (1) and put the fun back into being malfunctioning and defunded, bringing me to a place in which middle age can feel like childhood (but with sex, liquor and hipper boots, 11), where "we *pretend* history is the truck running us over." (Italics mine, 33). But part of what makes her faith in such "timelessness" throughout the book feel so *earned* is that it is not escapist as a transcendental ideological posture, but has more to do with health, humor, and a secret crush on everybody in the world—though with some jabs of tough love along the way to strengthen us to "face…the wind's teeth." (101)

In the wide range of aesthetic strategies and poetic forms Fuhrman brings into play in this collection (pantoums, sestinas, aphoristic one-liners, abecedarian, prose-poem "essays," Berriganian or Mayerian sonnets, etc.) such "timelessness" turns out to feel more alive, embodied, emotional, and present than the time-bound disembodied. Rather, it's something put on trial on an everyday basis, whether in the horror of an activist realizing s/he might very well have "a cell phone in [their] pocket instead of a heart," or "missing flesh...where a chest used to be" (48). Just because Fuhrman laments those who "mistake a beautiful etcetera / for a righteous plan" (51), doesn't mean she doesn't engage in activism

Fuhrman is well aware how the hostile external forces that we resist, fight, try to quell can trojan horse their way into us, and that externally directed anger (33, 36) may end up not harming any enemy but ourselves, while also making us less fun. At least that's what this line makes me think of: "Each day I woke to the sound of a monstrous bell. Without / noticing, I had become the bell myself." (80)

Reading lines like, "The world is burning, but everyone needs sleep," (54), other lines etched into my brain since college return, like D.H Lawrence's, "If we make a revolution, make it for fun," or Wallace Stevens' "The Revolutionists stop for orangeade." But even more I feel the spirit that Frank O'Hara (whose "Naphtha" Fuhrman rewrites in this book), Kenneth Koch, and other New York (School) poets tapped into and strove to embody. In Fuhrman's head-heart-hand poems, this spirit is alive and well and updated in a funky, at times fierce feminism that has healing potentials for that self-torturing little bell. Fuhrman's meta-political poems not only flesh out the second-wave feminist dictum that the personal is political, but remind me how defiant Kenneth Koch was in titling a book *The Pleasures of Peace* at the height of the Vietnam war and the militant anti-war movement.

In this collection, bodies, like hearts and spirits, are porous, whether felt in the contagion of a toddler's *transhistorical* "primal scream" (12) or in the transmittable pre-Covid germs in a stranger's sneeze, or in the joy of another (ahistorical) toddler smiling on the B train (5). Throughout, there are many images of outside and inside encountering each other or overspilling boundaries: oceans in bathtubs (14–16), water in iron shoes (44), currency made of pigeon blood spilling out in a bus (61), and what Martine Bellen calls "funicular modes of language transport," even in the most grounded poems.

The complex porousness between "outside" and "inside" is especially dynamic in the playfully engaging surfaces of the frame-shifting poem "The Happiness Factory." Set in a classroom and sustaining a conceit of poem-as "pigeon-shaped dwelling," it may be the best poem I've ever read about teaching imaginative poetry—I can't believe Kenneth Koch wouldn't love it—in part because it's no mere recounting of an experience, but also casts the reader into the role of the students listening to her embodied *ars poetica*, a pedagogy of fun that tells of the "purposeful purposelessness" of the sublime or "magical thinking" by showing it.

Even though the poem uses an "I–they" dynamic,

the speaker is less a dead lecturer than a kind of Zen master blowing the students' minds without any hint of paternalism or condescension. There's an awareness, on the part of the speaker, that the students are skeptical and that she has to seduce their imagination:

I know some of my students
would rather be asleep in bed, and that others are
daydreaming about pre-gaming with their ancestors.
They have a faraway look in their eyes as if their

great grandmother is holding their ponytail up
during a quick before-party hurl.

The outside is already inside, there in the here, memories and future projections in the 'now' of the class session. Reading this passage, I realize it's not fair to reduce the setting to the classroom because there are so many things going on here: a teacher imagining her students' imaginations wandering to time and space, a sense that you don't have to teach "imaginative flight," but tap into it. Later, when the skeptical students ask, basically, 'what's the point?', in the final three stanzas this teacher-speaker tells us:

I made up stories depending on who was in the room,
I'd tell them that one pigeon was being built to shelter
a future god. Another would be used to store a special
refrigerator capable of reproducing the food removed

from its shelves. I told them of "top secret" designs.
One would be so comfortable that its silk pillows
would instantly cure PTSD, and another would be
so quick it would travel faster than a rumor on Twitter.

I often said if we became experts at building
the birds it wouldn't even matter if our planet
died. The pigeons could be our new homes.
It wouldn't matter that none of us had the key. (65)

This is a teacher who can *read* her students, and
meet them where they are—whether their concerns
and anxieties are more spiritual, environmental, or are
more in terms of mental health or reputation. Fuhrman's
defenses of poetic imagining are so over the top (a self-
replenishing fridge?) that when I get to the deflating
punchline, "it wouldn't matter that none of us had the
key," I do not feel despair in the fact that we may not be
able to live there. Even if the (post-capitalist, worker-
owned collective) happiness factory cannot build any
inhabitable, bullet-proof happiness, you can still have
pigeon-shaped fun trying to.

Other poems also suggest a similar relationship
between fun and happiness, as if you can be fun, and
even have fun, without exactly being happy. In "Ode To
Unhappiness" (53), another poem that brings to mind
Kenneth Koch poems like "Locks" and "Thank You,"
Fuhrman praises the beautiful things that ordinary

unhappiness has given her, from "the cloud of spoiled milk ruining beautiful / bitter coffee" to "songs too remote / to be required to hear." This epideictic praise of unhappiness culminates in the last two couplets:

And for the warmth of your orange catlike
body, snuggling quietly between us,

The ghost mouse of the future, weirder sadness,
wriggling slowly in your closed jaw

Is ordinary unhappiness a cat with a not-quite-yet dead mouse in its mouth? Does "orange" suggest the shadow of Trump and Trumpism that haunts some of the poems in this book? Has anyone ever been able to rid themselves of unhappiness once and for all? Better to embrace a "future, weirder sadness" as more glamorous than the personified solitary "Happiness" in "Crunch!" (81), who doesn't seem very happy, or, if happy, not very fun. The praise of the ordinary can also get us to some of the sorrow that informs even the book's lightest poems, especially as regards patriarchy, which (unlike, say, the 'tech revolution') was as much a part of the old era as the new.

Many of the poems, especially in the book's third and final section, foreground gender and men's perennial attempt to flatten women's emotional intensity or seriousness:

In the Bible, Abraham thought Sarah was in a funk,
but she was actually shaking with grief.
(Lavender, 72)

She thinks "breakfast," but the world
hears "steak." She thinks it's time to tie

the ribbons on the invisible revolution,
but the world hears "party time,"
(Moveable Us, 87)

In one of the poems, titled "History Lesson," Fuhrman writes,

Women noticed that their tears
had the potential to be sexy if they wore
them inside out so the dry interior
hid the messy wetness of the drop's
skin (58)

The gravitas and the pathos in these excerpts deepen and ground the humor and sense of fun foregrounded in some of the other poems, which satirize various forms of the patriarchal poetry tradition: "The Poetry Reading" (74) or "Bro-Realism" ("You may be a bro, but that doesn't mean / your liver doesn't wear a pink feather beret," 92).

"Listen to the Rooster" (69) seems like a send-up of a Whitmanian mode, both stylistically and thematically as the 'barbaric yawp' of Whitman's incantatory abstract transcendentalism becomes a "rust-gilded squawk" of barren cowboy bro-poet cosmic slop, the "I" here a polar opposite of the more grounded "I" of the domestic poems in the first section of *To a New Era*. The poem "Old Weather" (70–71), with its barren bull, missing sky father, and steeple, which, "like any other work of beauty, / pretends to pray for the end of thinking," talks back to Wallace Stevens' critique of surrealism as merely inventing, and not discovering.

One of Fuhrman's most capacious meta-political (and meta-poetic) poems, "Broken Singularity: Kali Tribe Sestina," takes place in a fault-line of intersectionality between the artist and activist, personal and political, transhistorical and historical, narrative and lyric, thinking, feeling and praxis. While many sestinas get more strained, clunky, or lose their inspiration at the end under the constraints of "boxed being," the skillful transformations Fuhrman takes her six ending words through (and/or let them take her through) create a world that cannot be contained by any reading. Every time I reread it, I find something else I somehow missed, like a reusable mirror.

Most of the poem is spoken by a "we," in a detached meditative tone, looking back without regret, self-pity or snark, at an involvement in a utopian collective art movement, righteously struggling for "more post-capitalist travels" (56) against billboards and broadcasts of the oppressive status-quo systemic enemy that "put a cage around our hope" (56). Trying to read it in terms of a narrative, it appears there are three characters: the "we" speaker, their babies/children, and an implied "they" of systemic oppression represented metonymically as "billboard" and "broadcast." To this group, by the end, we could add an "I," a singular speaker who appears to be part of the "we," like when a choral piece of music breaks to become an aria (though we could say the "we" is also part of the "I"). While many political poems against systemic injustice take the form of an us-and-them binary, Fuhrman's addition of the children triangulates the artist/activist's struggle.

The contrast between the speaker(s) and their children is particularly nuanced. Is it a primarily generational contrast, like a 70s feminist art-pioneer wondering if their children were born with advantages they weren't (perhaps because of their labors in fighting against the billboard)? Or are "we" fighting primarily in an aesthetic and spiritual dimension ("for portable arias," 56), where our children are primarily fighting on a militant activist, social realist level, as is suggested when Fuhrman writes "placards, / not poetry, taunted us," in contrast to "our children," who "wrote transformative placards / in the womb."

Yet the children are associated with arias, as if they embody what the "we" is but longing, hoping, wishing, fighting for, as some artists speak of their work as babies, and have been known to envy their works for their revolutionary power to shatter "the space time continuum." The children, however, do not reappear in the poem. One could map the triangulation as less between characters and more between words: at one extreme the negatively connoted "billboard," and on the other extreme the positively connoted "aria" (which can also be defined as a written or spoken passage or emotional, dramatic text), and somewhere between them the word "placard":

We tried to convince ourselves the blank and spiritual placard
we held above the burning city was more than a placard.
We hoped its blankness could change minds.

The linguistic slippage that occurs in the word "placard" here attests to what Martine Bellen calls *To a` New Era's* "debate with language's complicated conundrums, histories and alternate histories," as well as Elaine Equi's praise of this book for its embrace of "our commodified pop-art present, turning its tools against itself."

Beyond this, "Broken Singularity" removes any more specified historical context, and it also purposely does not gender this "we," that is, if we ignore the title and its dedication to pioneering second wave feminist activist and artist Mary Beth Edelson (now 87), who referenced "Kali" (the goddess of destruction) in her anti-patriarchal art. So it's as tempting to locate the speaker *as* Edelson as much as Fuhrman herself. Since Fuhrman, in another poem referencing gender, writes "all context is a lie," (87), the speaker could be any contemporary who has found themselves operating in the interstices of art and activism, or anyone who ever identified more with a "we" than an "I" (as if the "we" is what caused the "broken singularity" of the title).

In the sixth stanza and envoi, as Fuhrman's words, soaring with an elegant, seamless use of enjambment portray and (re)enact a transformation in sinuous conversational sentences, a "radical change like a spell" seems to occur as the "we," following its children, vanishes from the poem. We are left with, or introduced to, a previously absent "I," alone, being inspired by listening to (rather than singing, or fighting for) a portable aria:

I could hear the music beneath the broadcast
and watch its notes wrap themselves in wet leaves, soft placards
encircling pain. I'd slip wishes inside the slim volumes of travels.
I wanted to believe in this, in nothing else, I wanted to hand
over my future in the present tense, to ignore the billboards
for war and shopping, but I knew I needed more than an aria's

reprieve from suffering. No song would be enough to broadcast
the reverberating empathy required to upend the billboard and the placard.

No open hand would be open enough. There is no travel but travel.

Not only does the "we" become "I," but active yields to passive, receptive. Words like "boxed-in," "envy," "fighting," "framing," and "raised fists" yield to the previously elided sensual beauty, pain, and suffering, as if to return to the lyrical singularity that had been broken before the poem began, but it doesn't end there.

In the envoi, the final sentence is the only one in the present tense, and its enigma recalls, but betters, Rilke's "Archaic Torso of Apollo." Travel here seems far less tourism than it does travail, work, labor. Is she saying we may need to feel the world as through an "I" to feel more reverberating empathy in the present than a "we" with a future-oriented, transcendent ideology of hope could? Or does she reject the narrative closure of such an either/or? It may be a both/and, not opposing the "I" to the "we," but repairing the broken singularity to reground a wider tribal "we." Part of what makes this declaration of "reverberating empathy" so earned, and so convincing, is that it is not merely a declaration, but is *being enacted* in the poem's equanimous and empathetic attitude towards the "we" in the first five stanzas, as if you can't truly be empathetic to others without extending such empathy to your own (or collective) past, as if to forgive it, laugh and cry with it, rather than dismiss it as something you've moved beyond.

Even though this poem dedicated to a painter avoids

using colors, "Broken Singularity" itself could be called a "ricocheting opalescent aria." In the end, she claims that no matter how artful and emotionally powerful an aria can be, it's insufficient and reduced to mere "song" by the end. It may not be sufficient, but that doesn't mean it's not necessary. And though I do not know the author's intention, right now I prefer the feeling of "reverberating" to "ricocheting"—the latter feels a little more like a bullet, the latter more like a spine tingle.

ANNE BOYER, GARMENTS AGAINST WOMEN
(AHSAHTA PRESS, 2015)

"We haven't had time to develop societal antibodies to addictive new things."
      Silicon Valley investor Paul Graham

"I am everyday people."
      Sylvester Stewart

Anne Boyer's *Garments Against Women* is a genre-breaking book with a purpose. Divided into four sections, the book eludes categorization as either poetry or prose. Boyer begins with a quote by Mary Wollstonecraft about a woman for whom reading, and more importantly, writing, is "the only resource to escape from sorrow," especially if she can create writing that "might perhaps instruct her daughter, and shield her from the misery, the tyranny her mother knew not how to avoid." Can writing do this?

The first piece of lyric prose in the book, "The Animal Model of Inescapable Shock," presents the unshielded misery today's social engineers tyrannically inflict on their subjects (For examples, see Silicon Valley guru Nir Eyal's recently published *Hooked: How to Create Habit-Forming Products*). Using the clinical language of causality and "if-then" clauses on which these techno-behaviorists rely, Boyer admits an emotional anguish that Eyal edits out in order to diagnose the social paralysis created by the people who brought you both Instagram and the widening wealth gap. The terror of this psychopolitics accrues until "eventually all arousal will feel like shock" (2). If we are trapped in Capital's infinite laboratory called "conditions," this piece offers no escape, except, perhaps in the question: "And where is the edge of that electrified grid?"

In order to take this question as not merely rhetorical, you may have to cross over this edge to elevate the ethical over the aesthetic that abstracts itself from it. "Some of us write because there are problems to be solved," Boyer tells us at the start of the second, much longer piece, "The Innocent Question" (3). One such problem is "the problem of what-to-do-with-the information-that-is-feeling." (3) In an equivocal system in which feelings become a crime, Boyer troubles every frame she can find. She announces confidently, "I think of all those things conferring authority and exclude them one by one, an experiment in erasing importance" (4). Among the many authorities she excludes is the tyranny of the word "happiness." In a thrift store, she finds a book called *The Strategies and Tactics of Happiness* by Maynard W. Shelley, written in 1977 (10). "I read some, but there are so many things of such importance about which I have never found a book" (5). For instance, "How will I pay to see a doctor?" (10) In certain contexts, however, questions like these— involving the information that is feeling—become taboo, or as Boyer puts it, inadmissible:

Inadmissible information is often information that has something to do with biology (illness, sex, reproduction) or money (poverty) or violence (how money and bodies   meet). Inadmissible information might also have to do with being defanged by power (courts, bosses, fathers, editors, and other authorities) or behaving against power in such   a way that one soon will be defanged (crime). (9)

With this detached tone, conversant with, but one step removed from, complaint, pain expresses itself in polysyllabic ideas. "All three of these (pity, guilt, and contempt) are feelings of power, are the emotional indulgences of those who seek it" (9). Compelling me to rethink guilt, Boyer excels when she admits class struggle into her nuanced work. "There are many things I do not like to read, mostly accounts of the lives of the free… the constrainingly unconstrained literature of Capital produced aimlessness, alienation and boredom in me when I tried to read it" (12).
"The constrainingly unconstrained literature of Capital," Byung-Chul Han would agree, is a phrase that certainly characterizes the Internet. As Boyer continues,

It is all this self-expression that makes me so ashamed. In the comment boxes of a   popular fashion blog someone suggested any documentation of individual expression is   in fact anti-social rather than pro-social, in that it is a record of individuation from the   human mass." (13)

Perhaps part of Boyer's point is that even that critique of individual expression is a form of individual expression.

When Boyer writes of those who "want 'only the best' and those who believe only-the-best is immoral," she provides a useful, more inclusive, antidote to the happiness evangelists—"I am the dog who can never be happy because I am imagining the unhappiness of other dogs"—and she does this without pity, guilt, or contempt (13).

Speaking truth of power in ways that some would find inadmissible as a conspiracy theory, she writes,

taste is a weapon of class: Those guys have gotten together and agreed on their discourse: it will make them seem middling, casual like a sweater. Who dips in or out of it? What does it mean to give something up? There is a risk inherent in sliding all over the place. As if the language of poets is the language of property owners. (14)

As the questions proliferate, Boyer admits this unhinged rhetorical slide almost defiantly as a necessary tool against Big Data. But we also see frustration with the very foundational assumptions of one's investment in poetry, in writing, in the specialized bubbles in which poetry often circulates. I may be reading my own similar struggles, arousals, confusions, into her in this piece, but, as a writer trained in academia, I can very much identify with the voice that says, "I have done so much to be ordinary and made a record of this." (14)

Did I mention she's often funny? Contrasting herself with a man who won a Pulitzer Prize in fiction, Boyer writes,

I would like to not know how to write, also to know no words. I believe this prize-   winning novelist believed that the mind had two places, the conscious and the   subconscious, and that literature could only come out of the subconscious mind, but that   language preferred to live in the conscious one. This is wrong. Language prefers to live   on the internet. (16)

In "No World But The World," Boyer, as immanent sociologist, brings in some feeling information concerning the insularity of what some call the poetry world. She writes in the past tense, "There were certain conventions at these times: to fly, to conference, to panel, to anthologize. In other circles it was to contest, submit, or award" (18). The poetical distinction here, in many ways, is a more accurate description of the division between late 20th century poetic niches than the distinction between schools and aesthetics.

The next paragraph troubles the frame with feeling information that probably would be inadmissible at a literary conference:

Poetry was the wrong art for people who love justice. It was not like dance music.   Painting is the wrong art for people who love justice. It is not like science fiction. Epics   are the dance music of the people who love war. Movies are the justice of the people who love war. Information is the poetry of the people who love war. (19)

Boyer meets the feeling of confinement under a regime of specialized genre conventions with a refreshing restlessness. By contrast, the last paragraph in this piece speaks in a more personal (convulsively subjective) tone:

My favorite arts are the ones that can move your body or make a new world. What at   first kept me enthralled wasn't justice, it was justice-like waves, and a set of personal   issues, like the aestheticization of politics and the limitations of reading lists before the digital age. (19)

I certainly have experienced dance music bringing people and communities together in a way that even the most thoughtful and empathetic poetry has not. Although one could say Boyer's own writing is the opposite of dance music, its solidarity with that non-poetic form comes through clearest when expressed in the conventions of idea-driven prose syntax rather than poetic syntax. It unites extremes, which have been divided by an enemy that dresses up as moderation, centrism, the middleman's rational mean—all the narrow choices that can suck us in as kids with their seeming breadth.

The final page of "No World But The World" offers a potentially liberating alternative to both the institution of the Internet as well as the elitism encouraged in academic-adjacent poetry and letters.

In conclusion, there would be no army of clay soldiers in the tomb, just this: an array of   dress forms.... There is no superiority in making things or in re-making things. It's like   everything else, old men who go fishing, hair extensions, nail art. (20)

This is followed by a page-long sentence with images of often-surprising and sometimes hilarious daily quotidian images of working-class everyday people as if she's found an out to make an in to dip out of the grid with. I'd love to hear a performance of this sequence being read with otherwise instrumental dance music, especially the rhythmic list of "things" with which this sequence ends, to clear the way for the more personal, memoir-like writing of the rest of the book.

+++

In "Sewing," the centerpiece to the book's second section, Boyer finds an alternative to the social media and high art of this consumer society that threatened to paralyze her (and us) in the book's first section: to side with practical craft as a less alienated labor more analogous to dance music. Boyer reminds us how the invention of the sewing machine was (and still is) threatening to the captains of monopoly-capitalism:

"One of the inventors of the sewing machine didn't patent it because of the way it would restructure labor. Another was almost killed by the mob" (29).

Against this backdrop, it's no mere fantasy to imagine oneself as the revolutionary Emma Goldman while sewing, even if capital has found a way to convince many to devalue this skill and buy overpriced garments made in sweatshops. Yet, if the first section of this book thinks globally, "Sewing" finds at least a foothold that can act locally. Even when she finds herself pressured by the needs of her daughter to buy footwear, she is able to provide a heart-warming anecdote that can shield the young from the so-called consumer instincts on which social engineers from Alfred Bernays to Richard Berman to Nir Eyal have preyed.

+++

Section Three's "Not Writing" is a public list poem that refuses of the authority of any who wish to lock Boyer up in either poetry or memoir. A litany of negatives conjures a space away from commodified space to uncover the changing weather of creation. The follow-up piece, "What is 'Not Writing,'" could be considered a manifesto against bourgeois notions of art as play rather than work, as Boyer fleshes out her definition of work in more convincing ways than the proponents of the free time theory. If I'm ever able to start a "MFA in Non-Poetry" program (which would include everything currently called poetry, but yet be more capacious to include what Thomas Sayers Ellis calls "Perform-a-Forms"), I'd be more than honored to include this piece in its reading list.

With "Venge-Text" and "Twilight Revery," the book takes on the tradition of the patriarchal love poem; as the speaker studies the dynamics of a romantic relationship with an intellectual, yet dissembling, control freak of a lover, she reminds herself, "This is just one available story. I have so far been able to construct 22." (50) This Petruchio- or Thursdale-like male who fights for control on the level of language becomes representative of the so-called philosophical male mode of the Euro-enlightenment tradition.

+++

The fourth, and final, section of the book consists mostly of a poor woman's "memoir," written for those who distrust that genre and understand that memoirs are traditionally written by "property owners" (71). Yet, amidst all the horrors the speaker recounts here of the inhumanity of the literary world, she manages to find some escape that may yet lead to genuine transformation:

I was poor, I was solitary, and I undertook to
devote myself to literature in a community   in which
the interest in literature was, as yet, of the smallest. I
believed that autodidacts   were here to teach
decency. I believed I'd lost my front. (80)

I can absolutely relate to what she speaks here. As
she recounts being rejected by, and/or rejecting, the
conditional love of the literary world, she finds a kind of
solace: "It appears she refused the ladder, but in truth she
refused the rope." (80) To liberty, then, not banishment!
Garments Against Women does speak the language MFA or
Poetics sophisticates could appreciate, and perhaps this
may yet help change the conversation, if not exactly from
within, at least close enough (as if she's giving it one last
chance to be real, even if she's saying goodbye).

"Bon Pour Bruler" (84) is a strong ending to anchor
this collection, once again exposing the inhumanity
of the European patriarchal voice, here through the
quoted voice of Rousseau. Rousseau's sexist account of
why a young girl decided to stop writing brings us full
circle, back to the quote from his contemporary, Mary
Wollstonecraft, with which Boyer began her book. Like
Wollstonecraft, Boyer refuses to be silent. By the end of
this book, Boyer seems to have found a possibility beyond
escape toward transformation in solidarity with a ragtag
group of autodidacts, sewers, and the "anti-literature" of
catalogues, as she emerges as a woman who is able to use
the various garments of her time (from high literature to
today's social media) against themselves.

Ultimately, Boyer's book provides a space to challenge the ways we think about writing and make it question its foundations and reground itself. If she can't change the giant frame of the oligarchy, maybe her voice could at least have some say in changing the conversation that is literature. If she can't escape the cage, she can at least uncage her mouth!

BRENDA HILLMAN,
EXTRA HIDDEN LIFE AMONG THE DAYS
(WESLEYAN, 2018)

I could begin with a bold politically charged statement like: Huey Newton, Bobby Seale and others have suggested that we can't do away with the exploitation of systematic white supremacy unless we do away with mind-body dualism, and *Extra Hidden Life, Among the Days* provides us with tools for doing so. Or I could start with Hillman's charming & audacious alternative to some of Whitman's cringe-worthy excesses:

the elevator stars. Don't look for me under
        your bootsouls, look for us spinning multiply
    with our poems   among elements
                & our imitators (142)

This (plural) speaker could be the extra hidden life or more specifically the lichen. This book—through words and actual pictures (which, as Cara Dees puts it, could be a "new form of punctuation"), has not only whetted further curiosity and wonder about lichen, beyond how introductory science courses would have it, but it's also made me confront my own city-centric worldview and skepticism of words of nature to actually get me closer to nature than other linguistic registers can. Hillman is generous enough to reach out to the skeptic:

but the humans love beauty & can be released from
their positions because so many have doubts about
doubts about what is called the natural world, far below
(165)

One of the ways Hillman is able to break down my
resistances to nature poetry (she's been retro-actively
termed an eco-poet for whatever that's worth, though
Hillman prefers poets who are willing to "abandon their
camps & are burning the maps to stay warm," 35) is due
to her ingenuous milking of the fact that *lichen* (in the
U.S., if not necessarily in the U.K.) sounds like *liken*.
Indeed, throughout *Extra Hidden Life*, lichen is being
likened, whether it's to punctuation & typography (as
in "fringe lichen with tilde-like edges," 15) or to simile
& metaphor themselves ("Ruffle lichen / spreading near
the lake like similes" ("Day 2," 57), not to mention that
like also means being attracted to. Beyond a merely comic
pun, this cosmic phonetic resemblance suggests a way out
of logocentric, dualistic metaphysics that officially and
subliminally define our epoch.

While it would be reductive to say that, for Hillman,
lichen is a metaphor for metaphor, or metaphor is a
metaphor for lichen, certainly such likening, such
kinship, is near the core of Hillman's vision in this book,
in which the field work—the (re)search—of looking for
lichen is one & the same with looking for something
(in the human realm) to liken it to. It's almost as if she
can't write about actual physical lichens without also

writing about metaphor & simile, as if to balance the 20th century modernist-materialist "no ideas but in things" dictate with a complementary "no things but in ideas" or feelings, or souls, as her image of the microbes on the photo of microbes ("So Bacteria Have Their Thunder," 18) goes beyond any simple transparent 1=1 referent correspondence for the sake of transference, synergy, and passing (psychic) energy across.

Some people think lichen looks dead but it is alive in its dismantling. Some call it moss. It doesn't matter what you call it. Anything so radical & ordinary stands for something (56)

To say, in prose, however, that lichen is likened to metaphor may be of no help if we rely on standard dictionary (or Poetics 101) definitions of what metaphor does, in which metaphor is a rhetorical effect that directly refers to one thing by naming another. Such definitions may reduce it to a symbol on a one-way street, and may ignore the more suggestive and mysterious (or seemingly contradictory) evocations of its etymology: to carry over or across, to transfer, to bear.

For Hillman, sharing C.D. Wright's belief in "words / as action   not contingency" (119), metaphor can be, among other things, "a form of action" (55) and, at its most powerful, makes "a human & nonhuman meaning…. / (not sure what nonhuman meaning means)"

(55), but with the proviso that metaphor cannot really be a metaphor if it's only a metaphor, that it must sometimes lose consciousness of itself as metaphor to do its work, that metaphors can become their opposite, and there's a danger in that, yet ultimately there's a sense that metaphor both is and isn't a metaphor for the harmony between the human and the non-human that is necessary for there to be harmony among humans.

Lichens are also personified throughout this collection, even when they're unlikened to simile: "Lichens are calmer than people / and similes calmer than that" (68). Often they're pictured as labor, with clear working class solidarity. In "Triple Moments of Light & Industry," a prose-poem ode to "tiny slave bacteria (in an oil refinery) changing sulfides, ammonia, hydrocarbons & phenol into levels of toxins the mixture can tolerate," she writes, "the bacteria do not experience hurt or the void, but their service is uneven" (45). On the other hand, in "Species Prepare to Exist After Money," she writes:

> Turns out bacteria communicate in color.
> They warn each other in teal
> or celadon and humans assign
> meaning to this, saying they are distressed
> or full of longing. (21)

Even the so-called hard sciences can't entirely avoid affective language when writing about the sex life of lichen. Yet, even before the human assignation of meaning, there's a pre-meaning sense that their colors are warnings. More often Lichen are personified as listeners, whether it's "*Xanthomendoza* / growing real gold radar ears" (61), or *hypnogymnia* with its "tubes & big ears listening in thin woods, / an undercommon in the trees"[4] (63). The photo Brenda took of the *hypnogymnia,* with its white tendons and tannish-brown belly against a crisp black backdrop, is almost as beautiful as the sound of its name, which suggests both *hypnotic* and *gymnastic.* Occasionally, lichen speaks: On (or in) "Day 3," "Lichen says / accept what is then break it down" (58).

In the book's central "Metaphor & Simile" sequence, Hillman extends the basic love-is-a-rose metaphor to liken the destructive/healing powers of lichen to the heroic figures of Rosa Parks and Roza Luxemburg, as well as living protestors. Regardless of whether it's accurate to say metaphors & lichen "stand for something," these women are certainly standing for, or better, are embodiments of, love & justice (as well as serenity-in-grief), "as lichen reads the stone, as Rosa rides the bus" (64). And it may stretch credibility to mention that Hillman also links these healing forces to "punctuation...trying to help you along," but such ruminations on, in, & through metaphor go beyond the traditional metaphysical conceit to sound the very depth of (our) being, emphasizing the possibilities

4 Hillman appropriates this term from Moten & Haney's collaboration, *The Undercommons* (2014), in which the term "undercommons" is primarily spoken of in human, social terms. I'd been so out of the contemporary loop that I was not aware of that book until Hillman turned me onto it, and I'm very grateful.

for freedom, justice, "unknowing beauty," and harmony.

I get the feeling that the capaciousness of metaphor (or call it myth) allows Hillman to find a way to integrate the two main ethical social roles the (lower case) "i" enacts in this book: the political activist and the poet. It's not that they have to be opposed to each other, though it's so easy to forget when tangled up in the confines of specialized definitions of the human that can't cross over to the nonhuman to save it from the inhuman.

Yet, none of this comes close to answering Forrest Gander's question: "What is the connection between the book's many references to lichen and our 'grief-stricken days'?"[5] After all, the book begins with a crisis and grief, a feeling that "humans were extra or already gone," (3), and a need to forsake human company (13), and certainly this feeling of crisis—both public and private—explains why she uses this Judith Butler quote as one of her epigrams: "Can we perhaps find one of the sources of nonviolence in the capacity to grieve, to stay with the unbearable loss without converting it into destruction?" (1)

Butler's implied definition of grief poses an ethos somewhat similar to that implied by Keats' ethical ideal of "negative capability" (if one may translate Keats' "living in doubt" to Butler's "unbearable loss" and his "irritable groping after certainties" to her "converting it into destruction"), though such an ideal is easier said than done, unless (un)done over and over. As Cara Dees puts it, "Hillman offers a response [to Butler], showing

---

5 https://www.nyjournalofbooks.com/book-review/extra-hidden

how grieving and living alongside the unbearable can reverberate with the struggle to save forests, animals, plants, and shores, democracy, and human life."[6] In negotiating this ethical dilemma, Hillman is clearly aware that "a metaphor might make more trouble when it tries to be...the grief of history" (78, ellipses hers), as she tells herself, "don't fuck it up / and try harder" (136). Is "try harder" the same as fucking it up here? Or is the ambiguity itself an alternative to "ghostly word weapons" (39), the violence encoded in our ostensibly neutral language? On the other hand, Hillman acknowledges, at a political protest:

> It's best to try no hitting first
> but each minute has a separate brain
> & if the cops start to hit, I'm no longer
> sure what I'll do. (42)

and she defends "unmedicated moody / rage" (47).

As Hillman harmonizes, rather than attempts to synthesize, this ethical dialectic, she may agree with Butler's (presumably rhetorical) question, but only by complicating Butler's terms, investing the word "destruction" itself with positive connotations. Thus, lichen is not only the "wife of decomposers" but also celebrated as "the figure of destruction" who "comes in many forms & lately wears veils that look like nettings or hashtags, *Ramalina*—a Kali figure of change & destruction" (73).

---

6   https://theadroitjournal.org/2018/09/24/to-love-despite-collapse-a-review-of-brenda-hillmans-extra-hidden-life-among-the-days/

Hillman has an acute ear for the moments or processes in which what may be termed "destruction" is actually more healing than what is being destroyed. We can see this when Hillman writes, "Disperse the self, / serenity & grief" (66), and when she channels the spirit of C.D. Wright speaking from the grave: "I just wanted to poke holes in their egos / sprinkle out the one big self," 125).[7] Such destruction can charm with bacteria's "power for changing not-life into lives" (22).

For the most part Hillman does not "tax ye elements with unkindness"—and readers looking for poems about the arbitrary cruelty of natural forces are likely to be disappointed, but neither is nature presented as benign. The destructive decompositions of lichen, or simile and metaphor, can be useful tools in an ethical process of unknowing. One of the best compliments Hillman bestows in praise of the late C.D. Wright is: "She helped you   unknow / The half true" (14). Elsewhere Hillman celebrates a poetry reading as a communal ritual of "unknowing beauty among / the brutal days" (55), for author, reader, and listener. "Day 4" opens with:

,   In the afternoon of our unknowing
,   we were outside. So were
,   other organisms: flies, dust,
,   punctuation. It's impossible to know
          how to live (60)

---

7 Hillman also turned me onto C.D. Wright's *One Big Self* as well as Garamond font.

Elsewhere, the unknowing of beauty (and the beauty of unknowing) is linked to the power of simile through the suffering of doubt: "a simile sets up space for you to doubt / ever getting past the suffering...Rilke" ("Day 2", 58, ellipsis hers).

The ellipsis could imply the despairing thought is completed before the intrusion of Rilke, but the line break between "doubt" and "ever" suggests that each line could also be its own unit. In this sense, setting up "space for you to doubt" may actually be one of the most profound functions of simile and metaphor, to allow the *ever getting past* the daily suffering. In "Day 14," Hillman writes: a simile sets up gaps for you / to doubt when there is disagreement" (76).

"Doubting" can save us from disagreements becoming destructive, and since most of us are born into a world of disagreements (a "breaking at the start of time," 12) , this doubting can be very similar to the "love that / broke the breaking" (12). When simile opens up to contemplation to calm us from reaction, doubt becomes more similar to wonder, and partaking in creation.

In perhaps one of the most poignant moments of lyric clarity (or confession) in the book, Hillman writes:

> Those who had tried
> too often walked
> with those who had yet to try
> as doubt can walk beside radical hope. (157)

What a beautiful personification of the compassionate

companionship, or marriage, of doubt and radical hope! As an older person whose professional and social life is largely among the young, I can relate to this beautiful defense of the much-maligned millennials. Radical skepticism, if taken to its logical conclusion even, has to defeat itself. While Craig Morgan Teicher calls Hillman's book "one uneasy answer," at times its healing power feels more like easy questions, listening, waiting for our response. & I like the way the book is able to move through grief and guilt, to embrace moments in which humans "didn't not feel joy" (153) without falling into the "false praise or bullshit" (74) of commodifying joy.

Nor is it mere wordplay to suggest to the reader that next time you go to a poetry reading, picture a reader as lichen and the book as stone, or picture the stone as the reader, and yourself as the listening lichen. The blank page could be stone and the writing lichen, or the worded page could be stone and the reading lichen, or the speaker may be lichen and the spirit of a dead friend can be live oak (139). Wood speaks as paper (136), and passages like

> larval forms of the obtuse

> ...love wood as I love paper
> sexy sexy sexy abstract beauty (140)

make it clear that for Hillman the abstract is always already grounded; lichens are an (abstract) artist, or even the unacknowledged legislators of the world, who listen.

MAW SHEIN WIN
STORAGE UNIT FOR THE SPIRIT HOUSE
(OMNIDAWN, 2020)

Some say a healthy body makes a healthy mind; others say great physical pain and illness is the result of a spiritual (or, more secularly, emotional or cultural) crisis. In contrast to such reductive narratives of cause & effect, Maw Shein Win's second full-length collection of poetry, *Storage Unit for the Spirit House* (Omnidawn, 2020), evokes the mysteries of symbiosis in the relationship between body & spirit. As Penny Edwards puts it, Win "invites us to reconsider and reconstitute the holding patterns that organize our lives, and reminds us of the power of the spirit—animal, human or *nat*—to resist containment.

Nats are god-like spirits venerated in Myanmar and neighboring countries in conjunction with Buddhism. Although each of these poems (rarely exceeding one page) stands on its own, they are loosely framed by a plot in which the speaker›s, and the reader's, task is to honor, appease, or liberate the neglected *nats*, trapped in a (self-) storage space, exiled from their rightful spirit houses, and thus (co-)responsible for the illness, injury, and disaster felt in many of these poems. The crises in this book are as physical & social as they are spiritual, or as Eve Wood writes, "Illness...pervades this collection, the sense that the body is at odds with the spirit."[8] Yet, since the illnesses are as much a result of being trapped

---

8 https://lareviewofbooks.org/short-takes/maw-shein-win-storage-unit/

in rigid containers (prisons, storage units, physical disability, wounded kinship, and social stigma), as in the ungrounded freedom of "extreme isolation (like) a radio between stations" ("Portal," 87), the forms of healing, release, and liberation are various.

"Storage Unit 202" (23) reveals the speaker—who had been previously more materialist, secularized, assimilated into American culture—realizing she must become more spiritual. This doesn't, however, entail atonement as a renunciation of sensual pleasures, as Win leaves ample room for linguistic play. "I drink moonshine at dawn" (23) may suggest, to a secularist, bootleg liquor—but what if it's actual moonshine? After all, liquor is called "spirits" and Dickinson tasted a liquor never brewed!

A similar use of the sublime pun occurs in the first two lines of "Water Space (one)":

> tree mouth
> of river (24)

suggests that, to a *nat*, a tree has a mouth, and can also be a mouth of a river, and that such an incantation perhaps has the power to liberate "mother trapped / in a tree." The lack of personal pronouns in these pieces may show perceptions the mother & daughter share (generational trauma, for instance) despite the differences and distances.

In Win's poems, a single word "has so many meanings that it's tempting to write a long, loopy paragraph on how gratifyingly evocative it is," as Barbara Berman remarks in *The Rumpus*.[9] Interpretation becomes less important than the word's generative power. The book's first section also introduces us to the saving powers of "reversibility" (27) on both image and psychological levels. On a psychological level, what's called shyness, social anxiety, and awkwardness that may get mistaken for being "idle" (17) by toxically extroverted cousins isn't attachment avoidance as much as "avoidant attachment."

And though this section began with crisis and disaster by water, the fiery colors of asters & star(gazer) lilies, snapdragons, and fuchsia (with its Mardi Gras-esque combination of purplish, yellow and green) bring an earthy warmth to free the "king drinking pear juice trapped in a glass jar" (22), the mother-spirit, spirit mother, and the "wildflower superbloom" from trampling tourists (23).

+++

Section 2 is framed by a prison tale, and the barest outlines of a human subject speaker, but many lines stand without an apparent frame and might be happier without a context, such as:

resting places

dandelion seeds

9   https://therumpus.net/2020/10/30/juan-felipe-herrera-maw-shein-win-and-john-freeman/

inside a head hewn out of granite. (41)

On a plot level, however, if Section 1 dwelt primarily on addressing the disaster and injury the *nats* influenced, many poems in Sections 2 and 3 focus more on illness and disability. I love the way Win is able to put the feeling of being a prisoner to physical pain into words:

> blindfold wound around a bleeding head
> sepia timecards & combination locks (72)

> the brakes of the car an unsettling sound
> detachment of hips dislocation of sorrow
> align the axle your fluids are down (59)

This could suggest a car accident caused the physical injury, but also that many of us in America are brought up to think of, and to feel, our bodies as a car (in which, in the words of Delmore Schwartz, "the ego is always at the wheel"). In the process of self-diagnosis that occurs in many of these poems, I also detect a critique of other literary and dramatic genres as potential causes of illness. The poem "Cinema" begins with the enigmatic couplet:

> the auteur pops pain pills
> hybrid, saga, biopic (43)

"Theatre in Three Acts" asks:

What happens to the body after soliloquy
mine in mottled fur coat (46)

These narrative forms of cinema are a kind of pain
pill and, as many (non-Western) healers know, pain pills
don't get to the root, or sometimes have side effects that
are worse than the pain they were taken for. (The same
could be said for novels or memoirs for that matter.) It
is as if the poem enacts the patience necessary to doctor
the more gregarious, gaudy, and bulky genres. "Spectre
Show" (45) delves more intimately, or personally, into the
relationship between a physical illness and an affective
state of mind, such as a childhood experience of being
shy. After being traumatized by others deriding her for
being different and introverted in the first section, a child
with "avoidant attachment" wrestles with performance
anxiety.

center of the panel   young
dance star rehearses

steel-encased contestant
clickclick   rushed to the hospital
dog bomb & ambrosia

artificial dreams
still-beating heart of a queen (45)

Similarly, "MRI Scan" (58) (which visually rhymes with the word "musician") suggests that the sound of a loud marching band—which in many moods can be a festive cathartic occasion—can also bring on rising blood pressure that is not good for one's health ("panic button / bang bang / last sensation"), especially in your 50s in illness when your body & soul are crying out for something slower & quieter. In the portal Win's poems sweep us through, it's never clear if this is actual music and if the music led one to the ER, or if this is the music of pain *in* the ER, or the cloying voice of a fire & brimstone preacher. I like the way Eve Wood puts it: "Win finds a strange redemption in the *imaging center* [emphasis added]." She also finds strange redemption bonding with her health care professional in a hospital over a belief in magic on the level of a single word (as spectres become sceptors):

trinkets & sceptres & waterfalls in Brazil
dragon fruit scooped into bowls
owls & blue spaces in parking lots a slithering towards
planted things (62)

+++

Like "MRI Scan," the later poem "Shops" (75) explores the relationship between physical illness and aurality (specifically music) with a wisdom equal to any community music therapist. It's like a sequel: If "MRI

Scan" were a song of experience (in its crisis of sickness & despair), "Shops" may be a song of higher innocence as it presents a playful dialogue that could be interior as well as exterior (but with ample white space to save it from sickening soliloquy). The voice that makes up the three stanzas with a justified left margin (that gets both first word and last word) feels healthier than the voice in the indented stanzas (which recall the sick voices of the breaking down body in Section 2, which deal with illness and disability).

The justified left voice begins the conversation with the healing powers of a synesthetic poesis:

> phytomineral etudes
> at the paw quilt shop (75)

What is the relationship between the adjective "phytomineral" and the noun "etudes"? Is it the music of the plant or the plant of the music? Is the paw quilt shop the antidote for what's diagnosed by a "CAT scan" (63)?

In the indented voice, however, we feel:

> nocturnal haloes
> mind fevers

It is the left-justified voice, however, that gets the last word. The barest hint of touch here could suggest a massage table, massage music:

smelling salts
air   guitar   &   filigree
[…   ]

the reverie of mobs as the architects
listen for their Ganesh ringtones

Perhaps this "reverie of mobs" could be contrasted with the revelry of the mobs in "MRI Scan":

band marches through the crowd

chimes gongs

a sound bridge (58)

Or perhaps Ganesh's spirit of new beginnings is meant to contrast with the "malediction but no misfortune" in "MRI Scan."

"Shops" uses a strategy Win highlights in section 4: reversibility. In Section 1, Win refers to the reversibility of a moon/coin (27). Though the word reversibility is not mentioned in Section 4, it's felt in Win's careful and brilliant choice to use an image as a title instead of words to frame this section: Mark Dutcher's rendering of a Rubin vase, perhaps the most famous example of an image that challenges traditional figure/ground and perceptual/conceptual relationships. Some refer to this as an ambiguous image; perhaps ambivalent is a better word, since there's always a split second or blink interposing itself between seeing the space between the faces as a vase, and the space surrounding the vase as faces. Win makes use of the affective dimensions of that pairing that may not be as readily accessible if she had chosen a duck/rabbit to illustrate the principle. How can a poet translate such an image into language?

In one of these poems, "Diorama" (74), Win writes: "how does a painting speak? language is the difference / among three things." In some images of the Rubin vase, the lips are almost touching (like in Keats' urn?), but in Dutcher's drawing, their symmetry is more "nose to nose" or "jaw to jaw." This perhaps could suggest a more negative tone, as if staring each other down, as in "Factory," when Win writes:

sound of coworkers arguing in the bathroom
or is it the other way around (72)

If the Rubin vase is merely luma ("black & white self-portraits in bathroom mirrors," 71), Win's poems in Section 4 become more chroma: dynamic, dioramic, open to more than a mere binary reversibility. Yet the "reversibility" here is not only linguistic and perceptual, but also conceptual and ethical, spiritual/materialist, personal/political, local/global, the public in the private, the private in the public, etc. Nor does the humor in some of these poems preclude their gravitas (the lighter the vase the darker the faces?).

The haiku-like stanzas of "Spirit House (four)" present a mysterious ritual. We first see "two siblings" as figures, or subjects, while the ground is a sense of danger:

sibling follows
sibling into
forest of thorn" (69)

But the line-breaks make it seem that this is not an image of two siblings, but an image of one. And that which the faces call the ground is really a vase:

volcanic relics
sister brother
blue-throated barbets (69)

Do blue-throated barbets really exist? Or is it an imaginary bird-dog hybrid? Does such an image have the power to focus on a commonality? Must we bring bird and loyal dog together to bring brother and sister together, to traverse the space between, the mystery of the two in the one which is three. There is not that imperial sense of dominion over nature, nor of the fear of it that probably spawned such presumption.

The image that ends this ritual:

distant blaze
candle wick floating
in bowl of oil (69)

is left purposely vague. Contrasts appear to be established in this conjuring, but are they the contrasts between distance and nearness, small and large? Blaze and its aftermath? Is the candle wick in a bowl of oil a positive image to put out the blaze? One doesn't need to limit an interpretation to appreciate its haiku like qualities.

The two stanzas of "Huts" (70) are also based on contrast, but here they're framed temporally and culturally as well as affectively. The first stanza seems to depict a childhood memory of a traditional, rural Burmese harvest festival, which seems positive (even Edenic, prelapsarian), while the second stanza depicts a present-day American, modern, urban cleansing ritual known as "going to the laundrymat."

The first stanza is an image of fullness, satiation, while the second stanza is an image of emptiness, longing, and wanting (for what's depicted in the first stanza). There's also a sense of a natural cycle and reincarnation in the first stanza:

butchers
will find gold hay
in their belly.

 In contrast to these cows, the speaker has
no breasts
but two dark
drops of hillside.

The absent is more present, the present more absent;
memory repels and attracts conjuring.

***

At other times, Win takes on the voice of a ludic trickster. As in "Shops," the dialogue in "Restaurant" could be interior and/or exterior:

I recognize her voice because it's my voice
I don't know that name because it's his name
I think your voice has a name but it's my name
She met herself in a restaurant. (73)

Is this epideictic or a redacted story? Notably, "Restaurant" is one of the few poems in this collection in which personal pronouns are central, and it could be read as a satire on an overreliance of them—yet any sense of scene, speaker, and setting yields to a meditation on names, voices, identity, possession, and *reversibility.*

I feel the fourth wall breaking down, sweeping the reader up in its lyric drama, when Win writes, "I recognize her voice because it's my voice." I wonder if I probably only recognize my voice in what I think Win is writing, and if any "reading" of this poem will inevitably tell you more about me than Win. When she adds, "I think your voice has a name but it's my name," is she chiding the interlocuter for imitating, usurping, her voice, or presuming to speak in her name? She could also be questioning conventional ideas of "authorship." I feel it would be closer to the spirit(s) of this poem if I were to say Win is not the author as much as plural and protean *nats* are.

The contrast between "voice" and "name" in this poem may be similar to the vase and faces in the drawing. Unlike the more emotionally neutral Rubin vase, however, I get a sense that the speaker shows a clear preference for the voice (vase) versus the name (face) and their possessive personal pronouns: "What will you bring to table? What is your sir, name?" (73)

Perhaps this "sir" is hollow(ed out), materialist, subject, unable to (embrace) change, trapped in a static sense of time, a reified sense of singularity (of perception and identity) who prejudges voices (of other or self) based on bulky externals—like say race or reputation ("names"). The "sir" is prevented from truly hearing and speaking (which perhaps could be translated to, "can't see the vase for the faces"). There's an ethical contrast implied between a voice of worried containment and a voice of *carpe diem* letting go, as if Win, or the *nats*, are saying: who needs a name if you got a voice?

***

The lighthearted tone of "The Parlors" (77) reminds me of the prose poems of Maxine Chernoff and James Tate. The poem's long-lined (by Win's standards) and short stanzas make a pact with social realism as they approach ethical contrasts in the more public socio-political terms of "we" and "them:"

a local reported to authorities that a moose
stormed downtown & broke the shop windows

ping pong was back
the bars, the halls, the parlors

In this juxtaposition, the first stanza represents the xenophobic, protective mindset of private property, which sees a moose (as a synecdoche for disorderly nature) as a threat. The second stanza represents a playful, aesthetic, comic (recreating) approach to the moose. This basic contrast is continued in the first two lines of the third stanza:

shopkeepers hid their porcelain figures

we wore bright colors to disorient the animals
wool rugs flapped open to take in the glass

The fifth stanza names "bouncing white balls," which may not only refer back to the ping-pong balls, but the movement of words on the page, and a gesture of trans-species solidarity with the freedom of moose-force, as if this moose is another incarnation of Ganesh (who we saw in ringtone form in "Shops"), the elephant god of new beginnings, remover of obstacles, patron of the arts and intellectual wisdom!

***

Section 5 takes a darker turn, and fleshes out in more narrative detail some of the disastrous memories and wounded kinships that were portrayed more impressionistically in Section 1, as if to circle back to the theme of freeing the mother trapped in the tree. The speaker, as a sustained "I," appears more in this section than the others.

A childhood memory in "Spirit House (five)" recalls the cousins in "Spirit House (one)" who gossiped, *"she is so idle, not as enterprising as her four sisters"* (17). I first read these cruel extroverted cousins as female, but in "Spirit House (five)," gender and various forms of toxic masculinity, are highlighted.

the neighbor boys, cruel

one left a dead kitten in a box on the doorstep (81)

Yet here the speaker can bear the stings of that memory better. Left alone, she finds what others call as deficit is actually a strength:

as a child I did not climb trees
instead I gathered leaves that flew to the ground (81)

This could also be read as a defense of transformative language, a beautiful childhood sense of metaphorizing, or a poetic laurel-crowning apotheosis:

I made home among the leaves
safely in gold, yellow, brown
invented a family who lived in a tree house
green twig, the mother
broken branch, the father

two ferns, the missing sisters (81)

If Win had put an exclamation point at the end of the last line, it would sound manically excited—but what makes it as sad as it is beautiful is that it's just left hanging, as if you can't metaphorize your way out of the prison of solitude.

In Shakespeare's *Richard II*, a king who tended to take social life for granted, arrogantly believing it was his birthright, now, left alone in solitary confinement, takes to similar metaphorizing:

I have been studying how I may compare
This prison where I live unto the world:
And for because the world is populous
And here is not a creature but myself,
I cannot do it; yet I'll hammer it out.
My brain I'll prove the female to my soul,
My soul the father; and these two beget
A generation of still-breeding thoughts,
And these same thoughts people this little world,
In humours like the people of this world,
For no thought is contented (Act 5, scene 4, 1-11)

I prefer the way Win does it to the way Shakespeare does it, largely because Win offers a feminist antidote to Richard's parthenogenetic patriarchal metaphorizing. The metaphysics that sees the soul as the father, and the mother as mere material (a vessel) may be, in many ways, the cause of the universal discontent (the global catastrophe of the 400 odd years since Shakespeare wrote). In Win's the father is a broken branch.

Toxic masculinity also appears in "Relationship" (85), first in the form of a direct quote from Freud: "love cannot be much younger than the lust for murder"; next through the word "lovelock"; and lastly through the use of the kind of Petrarchan language Shakespeare's male characters are often satirized by his female characters for using:

when they met it was murder
was it her eyes that slayed him
lambent grenades (85)

In "Den" (88), we witness a patriarchal police dad barking orders and a heroic, self-sacrificing mother. This could be Win's mother, to whom the book is dedicated, but I see my own mother, and many others, who decide to stay in a destructive marriage longer for the sake of the children despite the pleas of children saying, we'll be happier if you're happier....

In this light, the depiction in the book's final poem of a celebratory festive collective expansive spiritual *nat pwe* ritual seems earned after all the darkness that appears in this book. I wonder if it's also meant to signify that the mother can be freed from the patriarchal tree that confined her through the marriage ritual of her children. Here the book's title itself seems to reverse: to become a Spirit House for the Storage Unit. At the end:

cousin slowly opened a large trunk of teak & silver
strips

the nats flew inside, one after the other after the other.
(95)

They flew in, but Win doesn't say whether the lid was closed, or if they're free (at last). This refusal of closure can be a great liberation, or, as Amanda Moore writes, it can "offer comfort and continuity, an assurance of wellness and prosperity."[10] It also reminds us that there is no once-and-for-all healing of present or past, individual or collective trauma.

---

10   https://www.omnidawn.com/product/storage-unit-for-the-spirit-house/

ANSELM BERRIGAN
SOMETHING FOR EVERYBODY
(WAVE BOOKS, 2018)

Berrigan's eighth book is his best yet, bringing his "deregulated / words like snuff films for sound" (1) together with an appealing ethos of "a family and community member looking at the seams of public life" (in the words of Publisher's Weekly). As Berrigan puts the sense of magic spell back into the word charm, I sense somewhat of a post-punk ethos, as well as the Shakespearean foole at his most linguistically complex: "it's not / enough to know what things mean / beaten off to the side, fool. Sometimes / you gotta know what things don't mean" (36), and sometimes you have to let yourself write "gotta."

Framed by the poem "What the Streets Look Like," Anselm's book places itself firmly in the tradition of the New York School's epistolary peripatetic poems, as Berrigan wrestles with the temptations of nostalgia that gentrification and other paradigm shifts have brought, but can still warmly celebrate the natural in the city: "I have / a great empathy for pigeons after two months / at work in the unnatural country" (1) The title of the book may also be in dialogue with Ted Berrigan's *Nothing for You*.

Just as Brenda Hillman has her lichen and Lorri Jackson had her regenerative rats, Anselm's pigeons become an avatar for the how-nature-comes-to-us-in-the-city undersong in this book. I feel great solidarity and sympathy when he speaks of the sh*t he gets for "attempting to separate nature from naming," for I, too, have resisted looking up the names of birds and trees on the web in the belief that somehow naming them would corrupt the experience. And, in the city, nature may assert itself in ways no less mysterious than it does for the non-urban nature poet:

> the signs
> for the washing of hands instill
> a thickening resentment towards
> dirt's absence as we navigate
> the gaps between moments of
> silence ("Lengthening Arches," 39)

Similarly, in "Compatibility Modes," he addresses the accusation that some body-nature-discourse referential essentialists may hurl, that of forgetting "I have a body." Instead Berrigan suggests that true embodiment—in language—is more likely to be achieved by imagining

> an
> utterly alien
> eros by listening
> for possible methods
> of extraterrestrial sex (79)

Embodiment, and/or so-called self-care, is also a foregrounded theme weaving in and out of "Chases Dirt" (which I first read as "Chassis Dirt"), to comic effect: "All dem leettle pressurs make you give yourself too many corrosive gifts" (81). Against these toxic pressures, Anselm's poetry can be a medicine, and his ethos has earned the right to give advice: "When the pressure's on, fuck—read the space / To add room to a weakness" (81).

Many of these poems propose relational ethical binaries. "To A Copy" is the first of many poems addressed to an unspecified "you" (demi-othering), who is probably also a writer, and one accused of being an

> emblem
> of ideas with
> a capital I, you
> nowhere in sight, ceaselessly
> referred to as missing (3)

As such, this poem is both a defense of the so-called impersonal, abstract modes, as well as a respectful acknowledgement of the speaker's difference, or divergence, from them, like the feeling one gets after losing oneself in someone's book that shook you out of a habitual comfort zone, and a feeling of "but it's not me" begins to flow back in....

The title may raise questions of influence & borrowing & stealing, but only if we understand a world in which

> everyone who dies
> before I'm born
> keeps being influenced by me. ("New Note," 22)

Although Berrigan—with "3 and a half jobs" (42)—could easily qualify as what Alissa Quart refers to as the "precariat," and there are certainly moments of what she'd term "hysterical surrealism" in this book, and it would be a mistake to call it "apolitical," this book does not generally go after the more visible socio-economic-political atrocities. In "Lengthening Arches" Berrigan writes,

> but I can't help think these
> times infected by a deeper
> meanness than savagery. (39)

He lashes out more against what makes him *want* to lash out at his oppressors (and in the process sink to their level):

> This negativity has to stop shopping itself
> around I only only hold cruelty against the vast
> Nonbody grinding bodies into numbers (49).

He does not reduce his poetic investigations to anything as rigid as a position or stance. A strong sense of conscience and personal responsibility emerges as he does his best to avoid any accusation of special pleading:

> Afternoon come over & sit down forever tell
> me all the ways in silence we don't exploit
> our traumas together I'm a father not a leak (45)

I admire this book's audacity to aspire to the old New York School dictum about doing one's best to "refuse the right to exist" of contemporary zeitgeist global news atrocities (as well as exploitation in the workplace). If you must, you could invoke that overused Brecht quote (his biggest American hit, aside from "Mack the Knife" & "Whiskey Bar") about dancing in the dark times. In "The Parliament of Reality," Berrigan writes:

Loitering is a primary talent reframed
as needed between coming tensions: I don't want
the references, I want to be irritated & freaked out
uneven in the fur, away from live wave domains, pushed
up hard against this or that delicately figured
boulder, a sprained delicacy absorbing biogenetic
prepositions masked as populated frequency
the illusion of daily non-acknowledgement   (9)

This is music to my ears, and eyes. Call it escapist if you must, but it can be a pledge of allegiance to the powers of poetry to save us from the occupational hazard of the adjunct critical thinking mind, and/or the reactive/ reactionary mind strongly encouraged by Facebook, et al:

timing's ability to withhold
statements designed to
provoke reinforcement
I neither trust nor need (23)

"Tilebreaker" is another poem in which the speaker's persona-self unfolds in relation to an oppressive force, one who prefers to "bring fist down / to table," as opposed to through "the absolute mystery / of composition" Berrigan prefers. (6) In terms of the culture wars, you could say the poem navigates the space between so-called low culture (or is it youth culture?) like the Polvo song "Tilebreaker" the poem's title references, or Superchunk's record *On the Mouth,* and so-called high culture like John Ashbery's poem "The New Spirit." It creates "something tran- / sistant" (6), beyond "Complanation" (a portmanteau of complaint and explanation?). I especially love the phrase "joyfully conjures / embarrassment," which could describe the dominant feeling I get reading this book.

By contrast, "Precision Auto" (15-16) phrases the dualistic conflict in terms of art versus money, and how easily the corruptions of professionalism can be Trojan-horsed into even the most resolute artistic purist, a stance Anselm beautifully mocks in "Life Without Rondo" ("I'm implying / for jobs by writing you," 35). "Creative Response" takes on the theme of professionalism and flattery getting in the way of the creative life, especially if your job requires you to write recommendation letters. Why not write a recommendation poem for the pigeon?

Berrigan's theatrical willingness to let his speaker be as mean as he can be (like the "safety valve" theory of catharsis) is evident in quite a few of these poems ("and make my evil labors clear," 19; "Expect to be killed by otherwise / docile poets when they get inside / the etcetera zone," 30), and, just as O'Hara preferred the poem to the phone call, for Anselm poems often come best when one refuses a social engagement so as better to engage: "O Pierre! We should have come over for the midnight omelette, but do you know how hard it is to be alive and not steal the state mace with a mutating bag" (22). In a lighter vein, "I Felt Like An Amputated Leg" is a fascinating eight-page short-lined fast-moving lyric character description/portrait of a dandy or *fanfaron*.

Reading many of these poems, I feel that, yes, I, too, often come to poetry to be irritated and freaked out, and for the meanness that used to be called "poetic license" or at least "tough love." Like the conscience-scouring poems of John Yau, whose name is coincidentally mentioned in this book, Anselm's mastery of the accusatory mode can charm a social justice warrior out of taking themselves too seriously, as he recuses himself from feeling "like a / condescendant's / objectivity" (33) or "unsleeping / Munchkins demanding adult brooding" (50) to embrace the difficult work of so-called frivolity.

On rare occasion, this leads Berrigan to seem to cynically portray anti-Trump protesters like Wallace Stevens does in "The Revolutionists stop for orangeade":

Eventually the climate overpowers
Inaugural sentiment, breaking
All comers into lists of pursed O's
Melting down over candy
("Complementary Noteboke" 77)

Yet it also could explain why Anselm loves writing poems with elementary school children, in which political sentiment is shown to be compatible with play, as in "Poem For Los Angeles," written with Sylvie Berrigan:

Pigeon going around the garbage
Thinking about flags in the sky
Moving and thinking about being flags
And eating the pigeons all up! (17)

I'd be remiss if I didn't quote some of the quieter (less irritated, if not necessarily less freaked out) moments in this book, like: "I like to be entered / by worry" (59), and "phrasings, crosswalk-like / pauses, so we don't get hit" (52).

I like the strategic way Anselm brings pauses into the book's most ambitious poem, "Asheville," which begins as a long-lined maximalist tight dense unpunctuated knot flow, seeming to struggle with the pressures of decommodifying, self-loathing, or at least performance anxiety. I feel I've entered into a terrain where Beckett's "I can't go on; I'll go on" and "Fail Better!" (which

Berrigan mentions in the book's final poem) would not be unwelcome guest-hosts. I can't deny a perverse pleasure I get from being dragged through the agitated onslaught for three stanzas, before space enters:

> Again is always something
> I respond to arrangements (84)

One can picture a non-dualistic back and forth between the lyric voice that enacts silences and blank spaces, and the discursive, more skeptical voice that demonstrates how even the word "silence" can end up adding to noise. On the one hand, there's long lined music like:

…in exact detail I do not remember most of my
education but all of the feeling
all the endlessly fucking slow layering of every minute
micro-jolt accreting there's
not much about money to tell you don't already contain
in your bulby knowledge
shell the boundaries of boredom I found myself nodding
against a grain…."(84)

What kind of music is this? Fast? Propulsive? Pounding? Noise rock? Dance Music? The heightened ambivalence of the sublime mode (feeling) appearing as embrace in more guttural, Germanic, crunchy-consonant heavy everyday quotidian vocabulary as if to release negative energy stuck in some words?

I wonder how many different emotional tones and speeds Anselm performs it in. What kind of sheet music is this?

On the other hand, do the shorter-lined sections imply they're read more slowly, imply more weighted words, in dialogue with the longer-lines? For example:

the distance between

    those two positions

        is a little immeasurable

            but I miss the absence of the person

              who filled the absence of

        another person—I miss

          the second person

           & that missing sucks to say…(86)

By page, 88, the differences between the maximal discursive and the minimal lyric create a kind of mesh, to keep himself from reducing his vision to zeitgeist voice and genre eyes by including many meta-morals:

the projection of luck onto others a ghastly utopia so
says a bold divergence nudge
an American reveal a cop decked out in a complaint to
avoid thus fate we must." (85)

with laconic emphasis a turning point witnessed
avoiding masses in my habits" (80")

all I ever wanted will be ceaseless vibrations warding off
resentment behind the plain layers view." (90).

MARY DACORRO
TECHNICOLOR FIRING SQUAD
(2018, SELF-PUBLISHED)

Mary Dacorro's new manuscript *TFS* (for Technicolor Firing Squad) uses a range of poetic strategies to critique as if from outside, but also to speak from within, the seedy belly of the beast of the Military/Infotainment complex and the sinister, often subliminal, role it plays in identity formation. The personal and the political come together in Dacorro's edgy poetry; in contrast to most official psychological theories of human development that place an over-emphasis on the family romance, Dacorro understands and emphasizes the foundational role that immersion in various electronic babysitters from infancy has on our psyche.

The poems "Techno-pop Desires" and "Techno-tramp Disorder" forcefully confront the beast unleashed by 21st century mass-culture addiction in a perfect (combustible) blend of suffering and satire. Her wry, sidewise glance is as at home in the absurdity of electronic mass-pop culture as at a strip-club, or in an abstract emotional (American) city-scape, as in the sharp imagistic juxtapositions of "Metropolis":

> Twin towers that tremble into dust
> Fossil-fuel   apple-pie slush
> Endless freeways   ant-like cars
> Stupefied blow-out sales….

> Stadiums as far as the eye can see
> Slaughter-houses   slave-labor tenements
> Up elevators   up city halls
> Up shady and forgotten stories….
>
> Crass commercials curl the grass
> Along the concrete wasteland

On the other hand, *TFS* also contains sadder, more empathetic elegies, or eulogies, for the casualties of this culture and victims of hate crimes, whether LGBT ("Dear Fabian"), Palestinians ("Gaza Blood") or fallen soldiers ("Coming Home," "Memorial Day," "Collateral"). "Static" is the kind of beautiful "weary song" that comes out of the doom felt by many as we helplessly witness our towns becoming displaced by gentrification. Dacorro also gives herself permission to grandstand or scream in poems such as "Star Spangled Diatribe" and "Maga's Demented Fallacy." Yet, ultimately, Dacorro is able to scratch out an alternative to the unnatural and inhumane "American way of life,"—now revealed as

> Bio-gangersterism profit bound
> Sterling opportunities mimicking designs
> And energy of Nature.

Although Dacorro is well aware of the risk that writing about these terrors could make things worse ("This is what happens / When body politics / invade my solitude," there's still a sense of an alternative that is tenacious enough not to be fully drowned:

> Why can't we have a conversation—
> With the prairies and the forests
> From hubris to human
> Run business like a redwood ("Quagmire")

And, in this sense, the quieter poems that may seem slighter on first reading, like "Sleep" and "Incessant," gain more traction as a testament to her poetic faith. Ultimately, there's an exuberance and buoyancy (as well as piercing wit and humor) in this collection, with its vow to "dwell from dawn to gloom / in the atmosphere of human thought," ending with a powerful ode to "The Power of Books," and their "magnetic lure." And while many books are surely as toxic as a technicolor firing squad ("the lies of white history"), the book ends with a beautiful book-dance:

> Metaphors cross over like bridges,
> Syllables vibrate like pendulum oscillates.
> Up and down the musical scales,
> Black hole's terrifying pull, nightmares of $E=mc2$
> As the lightning pause before thunder explodes.
> As a fly to a spider, as a moth braves the flame.
> As bees obey, suck the sugary nectar.
> Like a spark tended by embers,

Power and wrench curiosity's questions
Like diamond blade cuts illiterate thinking
Suddenly open close-minded views

DANEZ SMITH
[INSERT] BOY
(YESYES BOOKS, 2014)

I was hooked by Danez Smith the first time I read him: "I come to you out of ink, of breath, of patience, & almost emptied of any belief that there is anything in this country that doesn't seek to end me, keep me and my black & brown loved ones from *living lives that are not designed around your comfort and benefit,*" he wrote in "Open Letter To White Poets,"[11] an impassioned plea to white writers to speak to other whites that he *"cannot reach because what I make is degraded… for its label of black art."*

Indeed, as long as white poets are trained in a world of segregated anthologies, canons and reading lists that will include the L=A=N=G=U=A=G=E poets but not the Black Arts Movement (except perhaps a Baraka that is 90% Le Roi Jones), as long as these institutions are not changed (and not with the tokenism of a minority scholarship for a talented 1/10th), this will remain the case, even if the mere fact that I became aware of him through a piece called "Open Letter To White Poets" may be seen as evidence of Smith's crossover success.

When I hear more whites in public poetry gatherings at least *entertain* the possibility that the Black Art tradition in America may even be superior to the white one, I'll think otherwise. In the meantime, I have the pleasure

---

11   https://empathyeducates.org/Journeys-to-and-through/open-letter-to-white-poets-from-danez-smith/

and privilege of being acquainted with Smith's debut, *[INSERT] BOY*, a powerful collection that is not primarily addressed to a white audience—nor need it be, despite the ghosts of Louis Simpson's dictum that "poetry should not be recognizably black" that still haunt the ivory tower (even as one of my black students told me that she wants to learn to "write more white like Danez Smith" before she had seen him perform). He's got more important things to do than to worry about his "white audience" or the "white reader," though that doesn't mean whites aren't invited if you can let yourself be put on trial at least as much as you are putting black folks on trial without even knowing it.

Smith's appeal to white poets may also be his appeal to straight and cis-gendered people of any race. And, because he's a poor, black & gay social realist (with a nod to James Baldwin), he can't escape bringing up identity politics along the way in his journey to piecing together an identity and a community from the fragments of the gerrymandered roles he's inherited. This community is not a republic of outsiders, though even the media will subliminally place them there. These are voices that America needs to hear loud and clear. It's hard not to trust the speaker(s) that emerge in this book, in part because Smith acknowledges his own failings. The book is a coming-of-age story and spiritual quest as much as a seething commentary on the catastrophe effected by the disease of contemporary racism and white supremacy. It works through these various lenses, and thus needs to be read more than once.

The book's six sections are mainly structured around different social roles Smith has played, often under compulsion. There's the public-political, yet lyrically subtle, poems he writes from the voice of a black boy or man that frame the book; the personal, lyric, universal tone in the poems spoken as a grandson of abused and abusive elders in section 2; the graphic, even lurid, disquieting symbiosis of personal and political in his first-person telling of teen prostitution in section 4; and the more mature and self-respecting attitude of the man who has "learned what love is / not" in the book's penultimate poems.

In *The Rumpus*' interview with Tyler Gillespie,[12] Smith admits that his book is a "failed attempt" at sectioning off, at dissecting, the body into discrete parts—but says that this "failure" is precisely what allows this book the power to cast away false gods, and "speak to one self at a time." So when he speaks as the self of the confused teen male prostitute, he doesn't judge it from the perspective of the older and wiser and stronger man he becomes in the poem's concluding section, but he gives him "a chance to say whatever it is that [he] needed to say." Thus, anyone looking for an easy, formulaic resolution of one's queer identity with one's black identity (to say nothing of one's poor identity) in this book is bound to be disappointed, but Smith is after something more urgent.

In another interview with Rigoberto Gonzelez,[13] Smith

---

12 https://therumpus.net/2015/02/the-rumpus-interview-with-danez-smith/

13 https://www.bookcritics.org/author/rigoberto70aol-com/

writes that he neither wants himself "nor the reader to be able to separate the black boys from the black bois and gurls of the world...I didn't want the narrative of straight black males being murdered to be the only black narrative in the first and last sections of the book, and in many ways I failed. Writing these poems made me question when queerness or race showed up. When I'm pulled over by the police for unexplainable reasons, it's not because I am queer, at least not how I present my queerness. When I'm in bed with a black man, race is the farthest thing from mind. When I remember what America does to black bodies, it's everything amplified."

Again, this self-proclaimed failure reveals the heroic nature of the task, a matter of life or death, in a defensive world of "#AllLivesMatter" or racist whites in the queer community who claim "#QueerIsTheNewBlack" as if equality for blacks has been won. So, even though the queer or gay is implied in the unspoken adjective of the book's title (with its sexual double-entendre), it's no accident that the poems in which "black" is the adjective frame this book (as racism frames America).

In "The Black Boy and the Bullet," these perennial enemies, black boys and bullets, become each others' doppelgangers. This metaphor, in Danez's hands, is more striking than Emily Dickinson or 2pac Shakur's eroticized guns. Here's some of the similarities he finds:

> both spend their time trying to find someone
> to hold them bloodwarm & near

> both spark the same debate
> some folks want to protect them / some think we
> should just get rid
>   of the damn things all together (16)

The literary device of personification, or objective correlative, has long been used to objectify, *to thingify*, the black boy, and Smith's poem can help undo that destructive metaphor that America lives by in ways that address these bloody times more than the historical black is beautiful movement of 60s biopics can. Since then, thingification begat thuggification, as is seen in "Alternate Names for Black Boys" (17). In this piece, Smith provides a list of 17 epithets hurled by whites onto blacks (ranging from the blatant slur of "boy" to the "guilty until proven dead" black beast or stud of the corporate media) to the more subtle "poeticized" manifestations of bias ("phoenix who forgets to un-ash") that infest this culture like the air that can't be cleared by smogging a car.`

As Smith find himself dug in deeper and deeper into this hell, he tries to not lose a sense of divinity while being subject to an onslaught of false gods:

> white folks are afraid when you speak....
>
> where you see God: they see tin man
> made from prison bars
> gorilla trained to shoot (18)

In "For Black Boys," another poem relying on contrast, the "normal" life of complacency and apathy is implicitly white (if not exclusively):

> Sean Bell got filled with a war's worth of lead
> & the marriage rates went up
>
> Bo Morrison got killed with his hands up
> & people invested in garages (21)

More horrifically, beyond mere juxtaposition, we may also wonder whether the inflationary corruption of the housing market *was complicit in* Bo Morrison's murder.[14]

Throughout this collection, Smith struggles with and provides alternatives to so-called standards of black manhood. This theme is elaborated in the creation myth "Genesissy," a poem written as a tribute to two murdered black transwomen, which queers the Biblical creation myth as it presents Jesus showering compassion on those perjured and murdered by racists and homophobes. It also contrasts Jesus with a "God" who sounds more like the media and who creates the stereotype of the hard and hetero-normative black male. By contrast, Smith defends the "sissy" ("Ugly rumor begat truth / truth begat the need to pray or run," 25) as Charles Bernstein would

---

14 For a white person who acknowledges this, as well as her own "whitesplaining," see Contrapoints podcast to other whites, called "America: Still Racist" https://www.youtube.com/watch?v=GWwiUIVpmNY

defend the "girlie man." Yet, surveying the ruins of black America, and of America itself, leads him to a profound spiritual crisis as he asks a question many before him have struggled with: "such cruel injustice can't come from God, can it?" Smith leaves the question open, an open wound that can come out and show (us).

In "Healing: Attempt #2," the speaker's prayers are interrupted by the discovery that "most gods are just another man who demands my knees & I know where that commitment leads" (47). Smith digs deeper into the master-slave dynamic that passes for religion in "Healing Attempt #5." As he finds himself being paid to cum into the mouth of another black man he can't see, he asks with a deadly serious gallows humor,

> and what is worship without a song stopped up
> in the throat choking the choir blue boy?   What   is
> worship without an unseen God to bow to? and what kind
> of servant would I be   without prayer? (52))

This stunning elaboration of the God-as-lover metaphoric conceit continues in the book's most graphic section "Rent." In this section, racism in contemporary America is most graphically understood as a form of prostitution. The white man pays a black boy to gratify him sexually while at the same time calling him the "n" word. The black boy consents due to economic necessity and because he doesn't want to die: "is it worth it to stop this history / if you ain't gonna eat?" (57) The moral question of our times.

While this interaction is not exactly rape, in some ways it could be worse, just as the interracial power dynamics set in place after chattel slavery officially ended in 1865 can be even worse, like being "promoted" from *raped* to *prostituted*. Slavery was not merely analogous to rape, but literally involved rape, and the free market of Jim Crow and The New Jim Crow is not merely analogous to prostitution, but prostitution lies at its heart—however much we try to cover it up. Danez Smith refuses to cover it up; consequently, his book has the power to comfort the afflicted and afflict the comfortable.

The poem "Mail" is written in the voice of a "rent boy" writing with sweet vengeance to the white wife of the man who is paying for him. Yet even here, the white man, not the wife, gets the brunt of the boy's anger, and a kind of inter-racial solidarity emerges: *the white man played us both*. Smith is extremely effective at grounding the master-slave dynamics (or battered wife syndrome) of institutional racism ("a body on top of three-fifths of a body," 62) in the lived experiences of this particular occupation, but he could be talking about any other profession, including the entertainment industry.

The war between the true God and the fake (tin man) one that takes its name in vain appears again in "Craigslist Hook Ups" as the speaker comes damn close to letting these false gods make him forget the true god. The god he begs forgiveness from in this poem is gendered male, but in "Dancing (in bed) With White Men (with dreads)," the god is female. After encountering all these false male gods" it is the invocation of a woman that liberates him, as Smith milks the sublime pun in Audre Lorde's name for all its worth:

Audre, the master's tools brought my house down.
I begged him with my own hands. I've been floorboards, wing nuts & slow blues at his pale hard feet....
I let him stay in my bed after he said race wasn't real.
(74)

Conjuring the spirit of Lorde gives him the speaker the strength to kick this white man (with dreads), and his post-racial lie, out of his bed. The speaker is still burdened with the double-consciousness of wanting—even needing—to speak as an individual, while also realizing that he will be read as a representative of his race, whether he embraces it or not—but Smith navigates it with amazing grace and tenderness. It is no accident that the next section contains some of 21st Century America's best love poems.

"Poem In Which One Black Man Holds Another" is a gentle antidote to the sequence that precedes it, as if he had to go through the sex worker hell to let himself deserve the deep spirituality of lovemaking herein evoked: "I am learning what loving a man is / not, that we don't have to end with blood. (89)

Here, speaking in solidarity with a community of other black gay poets, Smith begins with a New Orleans-style funeral for the boy, a beautiful, creative funeral that may have the power to truly transcend this hell in the personal spiritual journey, restoring a collective identity. The public addresses of the final section bring this collectivity to the fore—not that the healing process is close to being finished.

"Song Of The Wreckage," which utilizes a variation on the sestina form with eight stanzas, invokes Baldwin again: "how much time do you want for your progress?" "I am sick of running from the fire / this time." (93) As a public poet, Smith excels in the high oratory of these questions:

How many black boys stolen in the hot night?
From their own homes? From their own bodies?
How many black boys until we make history
finally let us in on the joke? How little progress
before it's not progress? How much prayer & song

must we stuff our mouths with before we lose
our taste for empty? (93-4)

In what broken home was America raised?....
If I play dead, will I be acting my age? (101)

Smith revisits the book's central themes of religion and music in some of this collection's most poignant anger:

Let me slow down this funeral funk song
the notes are all fucked up in my head. I mean a boy was
shot

someone stopped the music, raised a glass, toasted progress,
how the trees no longer bloom with sons, but the night
being a black thing is all I can guarantee of history" (95)

Smith's attitude toward music—especially rhythmic music—is complex, as he's aware of its association with blacks in America: "Sometimes all I need is music; other times fuck your song / What is your blues juxtaposed to the black & ruby-wet of night?" (101) He is aware of how music has been used as a soporific and appeasement strategy (as Malcolm claimed SCLC did), or to create minstrels to sing the corporate war song ("What kind of jam should we play? What song / gets the apocalypse jumpin'?" 107). Deeply aware of the cultural rape that is the Western (American) songification of black art, and reification of black spirituality ("How could we be only a song?" 111), still he sings:

Let them build a black boy's world. Rhythm to replace time
water free of the bloodshed, peaches were there was once fire
watch the boy gods care for the dark child they raised
from nothingness, how it started black—and by black
(108)

In the process, the poem offers a contemporary rewrite of James Weldon Johnson's "Lift Ev'ry Voice & Sing" for these bloody times. Instead of "let us march on till victory is won," we have "let them cypher until their song is the new sun" (108), and a potent prayer: "Pray the boys / sing, with chaos all around, & finally have a chance to be normal." (107). By the end, he's cleared a way for a world in which black men can say,

> I am not your enemy
>
> not poison, not deadly sin, not hungry for blood
>
> nor trying to trick you

to each other and mean it. Bonding on blackness (with no white middleman pimp), beyond sex into brotherhood, Smith offers a benediction in a world of malediction: "Bless the body that strikes fear in pale police." Smith brilliantly unites the rhetoric of the #BlackLivesMatter movement with the diction of old school black preachers. When he adds that he's seen "god in the saltiest part of men," (112) it may strike a Whitmanian note (it reminds me of Chris Nealon's "salinity" in *The Shore*). But it goes deeper, as it extends its primary solidarity with the black man to a wider love and identification with other oppressed people and non-human nature:

Do you know what it means to be that beautiful & still hunted

      & still alive? Who knows the story but the elephants & the trees?

Who says the grace of a black man in motion is
not perfect

As a tusk in the sun or a single leaf taking its
sweet time to the ground? (112)

From "boy" to "man," this book becomes a ritual—or
record of a ritual—of becoming a man. It's a special book
that cuts through the white noise of American culture.
And Smith's weapons are sharp and warm and shouldn't
be reduced to weapons. It speaks to a contemporary
reality in a way one doesn't need to be a poetic specialist
to appreciate. "It feels like common sense to feel a need
to be active & vocal in individual & communal ways if I
have any desire to see a more liberated way of living for
my kin and fellow folks."[15]

---

15   http://bookcritics.org/blog/archive/small-press-spotlight-danez-smith).

ALLI WARREN
LITTLE HILL
(CITY LIGHTS, 2020)

Warren took the title to "Moveable C" from Ornette Coleman, who, at the age of 14, "developed a lifelong suspicion of the rules of Western harmony" when he learned a piano's C is an alto saxophone's A. By contrast, Coleman, a practitioner of what's been called free-jazz, believes everyone has (and by implication should be allowed to practice) their own "moveable C." For a poem that takes its title from a musical term, it rarely— if ever—uses diction about music, but for those who work in words, this concept may suggest why two people could say the same exact words but mean something entirely different, or why one person's swimming may be another's sinking like a stone, or how the meaning of the word 'spring' changes from one climate to the next, etc.— as if moveable C suggests tone, moods, connotations, more than denotations (which sound too much like detonations).

In Alli Warren's book, a linguistic skepticism—or call it a healthy sense of the absurd—is often present towards everyday practical uses of language ("What of its slippages"—15), especially when considering abstract words like the present (since "the present is a tradition"… ,"I study the past to denaturalize the present," 11), or the expressions of love we post-boomer babies of mass culture were razed on:

Does "I will always love you" necessarily imply
imminent
abandonment?

To change things by changing their names?

To produce numbers and so produce norms? (11)

Coleman's quote may also shed light on Warren's imminent critique of capitalism, and how the "exchange values" and "accelerating clogs" (9) of our always already mercantile language get into our labor body in "office time." When granted an ostensibly autonomous sliver of free time—much of which is spent trying to shake off the soul-draining dynamics of the workplace in tender measures of nature reverence and hope, it's so easy to get sucked back in by an atrocious manifestation of injustice. Yet, even in the most despairing reportage, Warren is able to seem much calmer in her vacillations than my characterization makes it sound, as the presence of the spaces between the lines allow her to best effect a de-acceleration. It is partially because she does not underestimate a world in which "everything organized to deliver force on a routine basis" (16) that she is able to suggest alternatives to it...

In a blurb Alice Notley points out that Warren's "principal method is articulation of exquisite units of speech (thought) that, maintaining separation, are capable of connection…." Her lines at times seem to borrow as much from the 21st century form of discrete tweet or facebook status report ("Mandatory self-reporting is optional but strongly encouraged" 35) as they do the one-liners of stand-up comedy (or, at times, what Maxine Chernoff would call, "stand up tragedy") or a meta-koan. A useful comparison can also be made with Chris Nealon's *The Shore (Wave Books, 2020)*.

Through a conversational tone, and the illusion of polyvocal interior monologue, the speaker becomes more present to me than a more transparent one would. With an ear for condensed imaginative leaps ("drug-store talisman, pop-up dust bowl" 11), Warren can figure a cellphone in your pocket as "hibernating rust" (9) and puts the macro in the micro in language that seems like the name of edgy college rock bands.

Although one doesn't have to look for a forward moving narrative, on a thematic level at least, her artful use of spaces between lines—as both bridge and wall—become ever present as one reads and rereads her imagining possible connections beyond an implied vicious circle or narrative of decay. It's almost like what's unsaid between the lines is asking us: "does it really matter what the author thinks about the statements she presents? But can they be scaffolding for your thoughts and feelings today?" I like the way it makes me self-conscious of the reading process (and just because the spaces between lines *look* the same length doesn't mean they last the same length).

For instance, what do we make of a question like:

"Who is permitted unhindered breath?" coming as it does after a passage straight out of The New Jim Crow on racial profiling: "Orders are phrased as questions and compliance interpreted as consent" (15). Could we read it as ordering us to breathe as unhinderedly as possible? Or what do you make of the seemingly obvious contradiction between "there is a possible future in a tender measure" (13) and "demand a future equal to polemic" (14), as if she's clearly preferring the former and satirizing the latter. We could spend at least an hour tracing the lines of how she got there on the way to "some better measure might be underwater." (18)

It's also difficult for me not to draw a line between her admission of "self-disgust" (10) and her powerfully acerbic critique of the "everyday violence vigorously and unequally enforced" (12) by "self-satisfied men" ("He thinks we share a world, and my horror to the extent that we do" 12-13). If that's an either/or choice, bring on the self-disgust!

By contrast, on page 14 Warren writes:

the dead, electively present, conduit for all
the both/and meadow—beautiful and bleeding (14)

Is this attitude towards, or relationship with, the dead, an adequate opposite to the violence-inducing fear of death? Or is it the kind of necromancy that runs away from life and love? Is it still a refusal to let the mystery be? Or is the alliterative beautiful bleeding both/and meadow but fragile cover of the everyday violence of the cruel self-satisfied? Sometimes, it's difficult to read her tone, but I do not say this as a criticism. I read a line like, "My responsibility is to others first and from this I come to myself," (16) and say "Yes! That self-abnegating interdependence is good thing, right?" But then on page 18, I read:

The disorder? Global

Self-diagnosis? Nearsighted

    Since "the body clock rings in line with office time" (18), the conflict between economy and ecology
    becomes analogous to that between the performative self ("one's dress, demeanor, movement
        through public space, tone of voice, companions,"17) and body ("the bones remember, gather
        round the legible bones..."17) In this sense, the poem occupies and negotiates the contentious *eco*
        space between *onomy* and *ology*, ego v. eco, consciousness & behavior:

The function vs. the particular one who embodies this function. (18)

    This quote near the end of this 11-page poem reminds me of a passage near the end of the second 8 page poem, "Visual Letter"—

Strolling around like a subject

Speaking about a who as though it were a what (28)

Perhaps this is meant to be a portrait of a dehumanizing character, but seeing a "who" as a "what" could also be liberating to a person who says "I am a depressed person" rather than "I am suffering depression."

In the end, there's no resolve between the opposing impulses or voices, but what she does offer—"as gift more than condemnation" (as Notley puts it) is even better; an evocation of the "whale's heft" and a "hope we can be buoyant in the break, I hope we can be forked." (19) The word "break" itself has ambiguous and/or ambivalent connotations: it could suggest being broken ("the crippling caving/Unintentional day of silence," 11) is a condition for buoyancy, the unspeakable horrors of an un-representable present, the radical uncertainty of death. On the other hand, it could be time off from work, the death of capitalism, or a purely descriptive musical term when the issue of "movable C" is moot because the melodic instruments aren't playing, or is it working? Finally, this break could be the space between her lines, liminal between being self-contained and being capable of connection while brilliantly, buoyantly and generously taking the con out of context. (And who, or what is the fork if not a tuning fork?)

I love this little pocket-book book; buy it. Get your library to buy it...if they ever open again....

CIRCUITS OF R/ELATION:
A CONVERSATION WITH ADEENA KARASICK
ABOUT MASSAGING THE MEDIUM:
SEVEN PECHAKUCHAS (IGS, 2022)

Hi Adeena Karasick:
   When listening to songs, sometimes I feel the lyrics so deeply that I forget that if it weren't for the voice of the singer and the other less, uh, logocentric elements of the song, they wouldn't have had that power. I get a similar feeling a about your "fracturing of language and image" in *Massaging the Medium,* and how it "asks the receiver to not only think about the subject matter but to negotiate the multiplicitous modes of information when conflictual communication models are at play; how and in what ways is the media massaging the message as it hits various emotional, psychological and cognitive registers at once" (2).

So, after spending a few weeks slowly reading it, with an emphasis on the medium of language, its rhetoric, vision and performative meta-play, lately I've gotten into carrying it around with me when I'm taking a break from other books or student papers, to focus more on the construction of the images, to relish the color combinations and wide variety of images, the surprising juxtapositions and aporia they create or allow, but also the ways they seem to comment on the text at least as much as the text comments on them.

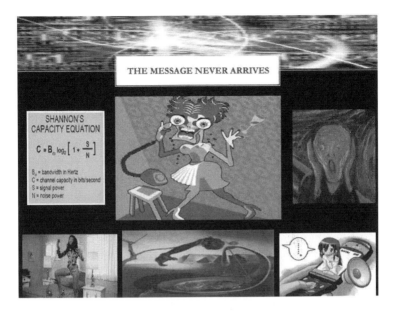

While the text in this meme (in Section 4 of the first pechakucha) can be taken as kind of title, or summary, of the text above: The Message Never Arrives (editing out the word "fully"), the seven (yes, 7!) images in the visual create their own media ecology like a visual poem.

Although one of these images is a yellow backdrop with black text on it, a mathematical equation whose "message" certainly eludes me, elsewhere a feeling of a spectral blue feels dominant against the black background. It appears in every image: the central cartoon of a pink female figure (apparently from the mid 20th century), the two distorted filtered classic European 20th century paintings, the scream motif that appears also in the last section of the pechakucha) seems to be introduced, and Flip Wilson as Geraldine circa 1970 (I'm guessing).

Blue even appears in the final image (if we read from left to right, top to bottom). This image is a 21st century cartoon image that seems to admit an anime girl crawling out of a flip top cell phone, like the first fish who flopped on land and grew legs. I see the fingers of the hand of her "user" or "creator" holding the phone. There is also some sort of electric megaphone speaker device overlaying the phone on the right side, but nobody seems to be talking on it. On the left side, there is a bidirectional dialogue balloon, in which apparently the anime girl and the unseen mouth presumably connected to the fingers of the user are talking—but there are no words in this dialogue balloon except a series of bullets with no bullet points, markers with no content. Furthermore, the anime girl is facing in the opposite direction from the dialogue box, as if trying to get away from her user. In the text above the meme you write, "The telephone is prosthetic and foregrounds the amputative present." I feel this image also is a powerful way to challenge the metaphysics of presence, as well as other themes throughout the book.

So, just using page 15 as a starting point, my questions for you now are: Many of these images seem to be found images, but many are massaged? Did you create some of the images? Do you devote much research to finding the right images to go with the text? or do you often find the images first before you wrote the text? Did the images go through the process of revision?

Hello Chris Stroffolino,

First let me say how i feel so blessed to have such a close and attentive reader—and it's hit you on so many levels, 'n especially rapt with the color palette, the intra-chromatic coding, as it were, which itself, another discourse; the resonance of textural modes, models, memes...even the recurrence of 7's which appear and re-appear; a *septenaria* of intermediatic textaticism, ha! So, where even to start, (in this amputative present of our dialogia ;)

Diving into this new form was such an investigative journey– First, as long as i can remember, i've been so keyed into both the visual and acoustic aspects of language, and get so much pleasure in highlighting its physical and material qualities. And so, with this project, extending this physicality / visuality through both representational and nonrepresentational images / references / textures, was a kinda thrilling exercise. It's not that the medium relies "even *more* on the visual," but thinking about how the [medium *is* the message] or [form an *extension* of content], or even Bernstein's "an extension of an extension," for me the visuals here offer another strand of the conversation—where together they become a verbo-visual convergence of multi-sensoric stimuli.

So, just using page 15 as a starting point, yeah, many of the images are indeed found, collected over time, but all massaged to various degrees, re sized colored and collaged, over-dubbed with various modes of defamiliarization. As you know, i'm so drawn to the "verfredungs-ty" feel of mashing up something cartoonish or animated or full of high gloss and juxtaposing it against the Shannon Weaver model of communication, on top of a video still of Beyoncé and Lady Gaga's "Telephone," mashed up with a Dalí painting reworked with a melting telephone in it, or asking the viewer to revisit Munch's "Scream" in light of the frustration of how meaning never "arrives." It makes me think back to my 2000 [book], *Dyssemia Sleaze*, (which Maria Damon also wrote about), and how obsessed even then almost 20 years ago i was with the concept of "dyssemia" referring to how information goes out but never reaches its destination. As a kind of centerpiece, that book *also* features a hybrid collage essay exploring how the Wall (The Western Wall in Jerusalem) is structured like a language—punctuated by a wild and subversive range of visual/ comic and destabilizing infusions—an early precursor i suppose, to this project.

So, you ask, in *this* book—did i devote much research to finding the right images to go with the text? Absolutely! I would write the text first, and then obsess over various ways to represent it. It was all created on old-school Powerpoint. Typically, i would focus on the language, the concepts and then just start collecting images from the web, from photographs i've taken, vispo videos i've created, from shards, scraps, fragments amassed over the years—and often very late at night, using a very lateral / paradigmatic process of play, of addition, subtraction, excess and engagement, focus on the variant ways i wanted a particular section of text to be represented. And yes, it would go through an infinitely circulatory process of revision as i routinely would finish one and then in light of what was created next, i'd go back and back and back, adding and layering and re-collaging.

One other consideration was, i was aiming for a very delicate balance of not wanting to be too literal, but yet giving enough information—due to the fact they were originally created for live performance; for audiences that were not necessar[il]y our typical academic literary crowd, but, geared for media ecology and General Semantics communities. And, as they were "live," the original visuals *were* moving, filled with film clips, GIFs and overlays, sonic montages, so it was quite an adventure to re-create that complexity and translate it to the page.

In many ways, the images themselves tell their own story. In a kinda Derridean *destinerrance*, all nomadic and vagrant, the visuals themselves announce themselves as a kind of polyoptically-based diasporic poetics that provides another narrative / n'errative. And like how a meme—a unit of cultural energy that virally replicates itself, ina kinda contagion, themes infect themes, icons, colors, codes repeat / re-produce, travelling, unravelling with and against and through each *slide*, all slippery, salient and speaking aslant—creating a s[y]mb[ol]iosis of verbio-visual space.

Hi Adeena—

I absolutely believe you succeeded in your "aiming for a very delicate balance of not wanting to be too literal, but yet giving enough information." I love when you say "in many ways, the images tell their own story" (and one, I'd say, that transcends any story anyone could make of them, yet I try coz it's kinda more fun than tweeting and texting). I feel it's a very social book. Not being able to see you perform in "real time," as your performance reverberates within and through an audience like a post-performance party, I guess my urge is more for a reading group to meet in a living room and look at the book and the images and shift roles from art-critic to social critic to standing up and intoning your words, as I listen and play piano, as my overly rigid mind enacts reductive meanings I make out of a few fe(s)tishized images...in n'errative fashion!

Anyhoo, I screwed up, and mistook the image of Beyoncé as Flip Wilson as Geraldine (images attached), which probably tells you more about my biases towards mid-20th century popular culture, and theoretical orientations I bring to my reading of the phonocentric pechakucha (I wonder how a 20-year-old may feel/think about these images of 20th century phones).

Thanks for reminding me that these are "*slides*, all slippery, salient and speaking aslant"; it makes me aware of the physicality, the tactility, of the slides I was "razed" with, little physical white squares with translucent images on/in them,—and the process of translation to an often larger than life screen as these pages, coming from the primacy of perceptual performance that—as Steve Hicks puts it—"transplants" the audio to the visual or "more specifically collapses the boundaries between," while managing to avoid etiolated forms of ocularcentrism. Since you mention that "the original images were moving," I definitely experienced a few of the stills actually moving, as the text moves through perspectives in interstitional trans-narrative time, I am curious if you'd want to say more about how the seemingly more static slides on the page in the phonocentric pechakucha moved in the "real time" performance. Was the text above the slide also projected on a screen, or read aloud? Did *you* actually present each slide in performance for only 20 seconds?

Hello Chris—

Oh man! First, let me just say i love how you say "it's a very social book...in interstitionally trans-narrative time"—and as such am so living [sic] the image of you playing the piano at this imagined post-performance after party as we negotiate light, relationality, meaning and being. So let me just take my imagined martini 'n say—yes! in performance each "slide" was programmed for only 20 seconds and i dare say it took a lot of practice! In early stages of composition, the text was so much longer, so it was a good exercise in condensation—which i actually loved [because the] maximalist aesthetic [created] a diminutization of words. Yet this constriction or compression of ideas made way for a sense of infinite expansion (as it opened itself to further connections, references).

The text itself was *not* projected but read aloud—though often at the speed of which it was read, it could have been helpful ;). But it seemed redundant and also posed the problem of where to look—at the images? at me? at the text?—and i didn't want (as you so eloquently alluded to)—to "fetishize the ocularcentrism of the text."

And in regard to your curiosity about the seemingly "more static" images on the screen, they rarely were "static"—as in almost every case, each micro element featured some form of animation—whether encased within a trance-y psychedelic gif or using a variety of design effects as they grew, shrunk, dissolved, spun, appearing and disappearing. Sadly, that's not evident in looking at it on the printed page—however it highlights how (between oral and textual performance), one is never a transcription of the other—that the textual surface offers so many other nuances, micro-connections, temporal and spatial negotiations and complexities otherwise not evident in a rapid-fire 20 second "live" carnivalesque presentation; or in the words of McLuhan, a hot medium—that engages the full sensorium.

Hi Adeena –

"Engages the full sensorium!" That's such a great way of putting it…the "outside inside" the book…but back to my scripted questions!

Although many of the images or memes you include in your slides are of 20th century phones, the written part of the text tends to focus primarily on the 21st century phone. At first, the text focuses primarily in the arena of what the 21st century phone and its various calls have done to us, how it has changed us; how it's "become a site of toxic addiction" (17) and is "increasingly dividing us" (33). Yet, unlike some other contemporary media studies and cultural philosophers I've read (say Byung Chul-Han in *Psychopolitics*), you do not emphasize a *feeling* of alienation from the medium; the text does not cast a relentless pounding feel of some theoretical prose, but, lined as poetry, becomes more effective because of the *jouissance*, a weaving of spirits and/or theoretical affective specialized orientations to evoke more liberating possibilities in the midst of this dystopian systemic psychopolitics.

In section 9 (page 20) you write about how using the disembodied voice phone medium of texting can actually kick "some age old Western teleological binaric distinction / to the curb". The images that "adorn" (Steve Hicks' word) this written text bring us back to a mid-20th century dualism (that is still predominant in certain circles) in somewhat stark, clear, contrasts. The 7 (but kind of 8) phones that take up the bulk of the space in this slide are all 20th century phones. 4 are black and white, two are color (I'm bracketing the midcentury human figures here). In the smaller bar above, there are the covers of 6 Derrida books, and 7 other books whose title is too small to make out (in performance, were they more visible?). In this visual, Grammatology and orality become highly segregated, and rigidly specialized, in contrast to what the "text" says. These juxtapositions can create a generative space of inquiry.

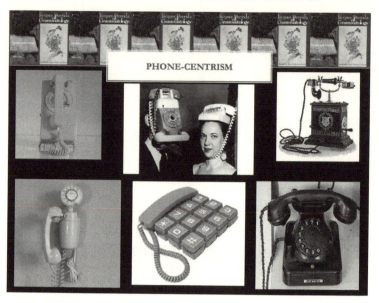

At first, I feel a voice telling me the 21st century medium can be a liberatory way out of such teleological binaries, but on remisreadings I acknowledge admiringly your *agency* in this section (this is first section in which the active "I" appears as subject), as if it is not "the medium itself" that does this, but the way(s) we (as media) respond to its call, call to its response...

Hello Chris –

Yeah, i wanted to explore from a historical perspective, how the telephone was originally perceived and how *now,* it's simultaneously a site of utility, amusement and complication — and thus erupts (as you so eloquently put it), as "a generative space of inquiry." Something i address both textually *and* imagistically and thus, the range of representations throughout the ages—visually highlighting ways that yes, the telephone's amazing and useful and a source of infinite connection and information *but yet*, contributing to ways we're all drowning in a sense of ersatz significance, that thwarts our ability to focus, analyze, filter, or synthesize information, short circuits thinking, often renders us "context blind," without patience (or ability) to sift through complex issues, and has become a site of toxic addiction.

CS: Yes! Yes!

AK: So, yeah, i was focused on how we got here — *and* embracing the telephone as a conflictual arena — highlighting how though (traditionally) grammatology and orality were segregated / seemingly oppositionary, the telephone as a medium in fact embodies the dissolution of this dichotomy; acts as a physical manifestation of subverting teleological binaries.

And also, i was so interested in dialing deep into the medialogical effects—highlighting how yes, it's a communicative vessel, but yet inundates, saturates us with a kinda technomediatic overload through not only the sheer excess of info, a scrambling of relations—and as such, though meant for communication, reminds us how the "message" never fully arrives (ie that you can't express "tone" in texting etc; how, there's *always* "noise" in the system); reminds us that no matter how tribally connected we think we are, social media is increasingly dividing us. All to say, the telephone is great, yes, a locus in many ways of absolute jouissance, but also so incredibly problematic and disturbing—not to mention the ways it's dumbing us down, changing our grammatical habits, contributing to memory loss; a source of anxiety, distraction, screws with our circadian rhythms ... So that's why there are representations of phones throughout the centuries (both 20th and 21st— some B/W, some in color, one say, on p. 12 a composite of both)—in one way harkening back to a more simpler time juxtaposed against what the telephone today represents. And also, *ahem* ;) i was just totally attracted to the kitchiness of some of them ;) And as such loooove some of the new Flip Wilson/Geraldine memes you brought to my attention.

And as you so aptly noted, it is in this section that the I is capitalized for the first time — graphematically embodying that sense of the enlarged subject—re-born from the snapchatty / tiktokin' meta twittering of narcissistic amplification—speaking to how (as you put it)—it's not "the medium itself" that does this but the way(s) we respond to its call or (in the words of Blondie) "call[s] me".

CS: I like the way you reframe my use of the word "agency," which may too much appeal to the rhetoric of a metaphysics of presence, as an "enlarged subject—reborn...from narcissistic amplification."

AK: And, oh yes, lastly, the books featured in this section included Derrida's *On Touching: Jean Luc Nancy,* Stephen Kerns' *The Culture of Time and Space 1880-*

1918, who reminds us that the telephone enables us to "be in [multiple] places at the same time," Derrida's *Of Grammatology* with the implicit pun of PHONEcentrism and Walter Ong's *Orality and Literacy*—which though in the book are not hugely readable, were definitely visible in performance as were projected on giant screens.

Hi Adeena –

Steve Hicks calls the first pechakucha a "back history of the telephone," but it is not a linear one. When I get to the final section (page 33), with its rising emotionally wrought rhetoric, as if musically building to an emphatic conclusion and a kind of cathartic affective release of tension (theatrically reading aloud to myself the alliteration can be fun), the last words are "*screaming* to be heard." If it is the phone that is "screaming to be heard," is the phone thus personified as needy?

Hi Chris –

Well, with all its algorhythmic amplification, i think, yeah, the phone *is* kinda needy, where not only are we via all our social media platforms *screaming* to be heard, but the phone itself, buzzing n vibrating and full of alerts and notifications, insistently ringing, pulsing, tracking us. Don't you feel your phone; with you, in your pocket, against your face, your legs, your chest? We sleep with our phones, eat with our phones. Our phones are alive with the sound of music ha! We take them on trips, on subways, planes and trains, they are extensions of our cars, our bodies. We physically attach them to ourselves by way of earphones. They *need* to be recharged. *Need* to be needed. And we speak into them and they (perhaps in the voice of Siri or Alexa) speak to us. Perhaps maybe needy isn't the best word but desirous. The phone is a desirous being in an ever-state of becoming, *de-sire. Siri. hmmm...*

Hi Adeena —

I think it's the first time the *word* "scream" has been used, as pathos enters the text that had generally been more tonally detached, investigative and informative before. The *image* of the scream had been used before, but the *text* spoke primarily of a "call." The image of the scream reappears here, an always already theatrical(ized) mannered scream in the upper right-hand corner, but there are three other images

In the upper lefthand corner, I see a mid-20th century business man, whose facial expression, loosened tie and slumpy jacketless shirt looks haggard, weary, worried, overstimulated by the act of trying to take four 4 calls at once, in a kind of horror that may not exactly be a scream. He's only holding one phone, but there are two next to his ear. The 2 other phones are either being held by off stage actors or props people, or in mid-air by their own volition

This image, in your text, "repeats/re-produces," through "travelling, and unravelling" a similar unit of cultural energy I felt in the first (titular) page of this phonocentric pechakucha (page 11). Placed in the upper-left hand corner (where the textual eye is trained to start?), I see a mid 20th century woman also with 4 phone receivers. She seems to be using her body to "take" these calls more than the man in the last image, holding 3 of them, and using her ear, shoulder and chin to hold one of them. Her classy shirt and facial expression also starkly contrasts; head tilted (partially to hold the phone), eyebrows raised, with a sidewise glance and an open mouth that looks anything but haggard and overstimulated (like the male on page 33). Her attitude seems more comic. Furthermore, she seems to have more, uh, agency, as one receiver is intentionally held *away* from her ear. I could read all kinds of drama into it; for instance, are the other 4 talking "behind this 5th caller's back"?

Another similar contrast occurs between the first and the last slide. In the first slide, which is mostly in monochrome, as to further the suggest[ion that] the text promises a historical narrative that moves from the past to the (multicolored pixelated) present, the only image of 21st century phones seems to occur as a palimpsested footnote, at the bottom and behind and almost *crushed* by the weight of the other, older, images: a pile of cellphones huddled and re-tribalized as it were; though a few seem turned on, I feel this as a "cellphone graveyard" and could get into the narrative of 21st global waste and environmental destruction of conspicuous consumption, or mortality.

The feeling of "cellphone graveyard," however mistaken, in both the title slide and the final section, affectively informs my reading, and could be read in terms of your post-Benjaminian *ruminations* on the relationship between past and "the present we walk backward into; a present / (which is also a gift)" and "the present is always re-presented in a messy prescience" (16) throughout this pechakucha, as well as the more elaborated critique of the metaphysics of presence more foregrounded in other pechakuchas in your book. Though the image is somewhat similar in the last section, and still the *only* image made up of 21st century phones, it is now foregrounded a little more at the top of the slide, and in color, alive with blue (again).

But most of the space taken up by this ensemble of images in the final slide emphasizes an ensemble of 4 or 5 (postmanic?) choreographed ballerinas on stage in what could be an outdoor theater at night (in the round, or at least a galaxy spiral); each have outstretched arms holding 5 midcentury 20th century phone receivers.

The dancers' gestures are an archetype of gracefulness, as it were, or statue of liberties with Bernaysian "torches of freedom" (phone as cigarette). The phones have no connecting wires, no base where the dials or keypad or ringer is, mobilized, dynamic, but impotent phones. If the phone is a prosthesis that amputates the present, the way this image amputates the phone could give the "present" back its legs and arms, a proprioceptively receivable calisthenic ensemble of heart healthy aerobics massaging the medium, a giving that could remediate the Husserlian now as the now of music! (jazz, Teruah!)—or is the black night of the sky merely a painted backdrop, "trending images on galaxy walls"?

In this, I can see this final slide as presenting (enacting) different *responses* to the call of the phone, call through the phone, the call *before* (and after) the phone (Teruah!) from a whisper or scream. Mortality comes "into play," (but) "permutated with the tetragrammaton" (to quote from a later piece). Since these ballerinas, like the cellphone graveyard, are an ensemble, are they more "retribalized" than the mid-century individuals in the upper left-hand and right hand corner? Does division retribalize us? Was this written before the increased pandemic web-dependency of "social distancing"?

Hello Chris –

Omigosh let me just say again what a pleasure it is to have such a close reader; all that you see, the connections you're weaving. And wo! before i answer, let me just say i love how you, like the phone itself connect the unconnectable calling into and across all the chapters, and (at the moment) struck with your musing of "is the black night of the sky merely a painted backdrop"—so deeply Benjaminian—making me think even the ringing of the telephone (the pounding insistence of its repetition IS always already a reproduction)...

Psyched with how you brilliantly connect the ballerinas of the final slide to the cellphone graveyard, seeing them both as an ensemble of sorts, raising the issue of tribalization. To address this, let me dial up ha! / re-call the recent Dean Fleischer Camp film, *Marcel The Shell With Shoes On*. In case you haven't seen it, it focuses on Marcel (a shell) and his mockumentarian, Dean, who are living in an airbnb. Marcel's family has been abducted, and Dean attempts to help Marcel by posting info online, endeavoring to digitally foster community—with the hope of finding Marcel's "abducted family." *But* what happens is, instead of actively helping Marcel in his quest, the mass of digital recipients narcissistically take [shell]fies outside his home — not so interested in mobilizing search parties, but garnering reactions on their social media platforms. Leading to an exasperated Marcel eventually blurting out "this is an audience NOT a community."

CS: Shell With Shoes! What a dynamic emblem of 21st Century Techno-Culture that has gone far beyond the pre-cellphone late 20th century *The Truman Show*.

AK: So, this is what i'm thinking, does being infinitely connected make us closer? Were we more tribally connected before? i dunno. Does division retribalize us? Well, it certainly helped during Covid when we were so alienated from each other (and when this was re-visioned for the book). But in a larger sense, to answer this, is to be able to define connection and division, which [is] itself an icky dichotomy because we are heteroglossic enunciative processes, our subjectivities and proclivities so fluid, in flux; our media, ever shifting; the info around us is ever-changing — and as you invoked my "Teruah," truth itself so very slippery and conflictual, so i'd have to say the phone facilitates this sense of us a retribalized "ensemble"—but maybe how like bpNichol says in *The Martyrolgy Book V*, "(every(all at(toge(forever)ther) once)thing," an ensemble of shifting symbols, of re-semblance, dissemblance — *a troubled tribal* :)) that's simultaneously trivial and *retrouvé* (recovered); all palimpsested and multiperspectival; in excess of its excess and become a nexus of synnexes, annexes, diexis, lexically sugared circuits of elation, colloccation, condensation and distortion, as we amble through this information maelstrom often with shifting allegiance and fidelity to an origin, politics, purpose or agenda; as "social actors." with our electronically shimmering communicative vessels of light.

Tr[i]bal tr[i]bal tr[i]bal since the day [she] was born ha!

CS: "Half-Breed" by Cher! Talk about a circulating

resonant meme! Do you have plans to perform any of these pechakuchas again?

AK: Well at the moment am recording the audio of one of them (the Korzybski / bissett) for an IGS Podcast; will perform a few of them at the launch scheduled at the swanky historic Player's Club (date TBA, stay tuned!), and also creating a kind of mashup of them to performed at the 24th Annual Media Ecology Convention in New York next June....

CS: Great! So...as a kind of Postmanic Postscript, you write, in the 5th Pechakucha: "Refracted Facts/ The Crazy Talk of *Checking In:* A Postmanic *Pata* Semantics," "All language is rhetorical rather than denotative and any emphatic statement carries within it a cultural, lexical and political history that reinforces, engenders, instigates, propagates a metaphysics of presence (i.e. the Husserlian "now"). And thus, it's crucial to continually contextualize, uncover the fabrication, analyze the violence that this initiates and sustains; seek out the hidden assumptions and reveal the inherent violence of this dichotomy, and not lose sight of the larger systems of subordination" (96, section 8).

I bring this emphatic statement "against" emphatic statements into play in this already long dialogue, as it could serve as a critique of some of the emphatic statements I've made in my little n'*erratives* of your images. Also, to acknowledge for the curious reader that the first pechakucha in *Massaging the Medium* that we've been focusing on is but one of 7, and that *Checking In,* the 5th section, emphasizes written language as a medium much more than it does the "cell,er,net" focus of earlier sections. I become aware of the careful placement of the ordering of the pechakuchas in *Massaging The Medium.* Is there anything you'd want to add about these int(er)(ra) textual juxtapositions on the macro-book level?

AK: First, let me just say, so fun how you gravitated to that particular phrase as it's just such a reminder of how (especially in the contemporary climate) that it's *so* important to try (as much as possible) to read things within a socio/historical/ethno/political context — and as we look backwards into the future, the present is always re-presenting…. With that said, in terms of looking back to the book's compositional makeup — after a seemingly infinite amount of shuffling and reshuffling, the text actually ended up being in chronological order — which not only uncannily seemed to thematically make the most sense, but secretly highlighted *to me* that forces beyond my control are navigating the work, ha! I like how though written within a 7 year span, the 7 pieces speak to and fold into each other in ever reverberant ways — ie how it starts with the telephone, calling into and across ways we communicate; moving through our imagination (always already an image'nation an emerge'nation); moving into a realm of how talking machines *seem* to be "mystical," but like language itself, actually refers to that which is "enigmatic," "obscure" (and sometimes) "logically inaccessible;" & how language itself *is* a machine — sentiments echoed through the pechakuchas on the poetics of bissett; Conceptualisms[s]; *Checking In*; *Salomé* — accentuating how all meaning making a kind of dance of desire "misce-en screaming in the polyglossic intertextual miasma."

CS: In Section 3 of *Checking In*, you write, "And, as the text tempts, tremors, terrorizes, teases, torments and titillates, we must learn how to loosen our grip" (91). That's very much how I feel after spending a month or so rereading the book. The image in the slide, perhaps, enacts this process. It is one of the images I had mentioned I felt, even on the page, was *moving*. First, I feel a macrocosm in the microcosm: Outer space in a web of blue and red capillaries. The woman seems to [be] gripping tightly, with both hands and feet, this web of capillaries (that also look like branches and twigs), like a circus rope dancer. No, wait, for dear life, as if afraid of falling into boundless time and space and end up like Bowie's Major Tom, but, on closer observation, and/or "after awhile," she doesn't seem to be clinging to these red & blue ropes, but more like a kind of swimming. Then I return to the text and read, "As Jack Kerouac might say, embrace its ripple," (liberating a madness of discourse where Fancy Bread rhymes with lead, etc)—okay... Thank You for your Teruah!

AK: Lol well re that quote, on page 91 about loosening

our grip, i was riffing on bill bissett's "text bites" (which actually appears on p.93 in the book), and just thinking through yes Meaning *can* be tyrannical — ie one *can* get locked into some limited context / "a metaphysics of presence" but i'm more interested in how we need not be trapped but traipse, trip through a trapeze-y cirque of carnivalesque dialogism where yes! we are suspended by threads / fabrications / interweavings; and it's always a dance of connection, disconnection, confection, predilection, webs of desire; as we (with loosened grip) ripple through pulsing space / time textatically moving through zones of resistance—experiencing the limit by touching it. And, yo, Sir Stroffolino, *thank you!* It's been my supreme pleasure — addressing / undressing all your probey swirls, re-marks, extensions. Who else gonna raise my Gaga to Major Tom, Cher...;

CS: And who else gonna raise McLuhan's *Medium Is The Massage* to Benjamin's "angel" with the phone's prose-ethic wings by invoking Hegel's "underground work of changing the ideological coordinates" as "technology exposes the real as a weaving of spirits" and make theory pataphorically crazy stoopid fun coz "truth is always already a point in space that contains all other points" (98)?

& who else gonna inspire me to play a dirge-like version of Blondie's "Call Me" & remember they also did "Hanging On The Telephone" as non-ocularcentric visions of mash-ups dance through stumbling finger-ear coordination before the arrival, in the ipod of memory, of Exene Cervenka's "Your Phone's Off The Hook (But You're Not)" &, as I gaze at the gaze your piano woman on page 51 through the unseen ears of the trumpet emoji on page 47 in the jazzination of my goyish shofar to ack(nowledge) or feel the spectral fluidity in the amputative present of your *gif* that could keep giving, who else could raise "forces beyond my control are navigating this work"?

Oh, and now that facebook is called Meta, as Google is called Alphabet (which I just thought they did so they'd be earlier in the alphabet than Amazon), I wonder what that does to the word "meta."

AK: metastasize? Ha!

Oh St. Stroff, what a treat to enter and journey with you through this extraordinary christoverse! :)))))
Rippling through and loosening our grip, touching each other through this spectral fluidity, reading your reading of me, i'm reminded how for Derrida, the whole notion of touch is characterized by an ontological in-betweenness, highlighting how no matter how close — one can never fully "be with." Or how for Thomas Aquinas "'touch' is not skin but the interplay of the senses" or for Walter Benjamin "touch is the optical unconscious," let me just thank you for this leave you with a "touch" of this uh Codette:

Touching in the Wake of the Virus

Between abstract impact contact tact
axes of attraction transaction infractions reactions
have you through the daring viscera apparati
apparition partition screaming *parties*
touched the improper inappropriate impropriotous
riotous
touched la cirque of skin sucked succour
swung scripts voiled squalls'
scalded s'écretes scandals contours entreés

For, what lets itself be touched touches its border
touches only a point, a limit, a surface;
as a tangent touches a line
without crossing it

SYNCHRONICITY:
THE ORACLE OF SUN MEDICINE
TUREEDA MIKELL
(NOMADIC PRESS, 2020)

It has often been said, "the teacher will come when the student's ready." In her debut collection *Synchronicity* (2020), Tureeda Mikell gives many examples of this process in her own life:

If I hadn't experienced migraines while studying
for three exams,
    looking for subject-connectedness in a circle,
reading a book
    given to me, titled Muntu, and find a quote that
read, "For the
    African, to disengage one subject from life's
circle would paralyze
    the rest," and have the migraines disappear
shortly thereafter, (155)

Sometimes a single line can have a force that comes like medicine. By evoking the ways in which standard English textbooks disengage the subject from a circle by making it an unmoved mover, Mikell also shows how sharing some words can make people feel less alone or less crazy, especially against culturally normative institutions that pathologize nature. Yet, as a healer, she also knows how deep these cultural institutions have their claws in us, even if we think we've escaped them once and for all, as if a pill can purge these demons.

Mikell's most salient critiques in her lyrical discursive poems (which at times straddle and at other times transcend the old page vs. stage distinction) are against normative institutions more than individuals: a spiritual realpolitik. As a word warrior who uses "wordplay as a weapon," as Judy Juanita writes in a blurb on the back cover, Mikell's struggle is often on the level of ideas and language and cosmologies, the metaphysical foundations of often-uninterrogated institutions, including The Big Food Industry/FDA/HMO pipeline, the church, the school, and the very governing principle of the English language itself, to name but a few manifestations of the diseased culture most of us are born into.

To see, to feel, evil as sickness, as Mikell does, shows tremendous empathy for victims under the systemic linguistic (manifestations of) regime that has done a number on so many of us. By "number on us" I mean cast a spell, even if it's a secular spell (commercial, electronic, etc.). Mikell, in this book, uses any means necessary to expose this spell in order to undo it to make room for deeper, more embodied, ones: "shattering myth with older myth," as Juanita writes.

Many of the poems involve a hilarious and savage critique of imperial Christianity that take up where Amiri Baraka's poems like "When We'll Worship Jesus," "Dope," and "Allah Mean Everything" left off, utilizing silly soulful puns and jokes so ridiculous they can make you cringe with awareness. For instance:

Why did the son of the sun worship with warship,
Prey on those who pray for peace,
Set sail for sale of piece with pair-of-dice for paradise.
("Spell's Labyrinths: Double Talk," 7)

Rhyme and reason come together—Mikell's no snob against nursery rhymes—but on a level of drabber discursive prose the wisdom here would take paragraphs to unpack. In lengthy pieces such as "Worship Warship" and "Questions for SS," she lyricizes rhetorical and oratorical devices as she interrogates the churchmen who mouth such sanctimonious pieties as "God is love" by syncretically juxtaposing the patriarchal church definition of love with both Aretha Franklin's and Tina Turner's anthems against the hypocrisy of the male use of the word:

What did you say, Churchman?
        God is love?!!
What love got to do with it?
Where the *respect* what we'd like to know! (37)

"Questions for SS" is an elaborate metaphysical/linguistic history of the character of "God" as revealed in the bible as reinterpreted by this Churchman. In her psychoanalysis, she convincingly characterizes this "God" as a bipolar narcissist and depressive megalomaniac, and asks such questions as:

Did you consider God a good model for your parents?
Did God sound like a loving god, or a bully? (96)

Did you feel an emotional disconnect from your soul?
Did you learn psych means soul/light in Latin?
Did SS break you from feeling your soul light?
Did your body feel less alive?
Did life become bleary or unclear?
Were you afraid to trust your insight? (97)

Yes, I say! As one "razed Catholic," I feel this is a better
and more embodied diagnosis of much American
pathology than Freudian psychology's emphasis on the
family romance. This portrait of "God" also shares much
in common with Mikell's dramatic monologue, written
in the voice of the corporate lobbyists and advertisers
who propagate America's unhealthy addictions to food
and drugs (whether legal or not) in "Devil's Advocate."
Such devils—such as Richard Berman of the Center for
Consumer Freedom, dubbed Dr. Evil by Rachel Maddow,
or the other *profits-over-people* engineers with their PhDs
in the manipulative psychic warfare known as "consumer
psychology"—may be very similar to that biblical junk food
devil Jesus tried to resist in his forty day cleanse fast. Yet,
even in this dark poem, Mikell hints at an alternative in the

spiritual psychics who say

our soul sends and receives
with electro-chemical impulses
that sense with intuitive release. (67)

Such intuitive releases abound throughout *Synchronicity* beyond the hell these God-devils make of the world, beyond beyond in the betweening, twining, twinning, the emptiness, or say the soul-sol, the serious fun of Isis trapped in a Greco-Roman dog-eat-dog-star world. One way to access this, as the book's subtitle announces, is through "sun medicine."

Not only is the sun medicinal on the most physical and visceral level, but also on the metaphysical level, as Mikell finds inspiration in a heliocentric tradition that first arrived, in English poetry at least, in Phillis Wheatley's vastly underrated "Thoughts on the Works of Providence" in the early 1770s.

For Mikell, there is a political dimension to sun worshipping. In her introduction, she writes, "Sun medicine is an antidote against oppression. It is an act of resistance!" In "My Sun," she offers prayer and devotion:

I will speak for you
Though scriptures mask
Your testimony from eyes (1)

These oppressive scriptures

Tell us

The rise of sun's daily light cannot compare
To god's son who died for our own sins and rose
From the dead who will return? (1)

In a world with "too many religious saviors, / too many competitive death plans," all the miracles attributed to a once-and-for-all Jesus, as Mikell alludes to in the phrase "[w]alk upon waters," are but etiolated versions of what we feel, directly in the activity of sunlight. And also, recalling Dickinson ("Some Keep the Sabbath"), Mikell writes, "I need not wait for your return" (2). In her celebration of the non-denominational sun, Mikell takes her place in the long line of wise healer women, a tradition that predates the specializations called poetry or religion.

For Mikell, beyond the Christian cartoon, "synchronistic occurrences stun the mind with recognition of a greater *collective* at work" (emphasis added). As Mikell writes in the introduction, "According to Carl Jung, synchronicity is an 'acausal connecting (togetherness) principle,'" but for Mikell it's also manifest intertextually.

The book's final poem, "If I Hadn't," is a list of synchronistic experiences the poet had through her life that not only allowed her to recognize a greater collective at work, but also shaped her character. Sometimes the juxtapositions between stanzas show how the same feeling can be experienced intertextually in different languages, vocabularies, or disciplines. For instance:

If I hadn't called and talked to a Zen Buddhist priest for

2

Hours, who assured me I was not going mad or crazy, nor had I
Committed a sin, but was merely entering my enlightenment,

If I hadn't commissioned my astrology chart to be calculated 5 times,
Aligning on earth as it is in heaven, as an active noun verb agreement system,

If I hadn't recognized, while studying organic and inorganic chemistry,
That iron is not only a common element found in the body but throughout
The universe, causing life to be pulled or repelled in some way" (156)

By the time I get to the end of the third stanza, I get a visceral feeling of a magnet(ism). Mikell's stanzaic juxtapositions between specialized disciplines (organic chemistry, Buddhism and astrology) enhances all three disciplines with an open-minded syncretic curiosity that finds common wisdom beyond our society's rigid specializations. And such healers can be found anywhere, including "those who the world has discarded" (156).

Some of the poems focus on how the language norm has either caused, or been used to justify, a disenfranchisement of people for possessing, or being possessed by, one form of "mental illness," or many. In a spirit akin to that of Emily Dickinson's "Much Madness is Divinest Sense," and Martin Luther King's call to form a National Association for the Advancement of the Maladjusted, Mikell quotes Elanor Longden: "Inner voices are a sane reaction to insane circumstances, not abhorrent forms of schizophrenia to be endured, but complex meaningful experiences to be explored."[16]

Beautifully empathetic poems like "Look At Her" and "Take Me Home Mama" show how western medicine, even if it were affordable, often makes problems or diseases worse, especially for poor black girls:

> Doctor's education lacking
> Neural ethnic mediation
> Does what he knows best
> Prescribes medication
> Yet,
> Forgets to mention drug
> Side effect could
> Make her see things
> That were not there (40)

This elegiac tragic poem gets worse from here. As against the mental hospital in which "Doctors make the conclusion / patients suffered delusion," Mikell, in "Eyes So Bright: Blues," is able to celebrate a man so diagnosed:

---

16   https://www.ted.com/talks/eleanor_longden_the_voices_in_my_head?language=en

But I felt in my heart
If he were in the land origin of his art,
He'd be a priest seer" (42)

Access to health care, life care, and healthy food is a
political issue, as the Black Panthers knew and know. A
recent documentary about Ruth Beckford, the Oakland
dancer and dance instructor who co-founded the Black
Panther free breakfast programs, reminds us that J. Edgar
Hoover considered the Black Panthers such a threat
to national security largely because of their survival
programs and not, contrary to popular belief, because of
their guns. In a similar vein, Mikell writes in "Life Light
Remembered" of her reminiscences of the Black Panthers
who "gave better care than Kaiser dared."

In 1994, 23 years after volunteering
At the George Jackson free health clinic,
The Tribune calls, asks:

How many guns did you have at the
Black Panther Clinic
I would have told them of certain grains
To regain genetic memory...
To reverse heroin dependence
Reverse curse of opioid addiction
Purposely placed in our neighborhoods
To weaken black power base (74–75)

That Mikell ends this poem by quoting, by chanting, Gil Scott Heron's "The Revolution Will Not Be Televised" highlights her contempt for this journalist's sensationalistic commodity questions in an attempt to get him (and the reader) to see beyond the media misrepresentation of the Black Panthers. You can televise the guns—if it bleeds it leads—but healthcare makes boring TV....

"It's On," another poem about the intersection between healthcare and politics, could be seen as a sequel to "Life Light Remembered" in that it recounts her racial reawakening not long after Clinton signed the Crime Bill. I imagine the speaker had been an activist at the intersection of healthcare and politics, but then as she got older, realized self-care was more important, in part because of the stress of the racial battles she fought when younger. Yet now, when a regal elder confronts her with white supremacists at least as bad as those she fought in her youth, she scoffs disrespectfully at the elder. Listening to herself respond dismissively to this news, "we've come a long way, haven't we?" (144) triggers a deeper racialized trauma inhabiting her body. In this intensely dramatic, play-by-play account, a confrontation with voices of urgency wakes her from sleep. She finds herself blindly reaching for a tape she hadn't remembered recording called *Neo-Nazi, the Rise*. This reawakens her memory to the collective voices of suffering of which she is part.

"I'm a synchronistic story junkie," Mikell writes in "Synchronicity and the Bird" (117). "It's On" is one example of a synchronistic story, and so is "Five-To-Six Hundred Years Old." In this poem, a spirit tells the first-person speaker: "What troubles you today has a past / five-to-six hundred years old" (64). Such a lesson strikes me as wise when applied to many situations in life these days, where it can break the spell of overinflated self-worries that can get us down. This historical emphasis can also undo the tyranny the contemporary present. Beyond its more universal applications, what makes this poem so powerful is its subtle critique of racism and sexism on an experiential level, even if it doesn't announce itself as being about race yet alone culture.

In the 21st century, 500 to 600 years ago would make up the bulk of the 15th century, the century that Portugal and Spain, for instance, helped get Europe out of the so-called dark ages by inaugurating the transatlantic slave trade with its forced immigration of black people, and its genocide of indigenous people in the new world. Those who survived the first onslaught now found themselves in a culture that did not respect their traditions, beliefs and manner of dress.

In the poem, the speaker, after noticing white people avoiding eye contact with her, wonders "Perhaps it's my African dress / Gele' head wrap?" (62) At this point in the poem, the speaker is visited by a spirit that tells her to go to Chinatown, ostensibly only for the food, but this could also be a proactive alternative way of acting on an impulse to get out of the constricting white neighborhood. In Chinatown, the merchant sells her food healthier than that she'd buy in the funeral that is a white supermarket. Equally importantly, in contrast to the suspicious glances, this merchant bows reverently to give her the food of respect (perhaps *because* of her African clothing?). Such everyday experiences of small positive blessings are searched for and found throughout *Synchronicity*.

In selectively quoting several excerpts, I underemphasize many deeper aspects of this multi-faceted collection, but whether Mikell is foregrounding religion, economy, health, education, or astrology, she relentlessly works on reconnecting the circle to a subject that had disengaged itself from it, a subject perhaps like a disembodied god. She effects such reconnection through the power of wordplay, including puns (for instance, the space between profits and prophets). In making room for anger, humor, sorrow, confession, confusion, curiosity, play, righteousness and tenderness, *Synchronicity* can help provide a foundation for a new, more empathetic and equitable society.

Synchronicities need not always be fortuitous in this collection ("the difference between a psychic and a sick psychic," 157), but when they are, there's a syncretic symbiosis or a synergy exceeding the sum of its parts that one can feel in one's body and psyche beyond the book's pages.

In his unpaginated foreword to the book, James P. Garrett writes, "We experience magic as she pulls us into the examination of critique of the meaning and mis-meaning of words and become a witness to the ways that she squeezes out and nourishes with her own juices the tiny bits of wonder they contain." Slowly, I feel this book is infusing me "with the courage to stand in the light of the sun and receive [my] oracle," even in a cold winter in America.

UNPARALYZING DISENGAGEMENT

"If I hadn't experienced migraines while studying for three
exams,
Looking for subject-connectedness within a circle, reading a book
Given to me, titled Muntu, and find a quote that read, "For the
African, to disengage the one subject from life's circle would
paralyze
the rest" and have the migraines disappear shortly after
    Tureeda Mikell, *Syncronicity* (155)

As he hammered his intellectual property lyrics
into a Peruvian folk song, Paul Simon sang
"I'd rather be a hammer than a nail." Migraine!

I once sang, "I'd rather be a wall than a hammer of a
nail." but really i(t) feels more real as a circle, a cycle,

aspiring spiralings, being many, seeming one—
underlapping ensembles of the social, the senses,
within us and without us, affinities more than influences

objecting objects circling subjecting subjugators circled
as stealer's wheels become healer's squeals
when winter feels like a wash machine in spin cycle
like life's circle is always a spiral when it's not vicious.

So, I get evangelically giddy when Tureeda Mikell
testifies to having found not only a diagnostic power
in the (grammar of that) sentence, circling (in) subjects
but, also, a healing global circulatory power!

So, when I write, "She reconnects the circle
to a subject that had disengaged itself from it,"
and you may ask "What is it?"

For me, I guess it's life's circle,
but should circle be used twice in a sentence?
Is it disrespectful to call life's circle an *it*?

And how do you read "looking for
"subject-connectedness within a circle?

2.

Intro Section 2

The essays in Section 2 are exercises in the art of close readings which academia encourages more than editors of poetry magazines looking for reviews of recently published books. In the piece on Tureeda Mikell which ended Section 1, I allude to Mikell's philosophical and spiritual affinities with Phillis Wheatley's "Thoughts on the Works of Providence." Yet many contemporary poets and academics are unfamiliar with this important, revolutionary, poem written 250 years ago, and may be pleasantly surprised by its brilliance and relevance to today's technocratic society (if you can get past the 18th Century diction).

In an era in which the American/English canon is more contested than it was 60 years ago, the need to (re)visit Wheatley as more than a token African-American slave poet is important for several reasons. First, "Thoughts on the Works of Providence," as a theodicy, allows us to understand sophisticated American poetry's beginnings long before Poe or Whitman or Dickinson. Secondly, it challenges the common misreading of her most famous poem, "On Being Brought from Africa to America" as a renunciation of the so-called pagan religion she knew as a child in Gambia before being abducted into allegedly superior Christian ways. Thirdly, for those interested in the legacy and influence of the British Romantics on contemporary poetry, looking closely at this poem, which some of the younger British Romantic poets had read, reveals what they took unacknowledged from Wheatley, as well as what they chose to ignore.

But aside from the canon/lineage wars, "Thoughts on the Works of Providence," also speaks to today's spiritual/religious/psychological crisis in ways that complement contemporaries like Mikell's *Sun Medicine* poems to stir a religious, even evangelical, fervor in me. Wheatley's poem combines both British/American philosophy with that of her native land in ways that, if heeded at the founding of this country, could have prevented much strife, and created more love. Its syncretism sets a standard that can provide a wider trans-historical and trans-cultural perspective. Its capaciousness craves further discussion, which I hope my modest attempt can help further.

In contrast to the essay on Wheatley's largely overlooked poem, the essay on Dickinson is a shorter essay on a much shorter poem. Brenda Hillman had sent me this Dickinson poem as a birthday present on the spring equinox in 2021. My essay was written as a birthday present to her in an attempt to respond in kind. I also engage notes from an unpublished lecture Hillman graciously let me quote from. I also converse with Susan Kornfield's discussion of the poem in this essay. I am always amazed by how many different ways Dickinson's poems can be read and felt and the generative qualities that lead for invigorating discussions, today, in the present, knowing that these poems can feel very differently in different moods.

Even though the essays on Wheatley and Dickinson bring in more dense academic vocabulary, these essays are intended to be a more conversationally impressionistic 'thinking through' the poems than academic strictures allow. Since both pieces are in the public domain, I include them both in full so you may read them apart from my commentary, which you may feel free to disagree with.

"THOUGHTS ON THE WORKS OF PROVIDENCE," PHILLIS WHEATLEY

ARISE, my soul, on wings enraptur'd, rise
To praise the monarch of the earth and skies,
Whose goodness and benificence appear
As round its centre moves the rolling year,
Or when the morning glows with rosy charms,
Or the sun slumbers in the ocean's arms:
Of light divine be a rich portion lent
To guide my soul, and favour my intend.
Celestial muse, my arduous flight sustain
And raise my mind to a seraphic strain!
Ador'd for ever be the God unseen,
Which round the sun revolves this vast machine,
Though to his eye its mass a point appears:
Ador'd the God that whirls surrounding spheres,
Which first ordain'd that mighty Sol should reign
The peerless monarch of th' ethereal train:
Of miles twice forty millions is his height,
And yet his radiance dazzles mortal sight
So far beneath — from him th' extended earth
Vigour derives, and ev'ry flow'ry birth:
Vast through her orb she moves with easy grace
Around her Phoebus in unbounded space;
True to her course th' impetuous storm derides,
Triumphant o'er the winds, and surging tides.

Almighty, in these wond'rous works of thine,
What Pow'r, what Wisdom, and what Goodness shine!
And are thy wonders, Lord, by men explor'd,
And yet creating glory unador'd!
Creation smiles in various beauty gay,
While day to night, and night succeeds to day:
That Wisdom, which attends Jehovah's ways,
Shines most conspicuous in the solar rays:
Without them, destitute of heat and light,
This world would be the reign of endless night:
In their excess how would our race complain,
Abhorring life! how hate its length'ned chain!
From air adust what num'rous ills would rise?
What dire contagion taint the burning skies?
What pestilential vapours, fraught with death,
Would rise, and overspread the lands beneath?
Hail, smiling morn, that from the orient main
Ascending dost adorn the heav'nly plain!
So rich, so various are thy beauteous dies,
That spread through all the circuit of the skies,
That, full of thee, my soul in rapture soars,
And thy great God, the cause of all adores.
O'er beings infinite his love extends,
His Wisdom rules them, and his Pow'r defends.
When tasks diurnal tire the human frame,
The spirits faint, and dim the vital flame,
Then too that ever active bounty shines,
Which not infinity of space confines.
The sable veil, that Night in silence draws,

Conceals effects, but shows th' Almighty Cause,
Night seals in sleep the wide creation fair,
And all is peaceful but the brow of care.
Again, gay Phoebus, as the day before,
Wakes ev'ry eye, but what shall wake no more;
Again the face of nature is renew'd,
Which still appears harmonious, fair, and good.
May grateful strains salute the smiling morn,
Before its beams the eastern hills adorn!
Shall day to day, and night to night conspire
To show the goodness of the Almighty Sire?
This mental voice shall man regardless hear,
And never, never raise the filial pray'r?
To-day, O hearken, nor your folly mourn
For time mispent, that never will return.
But see the sons of vegetation rise,
And spread their leafy banners to the skies.
All-wise Almighty Providence we trace
In trees, and plants, and all the flow'ry race;
As clear as in the nobler frame of man,
All lovely copies of the Maker's plan.
The pow'r the same that forms a ray of light,
That call d creation from eternal night.
"Let there be light," he said: from his profound
Old Chaos heard, and trembled at the sound:
Swift as the word, inspir'd by pow'r divine,
Behold the light around its Maker shine,
The first fair product of th' omnific God,
And now through all his works diffus'd abroad.

As reason's pow'rs by day our God disclose,
So we may trace him in the night's repose:
Say what is sleep? and dreams how passing strange!
When action ceases, and ideas range
Licentious and unbounded o'er the plains,
Where Fancy's queen in giddy triumph reigns.
Hear in soft strains the dreaming lover sigh
To a kind fair, or rave in jealousy;
On pleasure now, and now on vengeance bent,
The lab'ring passions struggle for a vent.
What pow'r, O man! thy reason then restores,
So long suspended in nocturnal hours?
What secret hand returns the mental train,
And gives improv'd thine active pow'rs again?
From thee, O man, what gratitude should rise!
And, when from balmy sleep thou op'st thine eyes,
Let thy first thoughts be praises to the skies.
How merciful our God who thus imparts
O'erflowing tides of joy to human hearts,
When wants and woes might be our righteous lot,
Our God forgetting, by our God forgot!
Among the mental pow'rs a question rose,
"What most the image of th' Eternal shows?"
When thus to Reason (so let Fancy rove)
Her great companion spoke immortal Love.
"Say, mighty pow'r, how long shall strife prevail,
"And with its murmurs load the whisp'ring gale?
"Refer the cause to Recollection's shrine,
"Who loud proclaims my origin divine,

"The cause whence heav'n and earth began to be,
"And is not man immortaliz'd by me?
"Reason let this most causeless strife subside."
Thus Love pronounc'd, and Reason thus reply'd.
"Thy birth, coelestial queen! 'tis mine to own,
"In thee resplendent is the Godhead shown;
"Thy words persuade, my soul enraptur'd feels
"Resistless beauty which thy smile reveals."
Ardent she spoke, and, kindling at her charms,
She clasp'd the blooming goddess in her arms.
Infinite Love where'er we turn our eyes
Appears: this ev'ry creature's wants supplies;
This most is heard in Nature's constant voice,
This makes the morn, and this the eve rejoice;
This bids the fost'ring rains and dews descend
To nourish all, to serve one gen'ral end,
The good of man: yet man ungrateful pays
But little homage, and but little praise.
To him, whose works arry'd with mercy shine,
What songs should rise, how constant, how divine!

PHILLIS WHEATLEY
"THOUGHTS ON THE WORKS OF PROVIDENCE"

Providence is the protective care of God or of nature as a spiritual power. A theodicy is the vindication of divine goodness and providence in view of the existence of evil, often appealed to against the backdrop of such questions as "if God is so good, why is there so much suffering, misery and injustice in the world?"

Even though Phillis Wheatley does not use the word "evil" in this 131-line poem apparently written when a teenager in 1772 or 1773, "Thoughts on the Works of Providence" is her theodicy, testifying to and celebrating a non-sectarian power and presence accessible to everyone, unmediated by man's institutions and inventions. I find it so convincing, even those of us trained in a highly secularized society and a church "Whose Words and Actions are so diametrically opposite,"[17] may be moved to encomiums of gratitude for the divine healing powers of nature (especially the sun).

Rooted in a need for a ritual to help her detox from the physical and moral sickness she sees around her as a slave in an alien land, the poem is also a subtle critique of the limits of reason. It starts at—or just before—dawn, with a 10-line invocation to the celestial muse to lend

---

17   1774 letter to Samuel Occom from Phillis Wheatley, quoted in Phillis Wheatley (1753–1784), An Introduction. John C. Shields. —This article was written under the auspices of a National Endowment for the Humanities Summer Seminar Grant. **Full Text:** COPYRIGHT 2001 Charles Scribner›s Sons, COPYRIGHT 2009 Gale, Cengage Learning.

a rich portion of "light divine….to guide my soul," and "raise my mind to a seraphic strain!" to sustain her in her "arduous flight."

Yet, immediately after she expresses this wish, the poem's tone and diction changes from rapture and an "I-thou" relationship with the divine "monarch of the earth and skies" to a less seraphic strain, in a detached scientific tone, describing the sun in the third person: "as round its center moves the rolling year." This center could either be the sun or the earth's axis; it could also be God:

Ador'd for ever be the God unseen,
Which round the sun revolves this vast machine,
Though to his eye its mass a point appears:
Ador'd the God that whirls surrounding spheres,
Which first ordain'd that mighty Sol should reign
The peerless monarch of th' ethereal train:
Lines 11-16

Before attempting to analyze these lines, I must acknowledge how Wheatley's high 18th century British diction stretches our mind in attempts to paraphrase it. Does she mean, the unseen God who revolves this machine around the sun even if we are insignificant in its eyes? Does "whirls surrounding spheres" suggest that, even if the then "new" science tells us that the earth really moves around the sun, on earth, it still *feels* like the sun is going around the earth?

In this blend of discourses, is she contrasting the "God unseen" with "the God that whirls" here? Can the rhetorical contrast between "Ador'd forever" in line 11 and "ador'd" in line 14 be translated, as if to say, "you all already know about the God unseen, but let me tell you about the god that *can* be seen"? The mention of machine suggests that the God in the first line is the 18th century British deist sense of God, the unmoved mover, who set a watch going, once upon a time, while the second figuration a more of a hierarchical law-giver.. It may seem that her attitude is more *both/and* than *either/or* here.

In lines 17 through 22, her praise of the sun employs the language of Enlightenment and the scientific revolution, but on closer reading may also subvert it:

Of miles twice forty millions is his height,
And yet his radiance dazzles mortal sight
So far beneath — from him th' extended earth
Vigour derives, and ev'ry flow'ry birth:
Vast through her orb she moves with easy grace
Around her Phoebus in unbounded space;
17-22

The vertical metaphor Wheatley uses to measure our distance from the sun implies that she's looking up— rather, than, say, a map of the solar system. In lines 21-22, there's a hint of an erotic, coequal relationship between the sun and the female gendered earth. It's the sun's role *on (in)* earth that's important. Wheatley's not, at this point in the poem, claiming that the latter view is necessarily better, although on the levels of phanopiea (image) and melopiea (music), feeling the cosmos this way inspires sensual and dazzling language that, like the earth, "moves with easy grace" more than the machine affords. This culminates in a return of a seraphic strain:

Almighty, in these wond'rous works of thine,
What Pow'r, what Wisdom, and what Goodness shine!
And are thy wonders, Lord, by men explor'd,
And yet creating glory unador'd!
(25-28)

The praise in the first couplet is quickly supplanted by what seems to be a question, even though she uses an evangelical exclamation point. Addressing the Almighty Lord directly as if to confide, she wonders about and laments men's lack of adoration, and devotion to the Almighty. If we read this contrast in terms of the debate between the language of the Scientific Revolution and the Puritan religious view raging around (and within) her, Wheatley seems clearly arguing against the deists.

The contrast between "explor'd" and "unador'd" could also have political significance in the context of European Imperialism, which Wheatley was all too well aware of, in which both Africa and America were "explor'd" for their "wonders," mined for their products. Wheatley suggests that had these men prayed to the sun more, and appreciated the present, a creation that we may partake in, every day, they may not have been so restless to explore (certainly folks in her native Gambia weren't trying to "explore" Europe).

Yet, her religious sensibility is hardly conventional. While many have used a unilateral metaphor, "God is (like) the sun," in which the sun, as "vehicle," is subordinate to the "tenor" of God, Wheatley does not simply invert it by saying "the sun is God," but rather finds a more bidirectional providence, by bringing the language of Christianity and the language of nature (and sun-worshipping) together, often in the classical pagan terms of Greco-Roman mythology.

That Wisdom, which attends Jehovah's ways,
Shines most conspicuous in the solar rays:
(31-32)

At the very least this suggests that if we want to know the wisdom and light of the unseen god, look at, feel, the light of the visible sun (or Sol, Apollo or Phoebus, as God of light, poetry, music and healing); trade your *contemptus mundi* for an *intellectus mundi*. It is not accidental that the word "soul" has "sol" in it.

After considering God and/as the sun as the source of vigour, goodness and benevolence, this theodicy now uses (in lines 33-40) a common strategy of Aristotelean logic, presenting an extreme thesis of a world with no sun, to an extreme antithesis of a world with too much sun. This allows her to find the wisdom in the erotic kinship of earth and sun in the perfect synthesis of moderation evidenced in the rolling year, and more specifically in diurnal cycles:

When tasks diurnal tire the human frame,
The spirits faint, and dim the vital flame,
Then too that ever active bounty shines,
Which not infinity of space confines.
(49-52)

One could read the first couplet as the slave's cry for freedom; if we had endless day, they'd probably make "our race" work even more. Yet, "that ever active bounty" is a force man can't rob or take away, however they try to mediate our relationship with it. More important is what it (or thou) does. Hailing the "smiling morn," (41), Wheatley writes:

And thy great God, the cause of all adores.
O'er beings infinite his love extends,
His Wisdom rules them, and his Pow'r defends.
(46-48)

She is not just referring to God here, but the smiling morn's God! Furthermore, this first mention of love in the poem suggests not only that God's love is infinite but the beings it's extended to are too.

Just as earth, the watery planet, can cool the unchecked heat of the sun, so does it (or she) give us night; the almighty's love and providence may also come in the form of sleep. In "Providence," she describes the power of sleep twice. Here's the first account:

The sable veil, that Night in silence draws,
Conceals effects, but shows th' Almighty Cause,
Night seals in sleep the wide creation fair,
And all is peaceful but the brow of care.
Again, gay Phoebus, as the day before,
Wakes ev'ry eye, but what shall wake no more;
Again the face of nature is renew'd,
Which still appears harmonious, fair, and good.
(53-60)

While the shorter "A Hymn to Evening," also invoked the healing nocturnal powers of sleep:

(Let placid slumbers sooth each weary mind,/At morn to wake more heav'nly, more refin'd;)[18], "Thoughts on the Works of Providence" replaces that poem's language of sin and virtue with the language of sickness and health. This praise of sleep could be especially radical, and subversive against the backdrop of a puritan work ethic in which wake up and smell the coffee was becoming the new imperialist national anthem, and even more for a slave who was called lazy if she "only" worked a 14 hour day.

Sadly, however, even the most peaceful dreams are not immune from "the brow of care." The matter-of-fact

---

18 Notice, she does not just say soothe, but sooth; one may remember that Apollo was also the god of prophecy.

acknowledgement that one could die at any second (58) is another motivation to praise for the 4th time in the poem (line 61-62). The way her theodicy is often punctuated by panegyric enactments by this point in the poem gives me an accumulated feeling that our praise and kindness may actually be a co-creative force in the divine cosmos as Wheatley figures it (more on this later).

The next extended passage starts with a provocative question:

Shall day to day, and night to night conspire
To show the goodness of the Almighty Sire?
This mental voice shall man regardless hear,
And never, never raise the filial pray'r?
(63-66)

Conspiring means to breath together; as in "Hymn to Evening," the sun is personified as "exhaling the incense of blooming spring" as it exhales our praises and prayers. This complementary relationship between night & day is a more Taoist (yin and yang) attitude towards holistic balance.

Her "filial prayer" offers a seductive invitation—80 years before Walt Whitman's loafing and inviting—to her congregation, to those she's trying to convert:[19]

---

19 Shields points out that the white preacher who baptized her Christian, Samuel Cooper,who held to no absolute theological principle but the right to free inquiry, was a rare white man who understood and appreciated Wheatley's "insistence on the equalizing results of conversion," as if Wheatley told him, thank you for converting me the your words so I may better convert you to the African spirit in a more tolerant, henotheistic way.

To-day, O hearken, nor your folly mourn
For time mispent, that never will return.
But see the sons of vegetation rise,
And spread their leafy banners to the skies.
All-wise Almighty Providence we trace
In trees, and plants, and all the flow'ry race;
As clear as in the nobler frame of man,
All lovely copies of the Maker's plan.
(67-74)

These beautiful personifications of the flow'ry race provide a respectful challenge to the "Great Chain of Being" metaphysics that dominated her time, a hierarchy in which man is more angelic, more angeleic than animals who are better than vegetation.

****

Echoing and contrasting with the earlier couplet:

That Wisdom, which attends Jehovah's ways,
Shines most conspicuous in the solar rays:
(31-32)

the next two lines:

The pow'r the same that forms a ray of light,
That call'd creation from eternal night.
(75-76)

provide a transition sentence, linking the "yet creating glory" of the daily rays of light in the present tense to a brief summary of a creation myth in the past-tense:

"Let there be light," he said: from his profound
Old Chaos heard, and trembled at the sound:
Swift as the word, inspir'd by pow'r divine,
Behold the light around its Maker shine,
The first fair product of th' omnific God,
And now through all his works diffus'd abroad.
(77-82)

How do you read the tone of this Creation Myth? I read it as a light that imposes order on chaos; an unmoved mover, swift as the logos; the word "product" recalls the earlier "wonders" (27) and "effects" (54). The capitalization, and personification, of Chaos suggests she is referring to the Greek Goddess Khaos, the first god, of the chasm of air.

Does gender come into play here, as if this creation myth is the dawn of the patriarchal gods? Notably, there is absolutely no sun. "Light" has become a symbol, a mere metaphor in a dark study, indoor church, or factory made by the Job Creator of capitalism. Certainly Emily Dickinson, who wrote "Some Keep the Sabbath" some 80 years later, would agree. Love, too, has entirely disappeared.

The next transitional couplet makes it clear she

intended this passage to be an account of the light of reason, or at least the way reason understands god, rather than God himself.

As reason's pow'rs by day our God disclose,
So we may trace him in the night's repose:
(83-84)

The him in the second line is presumably reason and not God, yet although the colon promises that what will follow is an account of night's repose, the following passage seems anything but. John C. Shields reads this passage as a description of sleep and asks, "Is fancy's queen here reason?" If it is, it's clearly a very lustful, unhappy, reason, and feels more like a nightmare, an extended phantasmagoria on what she earlier called "the brow of care"[20] (56):

Say what is sleep? and dreams how passing strange!
When action ceases, and ideas range
Licentious and unbounded o'er the plains,
Where Fancy's queen in giddy triumph reigns.
Hear in soft strains the dreaming lover sigh
To a kind fair, or rave in jealousy;
On pleasure now, and now on vengeance bent,
The lab'ring passions struggle for a vent.
(85-92)

The phrase "on pleasure now, and now on vengeance

_____
20

bent," recalls Shakespeare's lust sonnet" (129), as well as Harriet Jacobs character depiction of Dr. Flint in her *Incidents in the Life of a Slave Girl*. The last line of Shakespeare's lust sonnet suggests that the *hell* of lust may be caused by a too purely idealized sense of *heaven,* or, for Wheatley, the light of the enlightenment. It's tempting to say the earlier account of sleep was a slave's (more peaceful) sleep, while this account is the violence of a slave master.

While an earlier (53-74) 21-line passage showed the peaceful night waking to the filial prayer of day, conspiring together to show the goodness, in these lines the movement from light to night may perhaps conspire to show the evil, or at least the sickness, of the symbiotic relationship between night and reason's day in lines 75-82 And if the peaceful sleep in the first account revealed the almighty cause, the restless sleep of the second passage may be merely an effect of reason's God.

If, indeed, this passage is a description of reason's God in night, the flipside, as it were, of the light of lines 77-82, it could be read as a return of the repressed Chaos (78), who had been "vanquished" by reason's Light in day, as if in revenge against reason for making her tremble. If so, is it possible that Wheatley is subtly criticizing this idea of light as imposing order on chaos as a futile, self-defeating philosophy, and a sign of psychic violence and cosmic disharmony?

The fact that this restless description in lines 86-92 also contrasts with the earlier more peaceful account of sleep in lines 53-60 that engendered the beautiful panegyric daylight ritual of lines 67-74 would lend support to such claim. It's possible that these lines aren't even meant to be an account of sleep, but, rather, an insomniac, unable to stop the rushing onslaught of ideas and passions.

What pow'r, O man! thy reason then restores,
So long suspended in nocturnal hours?
What secret hand returns the mental train,
And gives improv'd thine active pow'rs again?
93-96

Reason, here, is not the power that restores, but the power that is being restored by a greater power. Her use of the word "balmy" is more in the achaic sense of foolish and eccentric, than today's primary usage as a pleasantly warm day (or it if's meant in the latter sense, it is meant ironically, as she earlier spoke of reason in "night's repose" ironically.

The questions here beget a gratitude spoken in evangelical terms to "O man!" (gender being as important as race and culture here) in the next passage:

From thee, O man, what gratitude should rise!
And, when from balmy sleep thou op'st thine eyes,
Let thy first thoughts be praises to the skies.
How merciful our God who thus imparts
O'erflowing tides of joy to human hearts,
When wants and woes might be our righteous lot,
Our God forgetting, by our God forgot!
(97-103)

This is the first time that mercy is mentioned in the poem, and a hedonistic mercy at that, and contrasts with the god that demands our suffering as signs of righteousness, the anhedonism of the puritan god demanding *contemptus mundi!*

In contrast to God as an unmoved mover, Wheatley invites us to consider devotion relationally; there is a mysterious symbiosis between mercy and gratitude (in French, *merci*) here. Does our gratitude cause the mercy? Does divine mercy cause our gratitude? Do we have the power to harm god? Is our gratitude *our* mercy? Is there any better way to think about our relationship with the divine or eternal powers over which we have no control? What way feels more free? Is nature telling us it's our duty to let ourselves feel overflowing joy?

Yet after all these wonderful feelings, the final couplet, with its negative contrast, reminds us of the very despair it is claiming to transcend, as a theodicy must acknowledge the negative to accentuate this positive. Our forgetting God makes God forget us. If the poem ended here, it would feel as tragic as the presence of "Winter" at the end of her "On Imagination." But there's two more sections: can they help our God remember?

***

Until this point, the poem had largely existed primarily in the sphere of ideas and feelings on a general, even universal, level of man and the divine, and not so much on a level of particular intra-human relationships in an everyday social setting, but the penultimate section of the poem seems, on first reading, to be such a dramatic break from what had been going thus far, as the (transhistorical) mental powers of love and reason, personified and theatricalized, take center stage:

Among the mental pow'rs a question rose,
"What most the image of th' Eternal shows?"
When thus to Reason (so let Fancy rove)
Her great companion spoke immortal Love.
"Say, mighty pow'r, how long shall strife prevail,
"And with its murmurs load the whisp'ring gale?
"Refer the cause to Recollection's shrine,
"Who loud proclaims my origin divine,
"The cause whence heav'n and earth began to be,
"And is not man immortaliz'd by me?
"Reason let this most causeless strife subside."
Thus Love pronounc'd, and Reason thus reply'd.
(104—115)

This allegorical dialogue between love and reason, both personified as women, can be taken as happening *within* Wheatley's personal psyche, as an interior psychomachia, perhaps analogous to the principles of justice v. mercy, the more autocratic vengeful Jehova of the Old Testament v. the more loving, merciful Jesus, or it could be read in gendered terms—even though reason here is also gendered female. The contrast could also be read on a genre-level: reason being more the province of prose philosophers and theologians, and love more the province of poetic license ("So let fancy rove!")

At the start of this dialogue, there's a clear imbalance between these powers. Love laments that there is a strife that reason has the power to end, and thus the power to cause. Reason has become a tyrant to (or forgot) love. When Love appeals to "Recollection," can such recollection heal the "forgetting" in line 103, or to show, or at least ask reason, did you reason away your love; did you not once love more than you reasoned"

Perhaps she's asking us to remember childhood innocence of playing (praying) out in the sun before adulthood came to chide this as childish or immature? Or perhaps, an earlier more spiritual time, of being connected to nature, now derided as primitive societies (whether seen in Africa or in the indigenous people being displaced), or, like the later Wordsworth (who may have read, and been influenced by Wheatley), recollect a pre-birth feeling of eternity. The way love talks about herself is very similar to the way Wheatley throughout this poem had personified the sun. This makes sense given that they began the debate by asking: *What most the image of th' Eternal shows?* And, it should be clear by now, that, on an image level, the answer is the sun. On the level of pathos and ethos, however, it is gratitude and mercy, acts of love!

This may be Wheatley reminding herself that love, ultimately, is more important than reason, or that reason is nothing unless grounded in love, or to take the highroad and meet others' hate with love. Obviously, she's very drawn to the temptations of the rhetoric of reason, which she's employed throughout the poem, but the fact that Wheatley has reason reply:

"Thy birth, coelestial queen! 'tis **mine to own**,
"In thee resplendent is the Godhead shown;
"Thy words persuade, my soul enraptur'd feels
"Resistless beauty which thy smile reveals."
Ardent she spoke, and, kindling at her charms,
She clasp'd the blooming goddess in her arms
(116-121, emphasis added)

suggests a very specific speaker and situation, that she is speaking to her human "owner," her mistress Susanna Wheatley, with the hope that if she herself—in her own struggles—can let love rule over reason's strife, perhaps she can convince her mistress. Earlier in this poem, reason's god had been presented as the unmoved mover. It makes sense that a slave-owner would worship (and see their reflection in) an unmoved mover, but, in this beautiful passage, reason is *moved* by love. The persuasive ability here is not to be found only in Love's words, but also in her smile. I can only wonder what went through Susanna Wheatley's mind when she read it.

The final 10 lines of the poem (122-131) conclude her theodicy:

179

Infinite Love where'er we turn our eyes
Appears: this ev'ry creature's wants supplies;
This most is heard in Nature's constant voice,
This makes the morn, and this the eve rejoice;
This bids the fost'ring rains and dews descend
To nourish all, to serve one gen'ral end,
The good of man: yet man ungrateful pays
But little homage, and but little praise.
To him, whose works arry'd with mercy shine,
What songs should rise, how constant, how divine!
(122-131)

To claim this poem had been talking/singing about infinite love the whole time requires a leap of faith in what is too derided, by reason, as the *pathetic fallacy,* the idea that non-human (and even non-animal) nature can love, but certainly such beliefs of a *filial* relationship with nature, a sense that we owe praise and gratitude to nature for showing mercy on us, or a sense that our praise and gratitude is a way of showing mercy to nature (and to ourselves), was not alien to the indigenous people of America, nor the ancient Greeks, nor the contemporaries in Wheatley's homeland.

Notice, here the absence of the word "God," as if she perhaps may finally convince her oppressors that you don't really need your "God, and Saviour too" to find the image that most shows the eternal. By contrast, this poem enacts what she prays for in "Hymn to Humanity:"

Each human heart aspire:
To act in beauties unconfin'd
Enlarge the close contracted mind,
And fill it with thy fire."

In offering an enlargement of the "close contracted mind" of the so-called Enlightenment by inviting us to feel the *or* in "God or Nature" as a more porous *and,* "Thoughts on the Works of Providence" is a fitting rebuke to those whose (mis)understanding of Wheatley mostly comes from her most anthologized piece which is often (mis)read as her renouncing the "pagan" religion of her childhood to adopt the Christianity of her masters and their preachers.

Rather, "Thoughts on The Work of Providence," establishes a syncretism that is ultimately grounded in a (transcultural) ethos of love, mercy and gratitude on both the mortal and immortal realms to achieve true freedom and filial equality. Without having to appeal to fire and brimstone and eternal damnation, Wheatley offers an evangelical, even proto-feminist, exhortation to, and a lament of, negligent, heretic man trapped in a overly laborious work-ethic as well as the age of reason to realize they too would be happier if they slowed down their strife causing ways.

In writing about her poem, "On Imagination," John C. Shields shows how Wheatley's thought "prefigures the Romantic movement" and that she "develops a theory of imagination, in 1773, that exceeds anything of the kind in the British Isles. Not the white man's religion, not his politics, and not even his poetics, as learned by this maturing poet, could answer her overwhelming need—to be free."[21] Yet, though Wheatley had a reputation amongst whites for being "uppity," does this poem seem uppity to you? Maybe it was just too subtle for first white audience.

Recently, my brilliant student Jocelyn Wallace writes that Wheatley was well aware that "she had a rare privilege for a slave at the time, and she had to be careful not to lose it. She had to be smart (about how she wrote), and maybe that's why she wrote more poetry and less prose in the first place. Poetry allows for more subjectivity, nuances, and individual interpretation." "Thoughts on The Work of Providence," operating largely in the cultural superstructure, is liberation poetics in its deepest sense of the word, and it seems to me that this message that went unheeded then is still unheeded by people with the power to put an end to much of the world's strife today.

---

21 Phillis Wheatley (1753–1784), An Introduction. John C. Shields. —This article was written under the auspices of a National Endowment for the Humanities Summer Seminar Grant. Full Text: COPYRIGHT 2001 Charles Scribner›s Sons, COPYRIGHT 2009 Gale, Cengage Learning.

VISITING EMILY DICKINSON
ON A SPRING EQUINOX

The Zeroes—taught us—Phosphorous—
We learned to like the Fire
By playing Glaciers—when a Boy—
And Tinder—guessed—by power
Of Opposite—to balance Odd—
If White—a Red—must be!
Paralysis—our Primer—dumb—
Unto Vitality!
   (#689)

Have you ever found yourself devoting hours to a single 8-line poem, and returning to it several days apart, and finding something new in it every time? For me, Emily Dickinson is one of the best poets of such inexhaustible mysteries. Her poems can suggest so many meanings that I find relevant to my own life, while still remaining mysterious. Take, for example, the dynamic phosphorescent sinuosity of the poem that starts:

The Zeroes—taught us—Phosphorous—
We learned to like the Fire
By playing Glaciers—

There is a detached, even scientific tone here, as she speaks in the plural past-tense about the learning process by linking zeroes to glaciers and phosphorous to fire.

At the time Dickinson wrote this poem Phosphorous matches were a cutting-edge state of the art technology. The volatile white phosphorous matches first sold in the late 1820s (barely preceding Dickinson's birth) and the less poisonous red safety matches were introduced in 1855. In this sense, we may take it as an ode to human ingenuity, and scientific progress made possible by the Arabic invention—or discovery—of the "zero." But such a materialist reading is not very helpful and overemphasizes the vehicle at the expense of the tenor.[22]

Yet, despite, or perhaps because of, this seemingly cold, detached tone, there is an implied sense of an emotional state prior to the occasion of the poem: a time when we didn't like (and maybe even feared) the fire, and tried to escape its intensity. Even the most rational scientific ways of putting describing characteristics of phosphorous are rife with anthropomorphisms or the pathetic fallacy of its volatility: "it's essential for life, but because it is highly reactive, phosphorous is never found as a free element on earth" (Wikipedia). Poetically, phosphorous, as light-bearer, is associated with both Venus and Lucifer). Is the moral here: Excessive cold makes us appreciate the fire we ran away from, come to terms with it, maybe temper it? Susan Kornfield reads it as "we learn to love

---

22 Thank you, Brenda Hillman for mentioning "Women workers in match factories were some of the most vulnerable workers in the 19th century. Handling the phosphorous caused loss of bone and crippling disability. Annie Besant, my favorite theosophist, advocated for the match girls at the end of the century. (notes from an unpublished lecture)

warm personalities after having been around their opposite.[23]" But these Zeroes can also suggest, as Brenda Hillman points out, "a spiritual state of nothingness," or emptiness: in this sense this poem, like so many of Dickinson's, can be seen as a defense, and enactment, of a *via negativa,* an apophatic kenosis, but not necessarily for the sake of renunciation or rejection *per se*, but a sense that excessive coldness (absolute zero) can become its own self-regulating cop.

The phrase "playing glaciers" sounds like the speaker(s) is in control here, faking the cold, playing dead, feigning indifference, perhaps, like it's a game, as if some formula or method can manage the madness of the fire (of extreme emotions). In this sense, it could be read as an ode to the necessity of (at the very least) a temporary repression, or a more Taoist acceptance of the natural complementarity of fire/ice, as Hillman also says: "fire and ice are presented not as dueling force, but as figures for a process of experiential learning." It seems fairly straightforward so far, but the poem gets stranger in the next 3 lines:

By playing Glaciers—when a Boy—
And Tinder—guessed—by power
Of Opposite—to balance Odd—   (3-5)

The rebellious or stuttering punctuation, diacritical long-strokes, and use of enjambment, create a tension

---

23   http://bloggingdickinson.blogspot.com/2012/07/zeroes-taught-us-phosphorous.html

between the line, the sentence, and the phrase that reveal and challenge how the meaning-making function wants to insert imagined periods and commas. Rife with push and pull, fragmenting, overlapping and underlapping, this poem almost demands a plethora of simultaneous interpretations. We could read a full stop, a period after the word "Boy" which would complete the idea implied that "Playing glaciers" is a childhood game, by paraphrasing "when" as "when we were boys," but since the speaker had been plural before, wouldn't this "boy" really be "boys?"

Gender seems to be important here; Hillman writes that the "Boy" represents her *animus*, and I wonder if Dickinson's saying that we, women (in the very patriarchal 19th century), have to pretend to think like a boy, and thus be cold as, say, *the glacier of reason,* which had been the tone the poem seemed to be speaking in in the first 3 lines. One may feel a need to be, or play, or harmonize, both.

We could also read the long stroke between "Glaciers" and "when a boy" as a comma or even a period. In this reading, there's a contrast between the "we" learning by playing Glaciers and the boy guessing, trying to figure us out: We (the girls) were playing glaciers, when suddenly a boy, and tinder…"[24]

---

24 Hillman, too, recognizes that "the sentence divides" here and that "tinder" can go grammatically either with the previous line, or 'to balance odd."

Furthermore, she also breaks the word "And" into at least two possible functions. We may wonder whether "Tinder" is the subject of line 4, starting a new idea and doing the guessing, or is the "boy—and tinder" together the dual, albeit enjambed, subject who is doing the guessing through opposites. Or is she using the passive voice (which seems plausible in a poem celebrating paralysis), and the "power/ of opposite" is the subject that is guessing the existence of "tinder" and "the boy."

"We can guess at the "tinder' that started and initially fueled the fire by how it subsequently burns," Susan Kornfield writes in her paraphrase of lines 4 and 5. In this reading, the tinder is the imagined first cause we're deducing from the fiery effect. But the tinder, by itself, can't cause a fire: it needs a complement or an opposite. In the first stanza, it was glaciers, but here it seems to be a boy. I imagine him striking a match, or rubbing two sticks together, say the stick of thesis and antithesis to ignite the transformative fire of synthesis! Yet "balance Odd" suggests a hint of a satire of the scientific/experimental logical language she had been employing.

This "boy" is trying to explain the mystery away through some simple ethical formula, but neither are a "boy" and "tinder" exactly opposite nor does this process achieve any easeful evening but a "balance odd." When it comes to the emotional life, as well as the ways of nature, all balance is odd, even on the so called "equinox" (the day I started reading this poem). I believe Dickinson either wants us to feel lost here, or is at least letting us know it is okay, as if she wants to paralyze reason, the prose-like interpretive urge, to the very limits of languaging, in order to free a deeper vitality.

If White—a Red—must be!
Paralysis—our Primer—dumb—
Unto Vitality!

The sixth line: "If White—a Red—must be!" is perhaps the most childlike ejaculation in the poem; its self-conscious reduction of the contrast between glacier and fire, and zero and phosphorous, makes me laugh. It could also continue the gendered theme: the white as "virginal" femininity and the red, the scarlet letter of lust. Yet, the fact that immediately after this line the word "paralysis" appears suggests that such a conclusion, though it may work on the level of science and dialectics, is insufficient in accounting for the emotional or psychic life. It is as if such thinking itself, in leaving no space for the mystery, can lead one to the ice of paralysis. If synthesis, it may stitch the heavens shut, like a funeral treading, treading, until a plank of reason, breaks (to paraphrase a few other poems).

Though the word "paralysis" echoes the earlier "glaciers," there's a sense of gravitas here, that she is no longer playing, that this paralysis has overtaken the (plural) speaker (the boy—and the fire—has finally disappeared)—like the "hour of lead" in her poem, "After great pain, a formal feeling comes." I read the diacritical mark here as forcing us to slow down, and feel the paralysis as a discrete unit before the poem again gives us a shred of hope by suggesting that no matter how horrific such a feeling of paralysis can be, it can also be a teacher. The use of the bookish metaphor here also suggests that this poem could be read as (about) the process of reading—the way we may lose ourselves, our desires, our fears even, and ability to speak, in the absorptive & disorienting process of reading.

While most readers read an implied "is" between "Paralysis" and "our primer," there is nothing to preclude she's saying "Paralysis! Our primer, dumb—." The speechlessness here is important, that Dickinson is writing about what can't really written about, but in retrospect, as the "hour of lead" is "remembered, if outlived" in "After great pain, a formal feeling comes."

Part of what I love about this, in contrast, say, to Whitman whose *Song of Myself*, was published not long before this, is that she celebrates the conservative (in the sense of conservational) tendency (that could be termed the yin) that tends to get drowned out in Whitman's celebrations of the "procreative urge…always sex" etc. Hillman points out the etymological roots of meaning involve "intention" and "opinion," while the etymological roots of "mystery" involve "silent" and "small." In this sense, Dickinson's silent and small mystery here is a fitting antidote to a world glutting on the procreative fire of "meaning." And besides, the fire has been here all along, in between—the phrases—of the cold-detached language that may, on the level of words, and meaning, feel like paralysis, if shut up into prose without her radical punctuation and use of enjambment that is more multi-dimensional than any emoticon. ☺

I could also paraphrase as, "the world is so out of whack today, wars, genocide, slavery—everywhere fire, fire, fire (hell, now oil, soon electricity) that the only way I can feel and celebrate vitality—a word these earth destroyers have coopted I say, coopted—is to use the moments when I feel most vital to celebrate what these fire-obsessed men would call paralysis!" were it not for the fact that I, having come to the poem with a feeling of paralyzing loneliness and/or depression, feel the speaker *felt*, or even *feels*, is conversant with, this paralysis: Perhaps it's important that she's no longer using metaphors of fire and ice to speak of such paralysis, but to see the vitality in fire as well as in ice.

I'd be remiss if I also didn't consider the possible double meaning of the word "unto," which could mean "until" (as in marriage unto death do us part") but also "to" (as in "do unto others"), the first meaning moving in time, the second meaning moving between people. I read her as saying "until" at first. In this reading, the paralysis teaches us to like the fire of vitality by overdosing on its opposite, an excess of repression (or what Rumi might call "the close contracted mind"). But if we consider "unto" as "to," she could be saying "we are speechless when confronted with another's vitality, another's fire." And in this it can also be taken as the give and take of relationships, of conversation, or at least reading and writing (including—perhaps—reading—oneself—)

3.

MUSIC IN THE SCHOOLS

At the YMCA, Henry Clement tells me he's just turned 88. "One year for every key," I say. He laughs & smiles as if it hadn't occurred to him, even though he started with piano at age 7 when he learned to play "Pinetop's Boogie Woogie" in one day.

He came to Oakland at age 35 in 1970 from Crowley, Louisiana deep in creole country. Before he retired, Henry was an all-purpose R&B multi-instrumentalist, session musician, singer, band leader, performer as well as vital organizer in chitlin circuit of the 50s & 60s. A self-proclaimed "weekend musician." he'd put backup bands together for such touring luminaries as Bobby "Blue" Bland and Sugar Pie DeSantos, but refused the unstable and often soul-killing life of touring in the Jim Crow south to work more modestly behind the scenes in Crowley and keep his community-building day job as a K-12 Math teacher as well as band teacher.

He managed to persuade James Brown to play a local gig for far less than he commanded to help raise money for the school's underfunded band. When they closed the black schools in 1970 in the name of "integration" as progress, he moved to Oakland to continue teaching and became a vital presence in the West Oakland 7th St. music scene that was also becoming a victim to "urban renewal." He had been ordained a Mardi Gras Big Chief (Takawaka) and evangelized the New Orleans tradition in the more staid Bay Area.

As a music teacher, Henry laments the loss of music in the schools programs for the more recent generations. I do too, but that doesn't mean I want kids to have the privilege and blessing of the kind of music-in-the-schools education *I* had in Pennsylvania in the 1970s. We can surely do better than force-fed Steven Foster folk songs (with no mention that his songs were written to be sung in blackface). We can surely do better than musical scores like football scores, a hierarchy of seated parts, as if the melody at the top of the pyramid, 1st clarinet and 1st trumpet, is better than 3rd clarinet, 3rd trumpet, because high fluid melodies matter more than staccato low notes.

We can do better than Handel's Hallelujah Chorus or soulful ballads that could make me cry if sung by a solo singer with instruments, but arranged for an acapella chorus flatten out affect. We can do better than military half-time marching bands that tried to veer into big band swing but never broke up into small-combos to build from the bottom or meet around a piano and just jam, or learn songs we actually liked to rock ourselves to sleep with, or rouse us in the morning as Parlia-funkedelic sang of Sir Void O'Funk. We can do better than music abstracted from dance.

I totally get why many veterans of music in the schools no longer play music. Maybe because music-in-the schools didn't feel like music. Thankfully, most colleges I went to, and, later, taught at, usually had a piano I could play between classes, but, alas, the community college I teach at, which up until recently, served a demographic made up of a plurality of non-white students, while it does teach some aspects of jazz, could do more to accommodate hip hop or at least go back to the important, and increasingly erased, tradition of the "New Orleans inspired R&B, funked-up soul & dance-floor-filling Zydeco" (Living Blues Magazine, 2015) that has flowed through Henry's music and pedagogical spirit since his first sides with Excello in the 1950s. If he wasn't retired, I'd ask him to come into my writing class. Maybe I can convince the music department to let me use one of their pianos.

GIL SCOTT-HERON'S MOVIE AGAINST MOVIES: "B MOVIE" AS SEQUEL TO "BACKLASH BLUES"

1. "Backlash Blues"

Shortly before his death in 1967, Langston Hughes wrote the lyrics to Nina Simone's "Backlash Blues." In this blues, Hughes/Simone directly address Mr. Backlash, as metonymic representative of systemic white supremacy, who operates through economic discrimination and segregation. Hughes also recognizes how "the military and the monetary get together whenever they think it's necessary" as Scott-Heron would put it in "Work for Peace" (1994). "Backlash" could be read as topical reference to the reaction to the Civil Rights and Voting Rights Acts, or heard as representing black and white relations since the 17th century, "your *mean old white* backlash." There is, however, also a threat in this song, as the speaker turns the power dynamic on its head:

(The world is) full of folks like me
Who are black, yellow, beige, and brown....
I'm gonna leave you with the backlash blues.[25]

Why is this karmic threat so important? Ibram X. Kendi points out that, after the Truman Doctrine in 1947 branded the United States the leader of the "Free World"

---

25 Nina Simone, "Nina Simone - Backlash Blues (Official Audio)." Youtube. Uploaded by Neil Simone, June 1, 2021. https://www.youtube.com/watch?v=0tllTDwQKV8. Accessed October 13, 2022.

in the context of post WW2 Cold War Geopolitics, protecting America's "freedom brand" became important in the propaganda wars:

"By August 1963, 78% of White Americans interviewed believed that racial discrimination had harmed the US reputation abroad.... Some civil rights activists recognized the incredible power Cold War calculations had given them to embarrass America into desegregation.... On April 12, 1964, Malcolm X. "offered his plan for the ballot instead of the bullet: going before the United Nations to charge the United States with violating the human rights of African Americans."[26] In October 1966, The Black Panthers wrote: "(As) our major political objective, a United Nations-supervised plebiscite to be held throughout the black colony in which only black colonial subjects will be allowed to participate for the purpose of determining the will of black people as to their national destiny."[27] Scott-Heron joins the ensemble at the end of one of his earliest songs:

> Who'll pay reparations
> Coz I don't dig segregation
> But I can't get integration
> Gonna take it to the United Nations[28]

26 Ibram X. Kendi, Stamped from The Beginning: The Definitive History of Racist Ideas in America. New York: Nation Books, 2016,367-76.

27 Black Panther Party for Self Defense, Ten Point Platform. Oakland: October, 1966.

28 "Gil Scott-Heron-Who'll Pay Reparations On My Soul (Official Audio)," Youtube, uploaded by Ace Records Ltd, Aug. 19, 2014. https://www.

In contrast to "Backlash Blues," the tone is less a confident threat, but more a cry of pain like Simone's earlier "Mississippi Goddam." As a direct invocation to "Mr. Backlash" who "never did sharing," the "I" in the song is as personal as it is the voice of a people. This is a man who, although only 20 years old, knows he can't get integration.

Throughout the 70s, Scott-Heron, Brian Jackson and the Midnight Band struggled to keep alive the flame of Hughes' and the Panthers' intercommunal[29] alliance with oppressed global colonial subjects of American Imperialism and Neo-Colonialism, and extend the tenants of the Black Arts Movement through activist-inspiring songs like "Third World Revolution" (1978) and the infectiously funky and lyrically playful "Shah Mot (The Shah is Dead/Checkmate)" (1979). Perhaps this bridge building is most felt in "Johannesburg" (1975) as he sneaks a direct challenge to America's freedom brand in the coda:

The Valley is like Johannesburg

New York is like Johannesburg

Detroit is like Johannesburg...

Freedom ain't nothing but a word

---

youtube.com/watch?v=QVoDV3icbgc&list=RDQVoDV3icbgc&start_radio=1. Accessed October 15, 2022.

29 Huey P. Newton, "Intercommunalism: February 1971," *The Huey P. Newton Reader.* Ed. David Hilliard and Donald Weise. New York: Seven Stories Press, 2002, 181-199.

Ain't nothing but a word...[30]

As it fades out, we could even detect a threat: "It could be you instead of me." Like Hughes, Scott-Heron believed in the laws of karma, as he addresses "America" at the end of "We Beg Your Pardon (Pardon Our Analysis)" (1974):

> Because we have an understanding of karma:
> What goes around comes around,
> Because the pardon you gave this time
> Was not yours to give....[31]

He also told Nat Hentoff in 1970, "I'm convinced that as our technology becomes unnatural, nature will defend itself and destroy those products of technology which intrude on her."[32]

In the decade between Scott-Heron's first novel, and the *Small Talk* book and album in 1970, and his 10th album (eight with Brian Jackson), *1980*, Mr. Backlash, or what Amiri Baraka calls the Sisyphus Syndrome, only increased his systemic stranglehold, working in just about every cultural and economic arena imaginable. For starts, new racist ideas began circulating. According to Kendi, most

30 Gil Scott-Heron, "Johannesburg," "Gil Scott-Heron & Richard Pryor, "Vimeo. Uploaded by Culture Cuts. https://vimeo.com/30013585. Accessed September 21, 2022

31 Gil Scott-Heron, "We Beg Your Pardon," *The Mind of Gil Scott-Heron: A Collection of Poetry and Music*, Arista AL 8301, 1978.

32 Gil Scott-Heron, "An Introduction," liner notes, *Small Talk at 125 and Lenox*, Flying Dutchman FDC-131, 1970.

white Americans started believing that "equal opportunity had taken over" and claimed the reason racial disparities still existed must be black people's fault.[33]

2.   1980

Scott-Heron works through appeals to logos, pathos, and ethos in the ideological superstructure to expose the many levels of abstraction through which Mr. Backlash operates. As bard of the 1970s backlash, Scott-Heron is perhaps its best immanent historian; as Tony Bolden argues, "he tapped into people's personal pain and anguish and transfigured these sentiments into public discourse shaped by historicity and conveyed in resonant styles."[34] Bolden also calls attention to Scott-Heron's prescient, prophetic foresight. Scott-Heron was acutely aware of the corporate media's framings of decades and the gerrymandering of time to create divisions. In "Corners" he refers to the turning of the decade as a "man-made definition…like an advertising sign" that "is meant to separate."[35] In "1980," a song later sampled by Tupac Shakur, he sings:

The robot mayor is there to shake your hand

33   Kendi, *Stamped from The Beginning*, 385.

34   Tony Bolden, "Funky Bluesology: Gil Scott Heron as Black Organic Intellectual," *Groove Theory: The Blues Foundation of Funk*. Jackson, MS.: University Press of Mississippi, 2020, 154

35   Marcus Baram, *Gil Scott-Heron: Pieces of a Man*. New York: St. Martin's Press, 181.

But he ain't never seen himself no earth man.
Heard a funny word he just don't understand
But he hopes that it don't mean you need a piece of
land.[36]

This quatrain not only satirizes the zeitgeist of the encroaching technocracy and the techno-futurism Arista Records was trying to force onto Scott-Heron's sound, but the "robot" and "earth man" could also represent the widening racial wealth gap during the 1970s. Presumably the word the robot mayor doesn't understand is "reparations," promised like that "Train from Washington" during the Civil War, but it could be any cry or demand for economic self-determination. "1980" suggests that technological progress accelerates social and political regress, as if by design. Brian Jackson writes in his liner notes to a 21st century reissue of *1980*:

To those of us living in 1979, it felt like 1980 was the twenty-first century. With 1984, the Orwellian dooms date, right around the corner, we were concerned…many of us still saw a glimmer of hope in the seventies. But now there really wasn't, as Gil laments in the song '1980,' 'Even no way back to '75, much less 1969.'" In this powerful chorus, Scott-Heron evokes the *feeling* of walls closing in by shrinking the space between years and varying the length of the phrasing. As Wikipedia notes, "the song also references the exploitation and eventual discarding

36 "Gil Scott Heron & Brian Jackson—1980," Youtube, uploaded by FreedysseusX on July 19, 2011. https://www.youtube.com/watch?v=b2R9OojBb8c. Accessed on September 21, 2022

of African-American innovation ('Boogie-Woogie's" somewhere in the lost and found')."[37]

1980 was written and released when many pundits still believed Reagan had no chance of actually becoming President. In "B Movie" (1981), which Brian Gilmore calls Scott-Heron's "magnum opus,"[38] Scott-Heron is not restrained by stanzaic constrictions as he speeds past the federally mandated speech limit like a moving target. "B Movie" also extends many of the themes of "The Revolution Will Not Be Televised" as it weaves an intertextual web of suggestions that invite, if not demand, an analytical response.

3. "Reel to Reel."

Timo Müller writes: "'B Movie" does not attain the poetic quality of earlier pieces. The language is distinctly prosaic: it lacks the semantic density, carefully orchestrated sounds, and inherent rhythm of Scott-Heron's early work."[39]

---

37 "1980 (album)," Wikipedia, the free encyclopedia. .https://en.wikipedia.org/wiki/1980_(album). Retrieved October 8, 2022.

38 Brian Gilmore, "The Enduring Howl of Gil Scott Heron's "B-Movie," Oyster Boy Review. http://oysterboyreview.org/issue/21/reviews/GilmoreB-Heron.html#.YyNuli-B1N0. Retrieved October 11, 2022.

39 Timo Müller, "Poetry to Music: Gil Scott-Heron's Intermedial Performance Aesthetics," *Poem Unlimited: New Perspectives on Poetry and Genre*. Ed. David Kerler and Timo Müller. Berlin: De Gruyter, 2021, 237

Müller's reading generally ignores the intermedial interplay in "B Movie's" carefully orchestrated four-part structure.[40] The first features the propulsive rhythm of drummer Kenny Powell, bassist Robert Gordon and Scott-Heron's deep baritone speaking voice that, on the page, because it doesn't rhyme or exist in stanzaic forms, gets translated into "prosaic." At the 2:50 point in this 12:14 piece, the second section is introduced with the entrance of the horns; eventually piano and guitar join in. The third section begins at 6:56, as he begins to sing briefly before switching at 7:30 to a mantra that swells to an almost apocalyptic crescendo. Even on the page, there's a semantic density of mercurial multi-disciplinary juxtapositions that can speak to many different audiences and leave listeners/readers plenty of space to question, analyze and feel.

"B Movie" also takes the satirical aspects of Scott-Heron's art to a new level, weaving together and updating threads from "the three major poems in The Blues series."[41] Reagan, like Nixon, becomes synecdoche. Although the title alludes to Reagan's notoriety as a mediocre actor, it also satirizes the official (American) reality. It "was originally titled 'Reel to Real,' but Gil felt that it might be too vague for some listeners. He toyed with calling it 'Reel

---

40 Gil Scott Heron, "'B' Movie (Intro, Poem, Song)," Youtube, uploaded by Gil Scott-Heron-Topic on November 7, 2014. https://www.youtube.com/watch?v=6JvpNY1QHzs. Accessed September 21, 2022.

41 Gil Scott-Heron, "Diplomacy can kill poetry," *The Mind of Gil Scott-Heron*, 1978.

to Real to Surreal."[42] "Reel to Real" designates a more dynamic *process* that applies not only to Reagan, but how rather than art imitating life, we have life imitating art, and not even very good art at that, but mis-infotainment, mis-edutainment. In "B Movie" the Reel passes through The Real to create the Surreal (or "Afrosurreal").

The first section introduces two main theses. Though he brings up the character of Reagan in the second paragraph, it feels like an afterthought, as his use of the vernacular, "But, oh yeah, I remember," gives his voice the authority of intimate straight talk. The main emphasis in this section, however, concerns the character of "America."[43] What does he mean by "America?" There are several possibilities that Scott-Heron considers with expert dramatic pacing and a gradual revelation of necessary information at first deferred, in ways similar to the genre of "detective novel," which he had used to structure *The Vulture*.

Consider the finesse of Scott-Heron's subtle rhetorical use of the pronouns "we" and "they." Aside from the "I," the first personal pronoun in "B Movie" is a passive "we," who has "been convinced." Scott-Heron does not here blatantly name who or what the persuader is. Since he

---

42 Baram, 192

43 There are similarities with the structure of "H20 Gate Blues," which announces the theme of Watergate in its first three lines only to devote the next 40% of the song to a more general analytical direct address to "America," "to direct attention to structural problems in America's political economy," (Bolden 163) before getting specific about Watergate.

separates the "I" from the "we," one may wonder why he doesn't say "they" instead of "we?" "The American people," however, is a "they." In the third paragraph, "we" is named America, but later in the same paragraph he changes America to "this country" and a "they." These rhetorical sleights help weave a spell that gradually others any listener or reader who might have been tempted to identify with the abstraction "America."

America is a contested term. It is only in the 4th and final stanza of this hornless introduction that a contrast between a "we" and a "they" become clearer. America is a *they* "who settled for Ronald Reagan—and it has placed *us* in a situation we can only look at." Who are *they* here? The 26% of registered voters (mostly white males like my dad) who choose Reagan in an election with a historically low turn-out? I first heard it that way, but, in the second section, other possible interpretations emerge.

4.   From Shogun to Reagan

Another title Scott-Heron considered was "From Reagan to Shogun," which reverses the phrase in the first section, "from Shogun to Reagan" (pronounced 'Raygun' on the recording). *Shogun* was an NBC miniseries that aired between September 15th and 19th, 1980, during the media circus of the election season. This memorable phrase calls attention to the similarities between *Shogun*, Reagan and the gun.

The late 1970s was the era of Hollywood blockbusters such as *Star Wars,* which dress the Manichean dualism of the old black and white Westerns of John Wayne in an allegedly kinder gentler techno futurism now that space is the "final frontier." Or, as Scott-Heron puts it, "Get off my planet by sundown." *Shogun*, as TV blockbuster in living color, also looked back to a mythical imperialist past: Richard Chamberlain plays a white British imperialist who comes to Japan during the 1600s and allegedly successfully assimilates into Japanese Imperial culture. According to Wikipedia, it was the first time the word "piss" appeared in TV dialogue; "I piss on you and your country." They also note that Japanese audiences felt the "fictionalization of events in the 16th century seemed frivolous and trivial."[44]

This conceit allows ample room to open up improvisatory socio-political interpretative space. Scott-Heron explains: "in the last 20 years, America has changed from a producer to a consumer. And all consumers know that when the producer names the tune...the consumer has got to dance. That's the way it is."[45]

---

44 "The Documentary The Making of Shogun noted that during the week of broadcast, many restaurants and movie houses saw a decrease of business. Many stayed home to watch Shogun—unprecedented for a television broadcast (The home VCR was not yet ubiquitous and still expensive in 1980)." This final fact also addresses the "We" who actions are reduced to be only able to "look at" the B-Movie that's relentlessly becoming our lives. "Shōgun (1980 miniseries)," Wikipedia, the free encyclopedia. https://en.wikipedia.org/wiki/Shōgun_(1980_miniseries). Accessed August 30, 2022.

45 Gil Scott-Heron, "B Movie," So Far, So Good. Chicago. Third World Press, 1990, 8-10

Ostensibly, he is referring to America's increasing dependency on Saudi Arabian oil, and the threat it poses to American hegemonic imperialism, but it could also apply to the increased Japanese "servicing' of the American Consumer (from Honda to Sony, years before today's China could undersell Japan by paying its workers less). This could also explain why NBC (owned by GE) would want to push a fictionalized historical account of Japan in the year from *Shogun* to *Reagan*.

But are the Saudis, or the Japanese, really the "producer" of the post-industrial consumerization of America? The fact that Scott-Heron doesn't say "we used to be *laborers,* and now we're consumers" subtly reveals that the dichotomy between consumer and producer ignores labor. In this scene-setting analytical introduction, the consumerization of America is offered to ground a besieged America's identity crisis (torn between, say, a diplomatic mother and a nuclear nightmare father) and explains the nostalgia epidemic for when America (dressed up as John Wayne) "produced."

In 1976, Scott-Heron said: [W]hite America wants to go back…before Montgomery. And there's a mania related to happy times before people started to challenge the status quo, when women cooked dinner and sewed socks, and black people swept floors and smiled. And I'm saying that we can't afford to go back there, we can't afford to allow that type if imagery, which is fascist if done to the max…."[46] Yet, even though all the men he satirizes in

---

46 Bolden, 159

"B Movie" are white, America is never modified racially; Scott-Heron's slippery signification highlights differing identifications of, and with, "America." On a surface level, racism is virtually footnoted as a theme; gender politics and the ideal of militaristic "manhood" become at least as important, as he camps Reagan though the Village People. Scott-Heron's nuanced subtlety, however, did not prevent backlash from the racist white students booing and hissing and taunting the band when they played at the University of Mississippi. "As their tour bus pulled away, gunshots rang out, bullets nearly hitting the bus."[47]

5. "Come With Us"

As "B Movie" transitions to the second section, Scott-Heron's voice becomes more animated and the tone becomes more satirical; the word "producer" reappears. The horns signify not only the collective, active, "we," the Amnesia Express (whose name relates to the theme of 'selective amnesia' in "B Movie"), but also the start of the movie, a *metadrama*. In Scott-Heron's satire, "minor characters" become at least as important as Ronald Reagan, as he turns the camera to a movie *behind* the movie. The first character mentioned is the *producer,* the exact word that he used to describe the Saudis earlier. He subtly switches the blame from the xenophobic narrative that blames countries like Saudi Arabia for robbing American

---

47 Baram, 199

jobs and standard of living, to the administration:

"The producer underwritten by all the millionaires necessary will be Casper, 'The Defensive' Weinberger." According to l-boogiewrites.com, "GSH takes the fear of societal change within Americans, and rightfully places blame on the government in the shape of Reagan, instead of scapegoating an entire race's cultural values and livelihood."[48]

Typically, a Hollywood/TV producer handles the business components of film production and, sure enough, Weinberger's "underwritten by all the billionaires necessary." Again, we may notice Scott-Heron's use of the passive voice ("underwritten by" rather than "the underwriters are"). Weinberger is just acting the part of a producer; the real producers are off stage, or capital itself.

As "B Movie" structurally peels off one layer of deceit and delusion after another, we see the identity of who or what "America" is undergo subtle changes through Scott-Heron's brilliant metadramatic cinematic slow zoom in to find devils in the details.

In Scott-Heron's account of the forces and characters behind the scenes of the media spectacle of the "Reagan Revolution," attention is drawn toward the less visible, unelected, underwriting billionaires. The "Reagan Revolution" was televised, but there was an untelevised "revolution" behind that. "The screenplay adapted from

---

48 l-boogiewrites.com, "Dissertation—Political Hip Hop-'B' Movie." https://www.l-boogiewrites.com/post/b-movie. Retrieved September 22, 2022.

the book called *Voodoo Economics* by George 'Papa Doc' Bush." Nor does he neglect the influence of "David Rockefeller of the Remote Control Company." While General Alexander Haig was *seen* "frantically declaring himself in control and in charge," this "Remote Control Company" is cool, methodical, and deliberate in its control.

6. **"As Wall Street Goes, So Goes The Nation…**

...and here's a look at the closing numbers— racism's up, human rights are down, peace is shaky, war items are hot." "B Movie" brings us back to the beginnings of the increased dominance of the globalized "post-industrial" neo-liberal elite in dictating not only economic but political and cultural policies. In 1971, not long after Scott-Heron's first album appeared, jurist Lewis F. Powell, Jr, hoping to be selected to the Supreme court, wrote to the U.S. Chamber of Commerce that the "American free enterprise system (has been under attack) from the college campus, the pulpit, the media, the intellectual literary journals, the arts and sciences, and from politicians. The response of business…is appeasement. In terms of political influence, the American executive is truly the forgotten man…"[49]

49 A.L. Jones, "An 'excess of democracy': How corporations killed the campus," Independent Australia. June 7, 2021. https://independentaustralia.net/politics/politics-display/an-excess-of-democracy-how-corporations-killed-the-campus,15165. Retrieved September 10, 2022

Around the same time Nixon emphatically told H.R. Haldeman, "you have to face the fact that the whole problem is really the blacks. The key is to devise a system that recognizes this while not appearing to."[50] This can be easily paraphrased as "let's make it worse by pretending that we're making it better," an argument that goes at least as far back as telling the first slaves from Africa that moving here was certainly better than their "uncivilized, pagan" land. The New Jim Crow was one way to that. In "We Beg Your Pardon America" (1974), Scott-Heron wrote of how pushers:

…push drugs the government allows
in this country to suppress the masses who then do time.

Mr. Backlash also wore the face of increased inflation. As Scott Heron wrote in 1973:

Watching the price of everything soar
And hearing complaints 'cause the rich want more.[51]

David Rockefeller created the Tri-Lateral Commission to regain control of what he and the economic elite, following

50 "The Haldeman Diaries: Inside the Nixon White House Hardcover—May 18, 1994." .https://www.nixonlibrary.gov/sites/default/files/virtuallibrary/documents/haldeman-diaries/37-hrhd-journal-vol02-19690428.pdf. Retrieved August 22, 2022.

51 Gil Scott-Heron, *The Mind of Gil Scott-Heron*, 1978.

Powell, referred to as "the crisis in the governability of democracies." According to Samuel P. Huntington, in his *Report on the Governability of Democracies to the Trilateral Commission* (1975) "a democratic political system usually requires some measure of apathy or non-involvement on the part of...a marginal population... Marginal social groups, as in the case of the blacks, are now becoming full participants. Yet the danger of overloading the political system with demands... remains. . . the authority of wealth was challenged and successful efforts made...to limit its influence."[52] This is the crisis of the "excess of democracy." "B Movie" code-switches these sentiments into the pathetic vernacular: Civil Rights, Women's Rights, Gay Rights...it's all wrong. Call in the Calvary to disrupt the perception of freedom gone wild. God damn it...first one wants freedom, then the whole damn world wants from freedom."

In paragraph nine, the word "mandate" (the first word of "B Movie") reappears; it turns out Reagan had a mandate after all, but it was *from above* rather than from voters. Scott-Heron dramatizes the voice of the corporate power structure speaking paternalistically to the chameleon actor who never could think for himself, and whose entire career was based on parts written by his bosses. I imagine Reagan asking, "What part do I play this time?" Gil, ventriloquizing his bosses, responds, "'You go give them liberals hell, Ronnie.' That was the mandate...with

---

52 Noam Chomsky, "The Carter Administration: Myth and Reality," Chomsky.Info. The Noam Chomsky Website. https://chomsky.info/priorities01/. Retrieved October 11, 2022.

the accent on the dupe." He also reminds us the meaning of fascism is a merger of corporate and state power, as he put it in "H20 Blues" (1973):

The Shock of Vietnam defeat
Sent Republican donkeys scurrying down on Wall Street.

Republicans are elephants, and The Tri-lateral commission is bipartisan. As Mr. Backlash works in increasingly convert ways, it's harder to fight an enemy you have to prove exists.

7.   Media as Misrepresentation & Addiction

The Tri-Lateral Commission worked both on a policy level and a propaganda level. In the 1970s, corporate mass-media was used to subliminally compel the "newly mobilized strata to return to a measure of passivity and defeatism,"[53] not just through propagandistic misrepresentations, but the addictive medium itself. And, even before Reagan became president, they surely applauded when *Shogun* had more power to keep people glued to their TV than TV did in 1970.

---

53 Ibid. See also the Government's 1968 Kerner Commission Report that argued that allowing more black faces, if not black views, on TV would create an illusion of "negro" (sic) enfranchisement to neutralize protest and rebellion, purposely neglecting to mention calls for black ownership of the media. https://www.blackagendareport.com/black-godfather-clarence-avant-and-ruling-class-use-black-pop-culture. Retrieved July 30, 2022.

"B Movie" speaks to how TV rebranded business more benign to create a "me decade." Adam Curtis's BBC Documentary, *The Century of the Self*,[54] shows how Madison Avenue engaged in a wide-scale effort to rebrand a "labor and business" dichotomy into a "consumer and producer" binary, telling people who had previously thought of themselves as workers that you're *freer* if you think of yourself as consumers, and in the process muddy the distinction made in Marvin Gaye's "Inner City Blues," which Scott-Heron also covered on *Reflections:*

> Money, we make it
> Before we see it, they take it.[55]

Furthermore, as Amiri Baraka adds, comparing 1965-1980 to 1865-1880: "For fifty years…after the Civil War, the media was filled with sick distortions and attacks on Black people (like today) to hide the heroic anti-slavery image that emerged as a result of the Black struggle against slavery…to justify the U.S. determination not to grant equality to the ex-slaves, and to use these demeaning portraits as 'proof' that Black people did not have the capacity for equality. Today we have the media in

---

54 Adam Curtis, "There is a Policeman Inside All Our Heads; He Must Be Destroyed" (originally broadcast 31 March 2002)[4] "The Century of the Self - BBC Two England - 31 March 2002" BBC Genome. No. 4073. 28 March 2002. p. 82. https://www.youtube.com/watch?v=eJ3RzGoQC4s. Accessed September 13, 2022

55 Marvin Gaye, Inner City Blues. Youtube, uploaded by The Universal Music Group, on November 12, 20202. https://www.youtube.com/watch?v=WRLwTO_T52U. Accessed October 23, 2020.

the same role." [56] Scott-Heron also had a century-bridging scope; for instance, comparing the white people who steal black music in 1970 to the economic theft and aesthetic etiolation of jazz in the late 19th century ("It Ain't No New Thing"). The media's sick distortions become even worse, however, given the electronic babysitter's power to addict children even before they can read.

In 1961, Marshall McLuhan wrote of a "particular form of self-hypnosis, Narcissus Narcosis, or syndrome whereby man remains as unaware of the psychic and social effects of his new technology, as a fish of the water it swims in. As a result, precisely at the point where a new media-induced environment becomes all-pervasive and transmogrifies our sensory balance, it also becomes invisible."[57] McLuhan was 50 years old in 1961, and had witnessed firsthand this process, with radio and Hollywood movies in the 20s and 30s and Television in the 1950s. Scott-Heron, born in 1949, was more of the radio generation for whom TV was not as primary a force of socialization as it would become for those baptized in it in the 1960s, 70s, and 80s, and was able to see more clearly this "invisible" process; Gil made the hidden persuaders

56 Amiri Baraka, "Black Reconstruction: DuBois and the U.S. Struggle for Democracy and Socialism," *The LeRoi Jones/Amiri Baraka Reader.* Ed. William J. Harris. Philadelphia: Basic Books, 2000, (545-560)

57 Marshall McLuhan, "Playboy Interview, 1961," *Adeena Karasick, Massaging the Medium. Forest Hills, IGS.*,2022, 146. Tony Bolden uses a similar analogy when he invokes Charles Mills: "The Fish does not see the water, and whites do not see the racial nature of a white polity because it is natural to them" (Bolden, 162).

and subliminal seducers visible, or, better, audible.[58]

"The Revolution Will Not Be Televised," suggests that the real meaning of television shows are the advertisements that are its lifeblood. What are they trying to sell? But it was also "about criticizing cultural racism, how black people viewed the TV shows they watched, which didn't include their views, let alone their faces."[59] How are they selling us back to ourselves? In "Madison Avenue" (1978), Scott-Heron sings:

They can sell sand to a man living in the desert.
They can sell tuna to the chicken of the sea.

Throughout the 70s, he uses media of music, the live show, the recorded artifact, word of mouth and the radio to delegitimize the corporate media, as he puts it in "Message to theMessengers" (1994):

We was talkin' about television
And doin' it on the radio.

58 Brian Jackson mentions they read Hidden Persuaders and Subliminal Seducers in college. "Brian Jackson on Writing Music with Gil Scott-Heron." Youtube, uploaded by The Red Bull Music Academy, November 4, 2015, https://www.youtube.com/watch?v=LR9XF3WYkxQ. Accessed on October 7, 2022.

59 Baram, 76. Scott-Heron brings up TV's power to assimilate black people into an "Ossie and Harriet" ideal. An alternative to this is Ruby (Dee) and Ossie (Davis), on whose brief TV show Scott Heron joyously performed. "Gil Scott Heron TV Performance (Rare) on 'With Ossie and Ruby,'" Youtube, uploaded by groovieloo2 A Strict No Coon Zone on Jan. 15, 2013, https://www.youtube.com/watch?v=1rYzdt0wzl0. Accessed Stember 26, 2022.

When word of mouth led college and black radio stations to play tracks from *Small Talk,* radio was neither as subject to corporate Remote Control as television was, nor as radio became by the time his record label *Arista* cut him off in 1984. But, as Scott-Heron puts it in "B Movie," the free press went down. Increasingly, as Nelson George shows, corporate media became the only game in town.[60]

The relatively autonomous chitlin circuit in which black entertainers, healers and the black dollar circulated was also a casualty of the 1970s backlash, as "urban renewal" was destroying small local performance venues in favor of the new industry standard of arena rock, and a bigger is better superstar 70s mindset, and the corporate media conglomerates were able to put black-owned record labels like Stax/Volt out of business. When The Midnight Band performs on one of their few TV network appearances in 1975, NBC listeners can hear phrases "they may not get the news" and "the news we get is unreliable, man." And, as Scott-Heron mentions in "Message to the Messengers," he received backlash for that.

Could "B Movie" even suggest a cry or demand for black ownership of at least one media conglomerate? Amiri Baraka's "A New Reality is better than a New Movie" (1975) is not only influenced by "The Revolution Will Not Be Televised" but also in dialogue with Scott Heron's later "B Movie." Like Scott-Heron, Baraka emphasizes the difference between the reality on the ground and

---

60 Nelson George, *The Death of Rhythm and Blues.* New York: Pantheon Books, 1988, 121-146

the surreal Hollywood trickle down aerial attack. A case could be made that the younger Scott-Heron helped give the elder Baraka the nudge he needed to transition from his Black Nationalist phase to the more capacious Third World Marxist phase.[61]

When I first heard "B Movie" as a teen in 1981, it had the power to wean me off an unhealthy addiction to TV and other forms of consumerism, yet reducing it to a historical-poetical artifact limits its power to speak to the present. And over 40 years later, the song still lives, not only because of the similarities between Reagan and Trump, but also because, as Judy Juanita writes, "Black people often serve as an early warning system for the American populace...the hardcore issues blacks have faced...define the newest America." Juanita adds that "being subject to cultural imprinting by television and advertising have made this nation a hotbed."[62]

"B Movie" also allows us to see the similarities between the fake news media of that time, and the social media mediated news of today. In the penultimate line of the second section, he says "no one is looking because, we're all *starring* in a 'B' movie." This line probably has even *more force* today than it did in 1981, as it could be a prescient characterization of 21st century cell phone culture. Many of us who loathed what television was doing to us were sucked back in to the new television of

61 Baraka, "A New Reality is Better than a New Movie," *Baraka Reader,* 254-55.

62 Judy Juanita, *De Facto Feminism: Essays Straight Outta Oakland.* Oakland: EquiDistant Press, 2015, 145-167.

the desktop/laptop/phone, as if we, like Bonzo, have also become Madison Avenue masterpieces. The other half, however, can never be told, but heard, experienced, felt in nervous systems or spirits.

8.   Song and Chant

Timo Müller claims "'B Movie' demotes the musical accompaniment, and returns to a distinctly verbal style" that has more in common with the *Small Talk* album from 11 years earlier, as if the musicians play a merely subordinate role.[63] The 3rd & 4th sections, which last almost as long as the first two, suggest otherwise by providing a radical ensemblic intermediality that cannot be adequately understood within an interpretative framework that separates "orature from literature" or attempts to reduce what Fred Moten calls an "ensemble of the senses" and "ensemble of the social" into a singular Euro-subject essence.[64]

As the movie trails off bleakly, a lulling song begins to calm the words into a meditative trance in a liminal intersection of escape and transcendence, as if you can be in the movie but not of it. Yet it only lasts for 30 seconds, as if the mere mention of "something's wrong"

63   Müller, 236.

64   Fred Moten, *In The Break: The Aesthetics of The Black Radical Tradition*. Minneapolis: University of Minnesota Press, 2003, 227. See also Thomas Sayers Ellis, "The New Perform-A-Form [A Page Versus Stage Alliance], *Skin, Inc.: Identity Repair Poems*. Minneapolis: Graywolf Press, 2010, 71-73.

plants the seeds for the song's destruction: "It won't be too long/ Before the director cuts the scene…." The cut is ambiguous and ominous. The song is *cut* short. We are cut short. Who is the director? It's not the earlier mentioned "Director," Attila the Haig, as much as *The Amnesia Express* underwritten by a groove-chant that can conjure a spell of nature destroying the technologies that intrude on her:

> Ain't really your life
> Ain't really ain't nothing but a movie.

While sacred chants rely on affirmation, Scott-Heron's chant is a negation of a negation. If saying it once was escapism, chanting it repeatedly, through doubled and tripled tracking in musical call and response, becomes haunting ritual and resistance. The meaning of the words is both amplified and purged, as if, even during the era of reactionary backlash and The Integration Trap,[65] there's also exorcism, and a belief in a "common sense" elsewhere available to us pulsing through. In another context, Harmony Holiday writes, "if you repeat the same thing enough it becomes real, takes shape, is forced into the material world and leaves you with nothing left to say…." Scott-Heron's chant could be read as an example of what Holiday calls "The Black Catatonic Scream."[66]

---

65 Oba T'Shaka, *The Integration Trap*. Oakland: Pan African Publishers and Distributers, 2005.

66 Harmony Holiday, "The Black Catatonic Scream," CanopyCanopyCanopy, Aug. 20, 2020. https://canopycanopycanopy.

L-boogie.com writes that the "military repetitiveness" in this final section gives us "time to reflex and process the 12 minutes of information given to us by GSH."[67] Forty years after first hearing it, I'm still processing it.

Although Scott-Heron's words sublimate his own personal pain, it becomes difficult not to hear his own music industry trauma, after a decade in the "instant high and constant come and go bizness (that's) got you hangin' out in places you got no bizness" ("Show Bizness," 1978), as if he's also talking to himself when he trance-chants, as the blues talks to, and through, its musicians. And, as he reminds us in "Bicentennial Blues:"

The blues is grown, but not the home
The blues is grown, but the country has not.
The blues remembers everything the country forgot.

---

com/contents/the-black-catatonic-scream. Accessed October 23, 2022.

67 L-boogie.com, "'B'-Movie."

"WE ARE NOT MONSTERS"—
ABOUT DAVID & ME—

An essay/review in the July 2019 *Spin* Magazine by Brian Howe, entitled "David Berman's *Purple Mountains* is a Welcome Return from an Old Master," promises to explain where Berman has been since he retired the Silver Jews a decade earlier. For evidence, he quotes lines in which the speaker confesses that he's "spent a decade playing chicken with oblivion" as well as other flaws confessed on the album.

Howe, who can turn a phrase with an adeptness at wielding words like weapons, but apparently never took a poetry 101 class to learn that the speaker isn't necessarily the author, takes this speaker's lines at face value to sum up a decade in which David was actively engaged in an attempt to resist and combat the injustice of the corporate destruction of the middle class at the hands of people like his father. Howe reduces David's very public moral crusade to "he hates his father."

Howe's erasure of David's political and moral crusade against the influence of firms like The Center for Consumer Freedom is especially egregious when he brings up the "surreal apocalyptic prophecy" of "Time Will Break the World." from *Bright Flight* (2001). The line that Howe quotes appears in the song's second stanza, which I'll quote in full to give a little more context:

It's so very cold in the mansion after sunset
The snow is blowing through the baseboard outlets
And I have no idea what drives you, mister
Tanning beds explode with rich women inside."

Howe claims the final lines "make me wince in 2019"—and is "old fashion…in some off-putting ways," implying that David's image of exploding beds in a tanning salon is an example of the kind of toxic masculinity that got Trump elected. It seems pretty obvious to me that this "mister" is clearly the man Rachel Maddow has referred to as "Dr. Evil," as David wrote in 2009:

He props up fast food/soda/factory farming/childhood
obesity and diabetes/drunk driving/secondhand
smoke. He attacks animal lovers, ecologists, civil action
attorneys, scientists, dieticians, doctors, teachers. His
clients include everyone from the makers of Agent
Orange to the Tanning Salon Owners of America. He
helped ensure the minimum wage did not move a penny
from 1997-2007...

In this essay's last paragraph, Howe finally cops to what a more honest publication would have made the title: *"Why we white men shouldn't identify with Berman's idiom anymore [in an era of Trump]."* I will grant that for Howe to question his own investment with that old fashioned toxic masculinity is a good thing, but Howe's critiquing David's "Privilege to fail" while totally ignoring that David, more than almost anyone I know, rejected and critiqued that privilege.

Meanwhile, I'm very happy to see the poet Sandra Simonds write:

Some really smart people on Twitter have outed billionaire heiress Elizabeth Koch's pen name which is "E.B. Lyndon." The billionaire class would like to comfortably assimilate into the arts on the one hand, while on the other fund climate change denial which destroys our planet. We are not okay with this and you shouldn't be either. If you come across this name in fiction, remember who she is and what her family has done and how she has done NOTHING to speak out against it. I am reminded of David Berman whose father was a fucking monster and how he fought against his father his entire life and very publicly. I feel like it honors him, in some way, to speak out about this. His fight was a valiant one. Hers doesn't appear to be. We can't help what we are born into but it's what we do with it that matters." [November 9, 2019]

Before he died, David had explained to me that what makes Richard Berman's Center for Consumer Freedom and his other tax-exempt lobbyist fronts so successful is that his 'argument' is able to operate on subliminal, pre-conscious levels that by-pass the rational mind, employing classic post-Bernaysian double-speak.

Richard Berman himself brags, "hit people in their

heart rather than in their head. Intellectual understanding is facts and facts trump other facts. Emotional understanding is very different—it stays with you. When I understand something in my gut, you've got me in a very different way. People remember negative stuff. They don't like hearing it, but they remember it....We can use fear and anger. It stays with people longer than love and sympathy."[68] This is why he's such a daunting foe. This is just one of the many things David taught me in the decade since he retired the Silver Jews. Keep this quote in mind as you read the following reflections on my dear friend David.

1. I can't talk about David without talking about me

In the fall of 2008 I had gotten the "big idea,"—perhaps because of multi-genre poet heroes like Amiri Baraka, or the fact that I was no longer primarily teaching literature and creative writing at majority white colleges, but had just got hired teaching composition and critical thinking at a 95% non-white community college, that if I ever was going to take poetry as seriously as I had done up until 2005, I was going to have to operate outside what Jennifer

---

68 BROKEN CITY: Washington's robust market for attacks, half-truths: A look inside an industry of distortion, where unnamed corporations pay richly to bend the debate their way By Michael Kranish GLOBE STAFF MAY 19, 2013

Moxley once called the poet's only club, and try my hand at a more sustained book of cultural criticism, or a book that might be useful to some of my students or other non-academic acquaintances.

I knew this would take years of re-orienting my writing and reading habits and/or sensibilities—while in the meantime writing journalistic puff pieces for *The Oakbook*, and music criticism for *The Big Takeover*. I had fully believed that various losses piling up in my life were indeed largely the fault of systemic economic forces—how the crash of '08 allowed developers to buy cheap and sell high and finally cash in on their 40-year plan to kick the black folks out, even if they had to take white artists and low-paying professions like college teachers with them. In this frame of mind, I was very excited when I read David Berman's statement in January 2009 in which he announces what I took to be a somewhat analogous re-orientation of his cultural work:

This winter I decided that the SJs were too small of a force to ever come close to undoing a millionth of all the harm (corporate lobbyist and PR wizard Richard Berman) has caused. To you and everyone you know. Literally, if you eat food or have a job, he is reaching you…. Previously I thought, through songs and poems and drawings I could find and build a refuge away from his world. But there is the matter of Justice."

Reading through our correspondence now, which up until that time had been primarily aesthetic or concerning our various personal depressions, etc, an email exchange in early 2009 sticks out, in which one of us says, "my cause is your cause" and the other responds "my cause is your cause, too" and maybe it's okay if I can't figure out who said it first, for I feel in many ways we had a symbiosis that went beyond simple cause and effect. Thus began a decade-long correspondence through email and phone in which David and I collaborated more intimately and intensely than we ever did through music.

It seems so distant now: 2009, before the Arab Spring, Occupy Wall Street, "Hands Up Don't Shoot," #MeToo, Antifa, etc., when many whites were still congratulating themselves for Obama, and the word *post-racial* was gaining currency, in many ways it felt like David and I were working in a vacuum. He sent me a quote by Jodi Dean that argues in an era of "post-politics"—

"Matters previously thought to require debate and struggle are now addressed as personal issues or technical concerns. We use expert discourses of psychology and sociology to provide explanations for anger and resentment as symptoms...to be addressed therapeutically, juridically, spectacularily, or disciplinarily, rather than being treated as elements of larger signifying chains." And even though we were both in therapy, and placing a degree of faith in the psychological industry, I wholeheartedly agreed. As

David commented, "I know it's not strictly either/or, but I aspire to her position of 'real antagonism or dissent'"...

One question David and I asked ourselves, and each other, over and over again, is 'how can someone who was known and established as an aesthete, and circulated socially in these contexts—[in the sense that art contexts and 'scenes' can often value the asocial social, the introverted extroversion of aesthetic object mediation] transition into the role of an activist, or militant, or private-public intellectual. What forms and what contexts are available beyond the roped off theme park of what indie rock had become, his candy jail analogous to my poet's only club...to help "actuate, rouse, or set astir" (as David put it on May 21, 2013) anyone against the business class's "implacable draining of the swamp of the commons." Can arguments work against the mojo of Washington PR firms that disseminate misinformation on behalf of corporate giants on a pre-conscious level? Would stories of mythic proportions work better?

We shared our struggles with strategies and tactics, through trial and error, overwriting and code switching, trying to synthesize the personal and political. I loved when he gave me assignments and took pride in the fact that it pleased him when I introduced my students to the works and deeds of Richard Berman and the Center For Consumer Freedom, ["I wish they'd teach that on TV"] as we egged each other on in our research. I fancied myself some front-line politico in the trenches of the cultural superstructure in my class discussions. When other acquaintances criticized David for his stand against his father, I told David I wouldn't judge him negatively if he had decided to make peace with his father and get some of the inheritance. He said something to effect of, "Me, Ha! Never!" and he stuck to his word…. He also was the one who helped me get a little closer to my Trumpian dad before he died by providing direct evidence on how his dad busted the union at my dad's factory back in the 70s, and I began to understand that David had a stronger moral conscience than I, as if that, as much as anything biochemical, could be a root of great depression.

Although David had renounced music at the time, I still clung to the belief that music has historically been a communal, grass-roots force with revolutionary potential on a local level that, regardless of whether its lyrics are political, could provide a push-back to the corporate cooptation of previous people's movements [often reduced to 'underground' 'coterie' or 'youth' culture]. I still believed more firmly than David that cultural revolutions usually precede political revolutions, and clung to fantasy of bringing artists and activists together.

By January, 2011, however, when college/community radio station, KUSF was privatized by Entercom, and my artistic warehouse space fell apart due, in large degree, to gentrification, I was losing my faith in that possibility, as the local music scenes seemed coopted by an every-man-for-himself—ism [not to blame the victim]. During this time of emotional volatility and increasing isolation in my life aside from teaching, David was my biggest cheerleader, who I believed and trusted because he also showed tough love, and called me out on the self-destructive "horseshit" games I play with myself—the over-analytical self-consciousness he too was battling with; he made me feel less crazy, and could acknowledge that in the ways the world speaks we were both crazy.

Although reticent to send the writing he was working on, he encouraged me to send mine, & when I felt most alienated from previous enjoyers of my written work, he made me feel I wasn't wasting my time on some quixotic delusion when I sent him my essay on the corporate take-over of KUSF: [69]

you really killed it on that one...

"schools going down, book publishing going down, and now college radio—
all the FRAMES are vanishing, all the contexts—
HAIL KOMKAST!"

people are about ready to crawl into their "I-pods" and seal the world off...

we're seeing the prequel to the matrix. how did they convince the bodies to crawl into the pods?
they baited them with gadgets.

---

69   http://www.bigtakeover.com/essays/open-letter-to-president-privett-on-the-sale-of-kusf-by-the-university-of-san-francisco

all competing institutions have been either bought or
neutralized by business.
public opinion has been tamed. next challenge: taking over
Perceived Reality. [Jan 26, 2011]

2.   David as Reader, Critic, Collaborator and Friend

We both felt that writing a book of prose—that would combine the personal and the systemic—was probably the best we could do, and we both probably felt we could meet our perhaps over-high expectations for ourselves. During this time, I valued David as a reader—in fact, just about the only reader—of my work. I loved David's keen insights and advice, even if I couldn't always take it, and though wary of flatterers, I trusted David's compliments because they always included challenges. Not only was he curious to see what I was working on now, but he asked me for a book of essays from the 90s that he hadn't seen before, which I was reluctant to send him:

i liked the two essays too. i know you fled
that headspace a long time ago
but i get excited by theorizing as i, unlike yourself, never
spent a long enough time
in an atmosphere that would have led me to despise it.

im as impatient with the music world and the world's
ever-growing music surplus
as you are with witty theory {Feb 16, 2011}

***

Even when we had our differences, they were informed by a unity-in-diversity approach, and a mutual understanding that our earlier work—for all its accolades—had left our striving for wholeness unbalanced, like had the roles had been flipped we would have done the opposite?

After writing the KUSF piece, my research into the corporate takeover of radio led me backwards on a protracted historical detour, as if somehow a century-long historical argument could ground my criticism of the present oppressors, and motivate others against them, better than if I just started with my personal story about my personal crisis, and the advice David gave on my overly ambitious book project gave me a glimpse of what he was struggling with in his own daunting project.

it occurs to me that the story you tell about your life,
about the struggle
between your attachment to music and your attachment
to literature,
is an incredibly valuable story.
I always enjoy your essays. I think if you made a small
adjustment in your methods you'd have great success
and could thus find a way to profit from all your dearly
bought experience.

Adjustment: Assume your audience is incapable of

getting all of your parenthetical puns and pop music/art/
theory references. Your mind is most likely too agile, and
too sensitive to parallels and cross-cultural connections
for the general reader to keep up.
Digression and referentiality is our post-modern
birthright, I know.
I just think you should go against the grain of hi-volume
multiplicity and see what happens.... [Mar 3, 2011]

Wow. You can really write history. I'm envious of your
clarity.
Did you research or does it just tumble out of you?
Was your mom exposed to beryllium?   May 8, 2011

Both of us were trying to write about the intersection
of the "family romance" with the systemic, but mine
seemed more like a cheesy conceit.

**I think with this material you have to separate the
worlds out.** *I either want to know about
your parents as parents first, without ref. to media, or hear
about your childhood relationship
to media with light reference to your parents. Otherwise the
strands are tangled.*

*I like this idea, the radio was my mother and the tv was my
father (and piano=g.parents) as a way to start, but then
when you start talking about your real mother and father i
stop caring about tv and radio (because*

233

domestic strife just trumps media analysis, renders it
comparatively dry) and the rest of the way
the two worlds are so braided together i don't get a clear
picture of either.

it's interesting because you're able to write the history with a
kind of clarity that
i'd like to see here.
it's almost like you don't feel comfortable
(i'm psychologizing here) letting the camera stay on the
painful scenes of childhood.

and that's okay, you can just write about you and the radio,
but you can't keep the reader
straddled between pathos and cultural speculation,
or, you can but you need to give us longer looks,
1000 words of one, then 1000 words of the other... May 12,
2011

+++

i'd be interested in reading about the warehouse fiasco
you spoke of...

i've also been beaten down and fed up. though my cycle
has been 2.5 years to your 7.

i was so naive to think i could write a non-fiction david
and goliath tale. ….

it's our postmodern birthright to tell a story about failing
to tell a story

so why not embrace it....

*i have millions of notes. now i've systematized them. next i
grow them.*

*i m slower than agriculture and i have lost all boldness and
nerve but we'll see if i can't*

get a little back.

*i just have to be careful to avoid self-flattery, self-pity and a
redemptive upshot...*

i just read mary karr's lit and patti smith's book.

*both drove me nuts for different reasons. but these are
massive successes*

so im learning what i can from them...

May 26, 2011

I asked him if he'd like to share any of his writing
with me ["it would help me feel less insane and isolated I
think" and he wrote back, "I'm the type who clutches his
pages until the last possible moment. Once someone else
sees them I tend to stop improving them." I admired his

discipline and patience compared to my flailing kitchen sink strategies. How many writers can "avoid self-flattery, self-pity and the redemptive upshot." What's left?

by the way
i can't remember if you wrote anything about the bad oakland experience
you've referred to some. if so send that too.   Jun 13, 2011

maybe im off, i just get the feeling that you think you're revealing more than you are.
like the PTSD. it wasn't mentioned explicitly but you seemed to think it was plain as day.
[Jul 11, 2011]

+++

As the above emails show, David, even during this time of mutual intense political muckraking into systemic injustices always tried to push me to get more personal, but I had to come at it from 'the outside in' as it were, so I sent him a Baraka-inspired piece about the destruction of the San Francisco R&B scene by Bill Graham and others in the 1960s, which many of my black retired teachers at the Y believed was part of the root of many of the problems— both culturally and economically—we experience today:

all this information is new to me

and again i am impressed at your ability to piece together

lost (to me) histories.

i am curious though,

as your reader who is always trying to get you

to get personal,

(your note about the loft fiasco hinted at such)

arent you dousing your urge to confront

with reasonable and collegial scholarship?

When you strike out at Bill Grahamism

with Sly's words

I want to put you on the analyst's couch and get you to strike

out at your oppressor in your time.

Maybe confrontation makes you unhappy or makes you feel like you'll

lose control but I'm wondering

if you aren't

managing anger at power,

as it exists in its current form,

with historical scholarship?

++++++++

i think it's good that your doing your writing topically
like that.
that's how im trying to think.
write chapters that can be stand alone essays.
allow the means to determine the end.
 [Aug 31, 2011]

His implication that I was "dousing my urge to confront
with reasonable and collegial scholarship" struck me
deep, in part because my old academic colleagues and
supporters saw me as not reasonable and collegial enough,
but though my life seemed to be falling apart around me
and I was becoming more emotionally unhinged, and I
still wanted to prove I can be reasonable and collegial, I
knew that there was some truth in David's criticism.

Perhaps my writing had become more bloodless—like
the 'old left'— when I turned away from poetry, or perhaps
because I could blame the anti-depressants I started

taking in 2008—after years of resisting—that may also numb ability to feel? I didn't know. I was confused, so when David sent me an essay by a rather smug white guy (not David) criticizing hip-hop music for being co-opted by the corporations, I disagreed with what seemed to be the white author's paternalistic dismissal of an alternative, or call it, underground, relatively autonomous form of hip hop—like say Oakland's Boots Riley or "Hip Hop For Change,"—that could be effective in helping push back against the corporate agenda. I wrote an unhinged, angry, letter striking out.....and in that sense strangely taking David's advice—to be less reasonable and collegial, but not so much at the seat of power as in the author of that article, and, by implication, David—

This led to the most volatile angry exchange David and I ever had, before or since, and to his credit, David was able to argue with my unhinged rant with much more of a collegial and reasonable attitude than I. I certainly wasn't trying to be a white guy criticizing another white guy as racist, especially given his critique of contemporary country acts ["How about "Lady antebellum" for poetic stealth//"Slaveowner's wife" is the japanese translation.....Aug, 25, 2008], though I can see how he might have taken it that way. Looking back on it now, I was making a mountain out of molehill and nitpicking, since we agreed with each other about cultural decay taking the form of "atomization of the listener and the depoliticization of youth culture" and his [rhetorical] question about Jay-Z:

Does he turn around and do something with it or just reinvest cultural capital in his own career, most usually by selling crime and capitalism and materialism and misogyny back to the youth.
>You think the apoliticism of american heavy metal
> didn't benefit capitalism in the seventies and eighties?
>You don't think Kanye West, who felt bad and apologized
>for when he said the truth about george bush, isn't promise unfulfilled and settled for?
Our political idols are just business people concerned about popularity, not the welfare of the weak..
Music hasn't changed anything since woodstock. And that was just fashion. What in the world has all the trillions of hours and dollars sunk into rap rock folk or film done to change a whit of the chamber of commerce's plan
to remake america as a business first last and always country. The chamber of commerce
has acutally changed all our artists into self-branding, self-interested marketeers of themselves.

This last quote reminds me of a quote by Amiri Baraka on the co-optation of hip-hop, "our enemies have created our spokesmen." And just as Boots Riley criticized the Black Panthers for not connecting up with a worker's movement, David adds, looking back at our college years in the 80s/early 90s: "I don't think students or artists of that era had even an inkling of investment in worker's rights. Academics, like artists and musicians, were seeking prestige." In this, he reminds me of my Marxist Feminist professor in 1996 who took a harsh stance against the merely 'ludic' revolutionaries that dominated the 'academic left' at the time.

If David sounds a little extreme, or is letting his anger get carried away, I can hardly blame him considering that my email was even more so. Yet, even if it's an occupational hazard of mine to appear more reasonable and collegial and desperately search for an exception so I could accuse him of hasty generalization, I can't deny the large scale of truth here in questioning our youthful faith in all those heroic rock and roll myths of what Thomas Sayers Ellis likes to call a large-scale cultural PSYCH-OP.

For David, in 2011 at least,

I don't have an answer what to do, but for me
music is totally captured by my father's world.
for me, making music is worse than doing nothing,
it's collaboration with the forces of control

that idea threatens everything you love.

your fear that i was being reactionary
was actually me trying to suggest that you are asleep to
your cooptation

so...as ive had to learn with other friends, w__, m__,
c__, b___,

telling others that present-day musicmaking is a silly farce

is ruinous to their visions of a future of meaningful musicmaking

i have no right to upset people like that....

so ill keep it to my book, where the upsetting will be calculated to convince....

And though it made me sad that he couldn't see any way to include music in his toolbox, or couldn't consider that there may actually be something, on a vibrational level, that could be physically and psychically healing about music [not that I was acting like any exemplary ethical ideal as I had gotten into too many testosterone-laden arguments with musical collaborators], I certainly respected his decision and wasn't going to try to continue to argue that point. Besides, he could make exceptions for friends. Though we fought against the Koch Brothers, he could still post a Kenneth Koch poem on his blog and enjoy my waltz version of it I had recorded, for instance. He also liked my song lyrics like, "your peace sign sure looks cute, but it still ignores the roots" and, "how crazy can you get and still come back?" He even sent a birthday email with a possible band name [though I only had an album, not a band]: "Wildcat Strikes!" or "The Wildcat Strikes."

He also argued that the so-called "me decade" was approaching its 5th decade, and tried to not lose sight of the struggles that not just "LGBT, blacks, Palestinians, jews and fems" have in common. Even in this midst of this volatile exchange, there still remained a willingness to continue to learn from each other, as I sent him Baraka, bell hooks, and Nelson George essays. When David argued that identity politics divorced from class politics was "a transition...to the everyman for himself society that we have now," and a boon to conservatives because it allows them to "buy off" the left with symbols of change, I told him about how they destroyed the black business district in Oakland known as Grove St, and then to add insult to injury, named it "Martin Luther King."—And he responded, "or unveiled a multi-million dollar statue to MLK made from Chinese slave labor."

thanks for the essay on creative writing/black arts.
i don't think it's naive liberalism.
Sep 19, 2011

Despite all this, he could still understand the need to pragmatically work within the system, and often lamented the loss of Al Gore as a key moment in the plutocratic takeover. Though he craved collective action and a people's movement, and searched for, and often found in his research, a new illusion to keep living for, David never really drank the margarita or kool-aid of any purported liberator or movement, or if he did, it wouldn't be for long—but he was always open, and entertained and was willing to try:

On May 8, 2011, at 2:10 PM, D.C. Berman wrote:

also, i've been in touch with this fellow, barrett brown. i don't know if this stuff is interesting to you.....

Date: Fri, 13 May 2011 11:01:15 -0700, Chris Stroffolino wrote:

I've been looking around the "anonymous" materials, and it seems they're into culture jamming—
But I can't quite figure out what kind of interventions they're looking for.
I'm curious, and they seem very righteous...
are you doing any work with them?

On May 13, 2011, at 11:25 AM, D.C. Berman wrote:

http://arstechnica.com/tech-policy/news/2011/02/ anonymous-speaks-the-inside-story-of-the-hbgary-hack. ars

this is my favorite thing they did...

i was intrigued by a book of barret›s
called flock of dodo's that was a hilariously scathing exam.
of intelligent design.

then i read this and got a kick out of it
http://www.dmagazine.com/Home/D_Magazine/2011/
*April/How_Barrett_Brown_Helped_Overthrow_the_*
Government_of_Tunisia.aspx

i told him i was too old and computer illiierate to help but i
like how he tries to drum
up interest amongst olds like me. he insists that being able
to program or whatever doesn't matter.

the hard part for me is...how can you get involved with a
group that has no evaluatable leadership.

i like what they did to the chamber of c. but how can i
advocate a group whose
so faceless. i like barrett but its hard to tell how
representative he is.
how can you ever know if power-crazy counter-creeps are
running the show?

Date: Mon, 19 Sep 2011 17:28:48 -0700

did barrett brown write you about doing something on
tunisia?

On Sep 21, 2011, at 9:58 AM, D.C. Berman wrote:

yes. i told him to keep me in the loop.

***

When Occupy Wall Street went viral and national, as if it was a better sequel to the "Obamamania" of 2008, part of me wanted to get my hopes up. My composition students and I were discussing and debating the Black Panthers' demand for reparations, and wondering if it should be updated. From most of my students' perspective, Occupy Oakland was mostly white-folks misappropriating the name Oscar Grant. "Black people have always been the 99% percent," and though I didn't go out with the extroverts mansplaining the human microphone in pithy soundbites, I found myself writing to what I thought was a kind of "official" website of the 99% movement to put the demand for reparations onto the list of demands for the July 4th convention planned in Philadelphia. In short, my argument, to my mostly white audience, was an attempt to see the demand for reparations would actually help liberate them [us] from the grips of the 1% too. At one point, I even got slightly excited that this "Get Money Out of Politics" website, started by Dylan Ratigan, was going to catch on. I sent David a petition:

On Oct 12, 2011, at 6:59 PM, D.C. Berman wrote:

i signed.
i sighed.
 you would make a really good organizer

I responded, "Like you, David, i can't organize for shit, but if i can at least give ideas that end up being taken seriously by people who can, I would feel "of use." Oh, and here's funny sequel to this story that I never got to tell David. A few years I got an email from the guy who set up the now long defunct "Get Money Out" campaign asking me for money because he's running for political office. I know David would appreciate in that "I told you so" way of his.

Perhaps by January 2012 I had written enough of the historical backdrop to be able to write a little more personally in a way David would appreciate more:

Sun, 22 Jan 2012 18:13:43 -0800
> > *I like much more than 20 % of what's here!*
> > *Concrete bits seem like your best points of entry to the past.*
> > *The Cohen essay is excellent.*
> > *The moshpit, the individual song. Going through the littlest doors.*
> > *The clove cigarette as madeline.*
Thanks David.
> > *Of course you're going to have to cut back but overwriting is a method*
> > *I wish I could put into play in my own deal.*
 Exactly that's what I've been doing—i suck at efficiency (can't even
afford to live in one!)

> > *Coming up with more solutions than you need is*
tactically smart
> > *(specially when you don't know quite where you're*
going).
it's very possible the 'outtake book' will be 'better'
> > *You should keep moving, keep writing, keep pushing*
> > *while keeping an eye out for an editor*
> > *(levelheaded and leftbrained) who can help you prune*
and rearrange.
ah, the elusive search for a left-brained editor or musical
collaborator. i've pretty much given up
> > *with my project, i'm just spinniing my wheels. i need*
some of your
> > *steampower!!*
On Apr 12, 2012, at 9:55 AM, D.C. Berman wrote:

you ever think of doing a 33 1/3 book for american water?

And perhaps by May 2012, David had let himself open
more to music again:

The other thing is that i'm much more in touch with
emotions
which i also like. (of course convential wisdom is that
anti-d's numb you out
so i don't know why i'm so tearful.)

It's been years since songs have had the power
to bring me to tears.

Most notably Johnny Paycheck's "Old Violin" whose lyrics
just kill me.
It's more than the self-pity it's capable of conjuring in a
person who feels
used up and "done" in a cultural sense.

It's that moment he softly says "I tried" in the middle of the
song.
Perhaps it is self-pity. But it flushes out my tear ducts that
have been dry
for many years.

I looked this up: why are tears so hot?

It's because they're at 98.6 degrees but your skin, your
cheeks
have a surface temp of about 90 degrees.
[May 28, 2012, at 7:26 PM]

chris, i think this is an incredible song.
never knew of it before.
it's everything a song should be
and it puts the lie to rock critic/musician/fan's
most unquestioned axiom: music and politics don't mix.

http://www.youtube.com/watch?v=_
DboMAghWcA&ob=av3e
[May 29, 2012, at 12:36 AM

A few hours later, David, perhaps inspired by my overwriting method, sent me a powerful piece of writing, in the form of a letter to his mother, titled: *Empty Military Cemetery on Memorial Day.* In this piece of writing, he masterfully uses "concrete bits," to give him entry into the systematic injustice of our time, putting into practice the advice he gave me on my own writing. Starting with the figure of the epidemic of veterans committing suicide— no doubt inspired by the song "Hero of War" that made him cry hot tears—David meshes the personal and the political, pathos and the speculative, in this epistolary missive that had the rare power to make me cry at least as much as any of his songs had. I have no idea if this was the kind of writing he was hoping to include in his book, but I think it should be sufficient evidence to counter the haters of David's political/moral/spiritual vision.

I told him that his refusal of his father's inheritance in contrast to his sister remind me of Cordelia and her two sisters in *King Lear,* and he wrote a very long email, which I'll only give a brief excerpt of here:

On May 30, 2012, at 11:54 PM, D.C. Berman wrote:

okay. im reading king lear this summer and im going to ask you about it when im done.

the first thing i did when i thought about writng about my father was to turn to the literature of father son-conflict.

what i wanted was a son who knowingly/willingly takes on a tyrannical father.

what i found was very interesting, or more to the point, what i didn't find....

i don't know if you saw a blog post i did a couple months ago where i googled these phrases:

"jews control the world" = 161,000 results

"illuminati control the world" = 140,000 results

"freemasons control the world" = 40,500 results

"the vatican controls the world" = 4,090 results

"fathers control the world" = 0 results

that kind of says it all for me. only the last phrase is a truism.
of course there are powerful women and powerful childless men
but nothing is plainer than the fact that "fathers control the world"
yet those four words have never been typed on any text book blog or whatever

that google covers.

the closest thing ive found to what i have experienced in dealing with my father

is moses and the pharaoh. im no moses but the pharaoh is my father.
a slavedriver. a tyrant. and one who cannot be persuaded. who stonewalls.

who needs ten plagues to get him to budge.

can you think of any stories im forgetting?

Reading these emails now, I remain fascinated by the eclectic range of materials David was trying to synthesize in his book. Because of the difficulty David was having synthesizing the wide interdisciplinary range of reading he felt he needed for his book, I suggested to David that he take some of his favorite quotes from the articles he sent, and posted on his blog, and make it a commonplace book. But even if David was, as Laura Anderson puts it, "More comfortable with lyrical writing and unable, as he learned when he tried to venture into reportage, to discipline his minds to other forms," he is perhaps "our premier 'private intellectual'—a great influence [in exposing] the scenes around Rick, but never a public voice." I have no idea if he made any arrangement to have any of his notes or [unfinished?] chapters published, but am very curious.

3. Homelessness, Mental Illness & A Good Caretaker

On December 18, 2008, David sent me a video for a contemporary country story-song from 2002 by Craig Morgan called "Almost Home."[70] It's a dialogue song in which the speaker thinks he's helping a homeless man sleeping in a snow by waking him, only to be rebuked by the homeless man for meddling and ruining his dream. Songwriter Morgan writes: "A lot of people ask me [...] was he dying or dreaming? It's funny how people have different interpretations. That's the neat thing about a song, and I think understatement is the key to a good song...leaving enough room for the listener to draw their own conclusion[...] so I never answer them on that. I guess it's up to the listener."

I wrote David that I admired it, and it made me cry, but that I had a weird 'reaction formation" to it, like I fear how that song can be used to justify the teabaggers/ birthers, etc., like the opposite of "he ain't heavy he's my brother." Of course, even though the song can be read the cynical way I read it, it could also be read personally from the perspective of the homeless man in the song, that a great dream is no less a *real* experience than what we call waking life. It can be about preparing yourself, or being ready, for death, and that in a society that fears and tries to deny death, perhaps this homeless man has something

---

70   https://www.youtube.com/watch?v=MtqxY3t74To&feature=emb_logo

to teach. Nonetheless, the song stuck with me, in dealing with heavier themes than most commercial music does.

When I became homeless in 2012, except for a van with a piano in it, I began to understand why so many homeless people are called "mentally ill"—*environmental factors* are important. If you found them a home, I bet that could cure, or treat, a lot of this 'mental illness.' It's not just the lack of basic necessities I took for granted in my life, but also the stigma of homelessness and mental illness that made finding a job and or apartment in a new town increasingly difficult. Meanwhile, parked in an oil-drenched environment, I certainly lacked that "high and dry" mindset needed to complete my prose argumentative book, and when I thought of all the things I needed to get some semblance of my 'life' and/or 'sanity,' back, it was so daunting I couldn't even perform simple tasks.

For 4 months, I could suppress these thoughts by playing the piano in parking lots for people, in the deluded hope that I could meet other musicians—first and foremost drummers—who were looking for a musical housemate. There were these moments of transcendent, transient, collective group karaoke singalongs, but it dragged on too long, and got worse, once word of it went viral on the internet. I felt boxed in, and understood more intimately the stigmas David had to deal with, often by well-intentioned self-professed journalists (except for Scott Timberg, who understood it in terms of the *Culture Crash*): the "mental illness," the romantic lifestyle choice of the heroic self-contained individual. Increasingly, I just wanted to sleep, and battled with suicidal thoughts and knew he'd understand. I wrote to David: "I fear I'm turning into that guy from that sentimental classic you love, "Almost Home," only taking solace in sleep and dreams, but it not translating back to practical..." David wrote back immediately: "don't fall under the spell of negative self-talk."

During this time, as I found people retreating and/or I pushed them away, and no sense of continuity in my life, David was just about the only old friend who didn't turn away, even while recuperating in a hospital after being attacked by a Rottweiler in a heroic effort to save his dog Gittel's life. If anything, my misfortunes & fuck-ups brought us closer together. I usually find that talking about the other person's problems can help me with my own better than if I talk about my own, but 95% of the time David would deflect my questions about how he's doing to encourage me to open up. He talked me through many desperate rants, on phone and email, and was a beacon on some really tough nights. And though we both had a hard time taking compliments, he was also my biggest cheerleader, and spared my musical activity from his critique of what it's become in late capitalist post-internet America:

no i don't have any plans for another book- or record.
there's never been so much interesting stuff to read or listen to.
when i started writing and songwriting that definitely

was not the case.

seems to me that all cultural producers at this moment
in time, from radiohead and jonathan franzen on down,
are part of a glut of unnecessary, confusion creating,
volunteers for a glamourous cause with no zero need of
the "help" they are desperately competing with one
another to offer. that would include the "cowboy
overflow" which is part of the overflow...

 (i don't categorize what you do as part of this glut- if
you start selling records and competing for publicity, i
will be happy for you, but you will be adding to the glut.i
dont' feel this way about live music which has a function
that can't be fulfilled by all the great musicians of the
past.)   Oct 24, 2012

The phrase *"no zero need of the help"* stuck with me,
and made me wonder: was I doing that too? Increasingly,
it was clear to me I was making music I myself wouldn't
even want to hear. Since I always admired David's "anti-
performance" refusal to tour, I was a little surprised to
see him spare the van from his critique. Of course, since
I'm not so good at taking compliments, I wrote back, "But
isn't a piano in a van, too, part of the glut? I'm wasting tons
of money on fossil fuel!!" The way I saw it, and perhaps
this goes back to my initial bond with David, "live music"
often meant the tyranny of the extrovert, while recorded
music at least gives the introvert a chance to be heard, as
college radio did for David back in the 90s. Today, given
the corporate dominance on music distribution channels,

and the uncurated glut on the internet, perhaps recorded music becomes the tyranny of the moneyed or the aggressive hustler. I was trying to appeal to the "fellow introvert" in David in an attempt to compliment him, or, slyly, get him to consider recording again.

Though I never got my house back, by 2015, I did get the job teaching, and met my first girlfriend in 5 years, a wonderful woman named Jodi:

you sound - more at ease with yourself.
have you been teaching kids?

Jul 31, 2017

But David had lost his mom…

4.   *The Purple Mountains of 2018*

David and I are both in different places, geographically and in terms of our mindset we shared in 2008-2014. We had both abandoned—or at least suspended—our ambitious cultural-political—systemic—personal prose books. We had both recently become celibate, and both were living in closets (for me, a step up, for him a step down). He had almost finished recording *Purple Mountains,* his first album in 11 years, and I had just published my first book of poetry in 15. He admired my new poetry for bringing back more of the "relentless" voice he loved about my 90s poetry, and I cheered him on with his new songs. On October 30, 2018, he writes:

If I send you a song on dropbox
Could you overdub a piano track on it?

Just an experiment with a song that
Needs piano to break up the repetitive
Ness of the guitar and bass part

My least favorite song on the album
Wonder if you could spice it up
I especially dislike my singing in the verses
So anything you can do to draw attention away from that

The song seemed finished to me. Those Woods guys (his studio band) really filled the space, and I couldn't see the piano or organ really adding anything. I suspected that David only offered me to play on this to help me get some work as an act of friendship and kindness, especially because I hadn't played piano in 5 years and was rusty as frack, but that wasn't the only way David helped me. I wrote back, "I love this song…it definitely gets to the state of mind I like to think I've been extricating myself from since I left LA….haunting." The song was "Story Line Fever," the only song on *Purple Mountains* that eschews a lyric "I" for a sustained second person address to a "you." The first stanza seemed like a better diagnosis of the "strictly physical" ailments that had recently gotten me in ER:

On occasion we all do battle with
a little motivational paralysis
you get trapped at the stage of analysis
where thoughts bout the shortness of life may beget
bouts of shortness of breath in your chest
doubts bout the worth of the nights you got left
crowding out all but the fear and regret...

One way to read this is that thoughts of mortality (as defeat) may create a tyrannical narrative—life is a story—impulse that can bury you in a plot that prevents you from living in the present. It could be body talking to mind or at least self. Another way to read it is as a critique—not just of soul-killing consumerism, as in "Margaritas at The Mall," but of an internet culture that makes us all commodities, the way the marketplace encroaches on private life, as well as what used to be a less uncommon commons. Lines like "Gotta combover cut circa abscam sting," could suggest an autobiographical reading, or at least reduce the song to middle aged white [Jewish] male midlife crisis, but in talking about one of the other songs, he suggests an alternative to this album's biographical narrative: 'if I'm just talking to myself in the first moment, the album can retain plausible deniability that it is an actual coming back, but in fact is an item of tuneful surveillance."

The way I see it, "tuneful surveillance" means it's less important what some biographical David Berman really thinks, or means, when he sings: "The end of all wanting/ is what I've been wanting/ and that's just the way I feel," but what we think, or feel about that. As David adds, "Search the song and you'll find no body on the premises. They really are inhabitable. You can move in right away." David often enjoyed hearing what his songs meant to fans, regardless of whether it was what he "intended."

The second stanza is the closest "Story Line Fever" gets to telling a story, about how love gets tangled in the seemingly inescapable marketplace of consumer society & commodity culture. The "you," as we find out in the third stanza, is both "seller and commodity," as well as shopper—and in this bleak vision of 21st century American culture, the figure of the "you" and his "love" is but a cipher of the socio-cultural backdrop:

> You took your love to the marketplace
> In the wanton corner of a western state
> Where every other shopper is a basketcase
> Just realizin' the horizon forms a frowning face
> Hanging around those haunts at night
> Where half the clientele was part-poltergeist
> Grinding an axe against all that exists
> Minus their protected exceptions to it"

Listening to it in light of my relationship with David, I had the distinct feeling that what I had thought was our deep connection in previous correspondence and collaboration may have been just David going out of his way to "slum it," as it were in my overly secular, always-already commercialized, over-analytical mindset that hollowed out the personal.

> yr paradigm has cooked your mind clear thru...
> its making horseshit sound true to you
> now its impacting how you're acting too
> now its impacting how you're acting too

In the last verse the song seems to give advice to the one with "motivational paralysis:"

> Turn your pedestal into a carving board
> If that's what the audience is looking for

I suppose the "if" could qualify this advice, by suggesting the "you" should just pander to his audience, but when he first sent it to me the advice was less qualified—"that's what your audience is looking for." "Carving board" could mean just get back to the work of crafting songs, and I think of David's love for his fans who didn't necessarily appreciate the high horse he had gotten on in his search for justice, but I think the visceral power of him singing affected me on a deeper, one might say, pre-conscious level, especially when I heard the rest of the songs on *Purple Mountains*.

David understood that the songs 'might read as suicide notes," and certainly—on first listen—I agreed with Jeffrey Lewis that *Purple Mountains* is "the saddest, most suicidal depressed record I ever heard," but I take DCB at his word when he says, "Mine is not a cry for help, but an offer to provide a kind of it." He refers to the first three songs on his album as "hopeless, helpless and hapless married to music that is cheerful, chill and cool....three stable art objects that can house the listeners mind from the storms of life at four minutes a pop."

Questions arise: Can love and sympathy be expressed in lyrics of seeming absolute social disconnection? Can songs "house the listener's mind from the storms of life" if the songs themselves are stormy? Why do we often call often call the gentle, quiet snowfall, a storm? Is the fear of death similar to the fear of winter?

Can "snow" serve as an image for "the weather of forever?" Even Brian Howe begrudges that David is "always so good with how snow falls." And calls the album's 4th song, "'Snow Is Falling in Manhattan,' the record's most artful moment, where Berman makes trochaic tetrameter straight out of Longfellow sound at once conversationally spry and intricately fashioned." I'd also argue it's a better winter solstice song than the loudly-honked "Silent Night."

David was always better at seeing the beauty and wonder of winter than I. While I am a cliché spring/summer guy with huge seasonal affective disorder, David loved "the purple hills,... the silver lakes/... the icy bike chain rain of Portland, Oregon," as if he needed what I call its harshness to balance out the destructive story-line fever of winter-fearing summer mania. Even in "Darkness and Cold," the lamenting heartache, "rolling through the holes in the stories I've told," can be a celebration of lyric cries of pain, married to calm, chill melodies—necessary to cool the "story line fever." David once told me, "I'm a sleepy person," and although the storm is called a "bad one," there's so much joy in merely looking [perhaps the only present "joy" on the whole album, a cheaper alternative to margaritas!] to—slow us down—to wonder.... [does the song *sound* like snow to you?]

But it's not really just about snow. I sense a wisdom here necessary to counter the 'move fast, break things' plutocratic technocratic 21st century constant manufacturing of desires, and their flipside fears, by sucking us in with the loss-leader of just enough immediate gratification to set us up for a state of constant anticipation of reward and disappointment.

There's also a relationship in this poem between people, or call them souls or roles, that suggests an alternative to the shopper-seller-commodity dynamic of "Story-Line Fever." One character is presumably homeless in the cold wind and snow, but unlike the homeless man in Craig Morgan's "Almost Home," the beauty is in the present—not just a dream of childhood, and this person *is* seeking shelter. The other character is a "good caretaker" who offers shelter and warmth, and I'm reminded of Alissa Quart's passionate defense and championing of what she calls "care-workers" or "the careforce" in her 2018 book, *Squeezed*. A good caretaker is a nice thing to find, and also a nice thing to be—perhaps not too dissimilar to the mother guardian in another song on this album.[71]

The penultimate stanza steps out of the speaker and situation, and their highly formal, impersonal tableau, or black and white minimalist art film, to offer a kind of *ars poetica*:

> Songs build little rooms in time
> and housed within the song's design
> is the ghost the host has left behind
> to greet and sweep the guest inside.
> stoke the fire and sing his lines.

Can a song be a good caretaker? Does the meaning of "ghost" change once someone has died?

This evocation of the host's ghost's power to sweep the guest in, to stoke the fire, is the charm of David's disarming intimacy. I indeed feel included in this song, as a guest, or even patient. Notice the absence of a personal pronoun to describe "the fire"—not mine or yours. I first took these lines to suggest that the song lyrics can be shed skins, like what John Ashbery calls, "Saying It io Keep It From Happening" or what music therapists might call the cathartic powers of the blues, but these days I tend to think about it more in terms of an afterlife, or at least an astral plane.

"Story-line Fever" had its "part-poltergeist" Facebook friends, but "Nights That Won't Happen" (with its ghosting of white satin the color of snow) sings "ghosts are just

---

71

old houses dreaming people in the night," and "death is the black camel that kneels down so we can ride," I feel intimations of immortality, and when he sings "when the here and the hereafter momentarily align" I'm reminded of "We Are Real" from *American Water* (1998):

> when off and on collide
> we'll set our souls aside
> and walk away....

And this non-static sense of an afterlife reminds me of some of Gillian Conoley's poems, and of what Judy Juanita told me when she helped me decipher the postcard David sent me on the last day of his life: "sometimes when someone leaves us abruptly, it's because they have somewhere else to go." In the final verse of "Snow Is Falling in Manhattan," David sings:

> Snow is falling in Manhattan
> inside I got a fire crackling
> and on the couch beneath an afghan
> you're the old friend I just took in.

This is the first time an "I" and "you" dynamic enters the song, and there's a quiet astral plane braggadocio here that puns on the phrase "took you in." And here I am, sitting in my car, bundled up in a hat and coat, on a cold December Oakland rain over 4 months after you died, not even listening to your album, but just slowly reading a light blue lyric sheet, I want to exclaim! "Yes, indeed, you fucker, your beautiful fucking soulful fucker, I fucking BELIEVE you!" I do feel sheltered & warmed, quite physically, in your little room, with a warm crackling fire. You don't even have to use the word "soul" to teach me something about death...and provide an antidote to what made me skeptical about "Almost Home." *Purple Mountains* does manage to "avoid self-pity, self-flattery and the redemptive upshot" and its *agape* may very well work to counter the scurrilous techniques of the manipulative mouthpiece who said that "fear and anger stays with people longer than love and sympathy."

5. Coda: "We Are Not Monsters."

He sent the album on February 12. I was floored by its conscience scouring, soul reckoning, emptying out of blame, the lack of a cry for help, the via negative kenosis, the cliché of absolute isolation as ideal form. I told David it was perfect timing, since I had just come out of ER with a near-death experience, coupled with the fact that my closest friend, ex-girlfriend, was incommunicado in a hospital and I had no idea if she was still alive in the dead of winter; it made me feel less alone...

I couldn't shake the feeling that neither David nor I were long for this earth, and felt a need to respond better, "in kind" even if only as therapy, to pay him back by helping myself, and I can personally testify the scary power of *Purple Mountains* got me writing my first songs in 8 years, something I never thought I'd do again.

When the opportunity to play Greg Ashley's grand piano availed itself, I found my whole being vibrating vamping on the hypnotic 2 chord progression at the end of "Story Line Fever"—not so much to memorize David's plodding staccato *parlando* delivery of words as to "digest" them—and it awakened my vocal cords to groggily scream the repressed pain of a degenerative spine from too much sitting.

Though David had never once lorded it over me with his superior craftsmanship, and liked some of my songs over the years, I knew I wasn't really a good lyric-writer, in part, as both of us agreed, because of my poetic training and interests, and my over-self-consciousness. I won't blame my vocabulary though; David was always great about sticking in at least one surprising polysyllabic over-sophisticated word in a song, but *Purple Mountains* gave me an idiom that compelled me to confront a photo album of my past meannesses, and come clean about my flaws in a way I couldn't do in poetry, with what even my internal severe linguistic skeptic would probably have to acknowledge as anguish.

As I thought of what I would bequeath if I were to die now, and not just on a "material" level, all I could see was flaws: the eating disorder, the nature deprivation, old man defenses, out of touch with senses, obsessive need to create, cheating on lovers with jobs:

a search for moderation that's been known to be extreme:

     one year mourn a militant another an aesthete.

That final vacillation David and I shared.

How becoming a critic hollowed out my ability to write poems, as if beating myself up for being self-indulgent was any less self-indulgent than had I just let myself be self-indulgent in the first place:

was I so goddamn woke I could do it in my sleep?...
Spent years building a megaphone, but forgot what I should speak?

And, most importantly, here's my bad social behavior:

In this one, friends are fighting & I couldn't come between
     Here's 5 where I lack follow-through, 15 where I'm too mean

Perhaps I mistranslated what I read as David's faith in cathartic purging as: *"I don't know, must I expose it?/ Yes, or no, just to depose it."* David was glad to hear he got me writing songs again, and offered to listen and offer advice. I didn't want to send him any of the "lighter" songs I was working on because I felt David wanted me darker, and more serious about mortality, and soul-reckoning than

I'd ever been before. Because I was still embarrassed by the song most inspired by his—fearing it might come off like a watered down unintentional parody, I sent him a low-fi crappy solo-piano demo of three of the other slow, either sad, darker, or tender, melodic ones I wrote after, both addressed to women in the second person "you," relationship break-up attempted praise song in which the male "I" is also trying to not blame the woman, but realize his own mistakes, a more clichéd mode than David's.

Purple Mountains doesn't really have a breakup song that addresses the "you." Even "She's Making Friends, I'm Turning Stranger" seems to me more of a praise to the woman, or expresses an introvert/extrovert love relationship, ending with "She's my friend, and I'm her stranger."

4 days later he wrote back:

both sound promising.
can you send me the words?
no matter how provisional.

In all our years of exchanging songs with each other, one interesting difference was that David always needed to see and send me lyrics on the page before he could really listen. I was the opposite. When David would send me lyrics, I was always afraid to offer any critique until I heard the music. That's probably part of why David is a better lyricist than I. Although his melodies are at least as catchy as mine, I always saw David as a "Word first" guy. A day later, he sent a list of corrections—many emphasizing the all-important little words:

i cant be sure any of these corrections are right
for you.
and the corrections with ? are just a guess
and may not be an improvement.

the second song i think you should do
the no no no part two times. the part is very sad
in a sister lovers kind of way

+++

On April 28, I wrote:
Thanks for your help with my songs again—
I think repeating those no no nos in that song can work——

Chris
Yes yes yes…

+++

On Apr 29, 2019, at 11:32 AM, D.C. Berman wrote:

the no no no part
is the place to put the pain
and loneliness

you swallow in the verses

He soothed my worries, and gave me confidence, and I didn't need to bug him with the other songs, but a month later, I finally got the nerve up to send him "Sitting," a song that still had the power to scare me:

May 28, 2019:
one of your best songs it sounded like

what are the words?

May 29, 2019

just as i suspected.

its great piece, chris.

i see nothing i could suggest to improve it.

congratulations. could be your best song.

Thanks David. It means a lot, especially coming from you.

***

On July 18, 2019, David sent the *Spin* Review, with which I started the essay, asking:

why does it matter than I'm a white male
or that other white males might relate?...
isn't this "the stuff that get trump elected" ?

I immediately wrote David a passionate response of support: "Who gave this smug heartless critic the key to the "ethical norm" judgment throne??? So, what's his "properly well adjusted" ethical alternative? ...—Fuck this, and fuck him, and fuck *Spin*...."

I keep going back to David's beautiful portrayal of the epidemic of veterans of war committing suicide in "Empty Military Cemetery On Memorial Day." For some, to express such deep sympathy, empathy, and agape for these soldiers is on the "wrong side" of identity politics, even though many soldiers are not white male.

Furthermore, I'm just being descriptive if I say David generally *liked* music by white people more than he did black music, but, in contrast to the millions of whites who love black music but not black people, David loved reading and learning the perspective and generally agreed with the writings of the black and feminist intellectuals and revolutionaries I sent him. On one level, this just comes down to the national city-country divide that is often watered down as the less accurate "blue state/ red state" divide—David was operating in a red state, and I was operating in a blue state. Where I lived most of the veterans I knew were not white, so I tended to emphasize racism more than David. Yet we had a unity-in-diversity attitude against the common enemy, like Richard Berman who literally makes a killing off dividing the poor and oppressed from each other. David never gave up that cause, but knew it doesn't always have to be politicized, and I've seen, over and over, David's art and cultural work did have the power to bring people together and…

I had sent David a blog entry that in retrospect seems rushed, but I took David's cue about the album's theme of "male failure" when I wrote that "I as a 50 something male can relate." After reading Howe's piece, I was afraid it would offend David: "If you want me to cut it, I will."

On Jul 19, 2019, at 10:52 AM, D.C. Berman <dcberman@ outlook.com> wrote:

leave it right there. we are not monsters.

This reminded me of when he signed an email, "your brother in misery." That was our last exchange aside from the poetic post-card he sent the day he died, an image of distant snow-covered mountains, and in the foreground, the alliterative beauty of Lundy Lake. On the back, he wrote, nearly illegibly, "a perfect wedding for a Wednesday." On the day of his funeral, which I celebrated alone at the piano, I heard a voice say: "If you're not going to let me go yet, at least play some music of the spheres like the long instrumental of Lou Reed's "The Ocean" at U-Mass back in 1993." Then a pretty melody came to me, and maybe in it I could *put the pain and loneliness* [I'm] *swallow*ing in this attempt at "reasonable and collegial" prose.[72] I haven't tried to write a song since...

***

"*I'm just remembering*
I'm just remembering..."

---

72   https://www.youtube.com/watch?v=pUqkwmyUOJs&t=15s

4.

GILLIAN CONOLEY
A LITTLE MORE/ RED SUN ON/ THE HUMAN
[NIGHTBOAT BOOKS, 2019]

This *New & Selected* collects poems from Conoley's seven books, from 1987's *Some Gangster Pain* to the present. Wide-ranging stylistically & tonally, its richly varied music may appeal to different readers. We are invited to read it chronologically, from tight early lyrics to middle period fragments to the sprawling, yet precise, new (de)compositions that transcend the distinction between lyric, fragment and narrative. After doing that once, the back and forth may be even better. One may find what Tongo Eisen-Martin (in a blurb) calls a "singular energy" reverberating through the decades.

Compare, for instance, on a microscopic level of a line or a couplet, the languaging of "where silence/sends word" [96] in an earlier poem to a later poem in which silence sends "a hatchet with which to chop at the frozen seas inside us" [273]. In the painterly terms of the book's title, the latter line puts a little more red on the sun. Silence may also send loafing, inviting words of lung-like liminality:

soul made   to deflate, inflate
            to transfer   like breath to a summer-
hammock [311]

Such transfers abound in this collection. Just as this

couplet could be read either horizontally or vertically, the transfers can be between the human & the non-human, life and death (or immortality), the ways the dead and living, night-wounds and day-wounds [155], belief and doubt, converse. In one of the 43 new pages of poetry in this book, as Conoley meditates on her relationship with a "weak black bee," she asks:

I wonder if courage in one world
can create an expanse in another
          Is it akin to lovers who are alive in each
other? [281]

This has similarities with many of the earliest poems included in this connection:

If I nap in this light my grandparents rise
and mix their dominoes, their hands
rinsed of sun but bone pure.
What if I left with them,
and shed my body? Would I
hear a single, melodious siren
singing the power,
the glory? Or would I
live on, as the earth continues,
in death's sediment, face to face,
these melodies strewn through me." ["Suddenly the
Graves" 8]

Even the dead live "in death's sediment;" death is no "final resting place/no closed down factory" [68], no once-and-for all transition, and ancestors' spirits persist in the matter that sometimes becomes us. In "My Sister's Hand in Mine," inhabiting the soul, or at least the shoes, of the dead can also serve a kind of practical purpose in getting us beyond feelings of nostalgia and loss that even little kids feel:

> the past was a souvenir
> that could propel us
> from one void into another
> until we grew up
> like women who sold perfume
> walking around
> in their dead aunt's shoes...   [31]

As she announces her need to embrace death's 'common deep' as a positive force in life, listening to the "cry/ not of the living/ or dead, but the narrow between." [5], Conoley lets it widen, trying to heed the voice that says "let us place no more constraints on the eyes of dead" [243] and if that doesn't work, there's always a "Pale kimono in the closet in case we had got blasé/ about death being loose in us." [193]. It helps me when experiencing what's often reduced to grieving or mourning against a backdrop of estranged secular humanism [childhood "streets/ that claimed my home/ was invisible," 13] that elevates reason over body and death.

The dance between the souls of the living and the dead get more intimate in the poems from *Beckon* [1996]. Because "We Don't Have To Share A Fate" says "we don't have to draw shameful conclusions,"[57] it's tempting to read this as an un-judgmental address to one who committed suicide…. to be as respectful as possible to that decision while avoiding the temptation to feel guilty for not wanting to follow suit:

After the shutter releases,
I want you in the multiple, [57]

Avoiding object fetishization, respect turns to eroticism as the speaker seems to find the entire world in their relationship. "Painterly, Epigean, Dream's Hangover," from *Fatherless Afternoon [Profane Halo, 2005]* contrasts two styles of grieving, without necessarily judging either:

A griever in a party hat
                    come to lay like a corpse
                    before the weeper.   [149]

This stanza itself may seem incredibly witty and comic at first, but the next line makes it clear which mood the speaker is in:

"Stifle me not with the opposite."

I almost hear the exclamation point here, a "put the

lid on your wit! and let me be alone with my fructifying tears!" In this dialogue poem, grieving occasions moral reckoning and a sense of futurity leading to presents as the speaker lets the spirit of the recently dead be selfish enough to help her live more fully in emptiness than before in glut. Yet no clear distinction between living and dead takes hold. Who's telling who "It's bewildering but I can get you out of storage." Or perhaps the "weeper" is the living and the "griever in a party hat" is the dead trying to cheer her up? Is it the voice *of death* that's "way beyond the elucidative stage' to end with a beautiful, or at least awe-inspiring unfinishing…to undo the merely Epigean surface of the doubting newspapers of life?

"Thank You For The Afterlife"—a new 6 page poem— is an adventure in conversing with a dead "mother figure" and/or the "Creator." [290]. The relationship dynamics seem more volatile and antagonistic. The life of the dead is figured to be at least as lively or even restless as the death of the living:

Celestial nest, also like stress, hormone,
breathing with high peaks

skeletal sensory too, combustible planetarium,

an interstitial musculature where

ceiling angels peel and flake a weather

turned glassy in which you

are the shaken narrator   bundled up

taking a few trips   around the block, running one
loose hand over

the increasingly familiar hedges (293,4)

Yet Conoley often lets herself make room for the materialist and skeptic voice, "in this missive oblivion/ where synapse thinks it saw a spirit"[291]—at least until it threatens to tyrannize. Many spirits could be read into this mother figure:

For what have you done

that so many run to surround and warm

you, a boy and a girl so porous with the air,

lunar, earthly, I try very hard to never close the parenthesis on you,

it's one way to atone

for perhaps you are just swimming

slowly   to another scribe waiting

sort of perpendicularly   in the lake   near the shore
[294]

There's also a critique—in the collection's most expansive, previously unpublished recent poem, "Preparing one's consciousness for the avatar,"—of the still economically and politically dominant Euro-centric patriarchal ethics-cloaking metaphysics at play, and part of what makes it so affectively effective is that it lets itself relent.

She accepts a working definition of avatar as "manifestation of a deity or released soul in bodily form," a soul that *crosses down*. By contrasting it with the word "atavistic" which is rooted in the word "forefather," Conoley warns us that much of what may pass for an avatar may be merely atavistic, but how to tell—I mean figure—the difference? Throughout the poem, she offers a series of ethical contrasts, from a game of cat and bird to the difference between the atavistic "Frankenstein bewildered at his limp" and an avatar she finds in "the young muscled amputee in basketball shorts   heading cheerfully" as "world welcomes more   world   in sun" [305]

The atavistic Frankensteinian god scientist brain becomes cutting edge, 'state of the art' in the figure of David Hanson, of Hanson Robotics, reproducing the facial expressions and voice of an internet billionaire and transhumanist techno optimist who defends robots on the grounds of immortality and ending world hunger. To Conoley's speaker, it's the same-old-maleist atavism…on steroids as it were. Though the techies may invoke the disembodied possibilities of the post-human, from the perspective of what the collection's title poem calls "the first germ of life/afloat in the swampy gale" [142], such post-human is, if anything, human all too human. To reduce this section to its argument, however, ignores the alternative figure she presents near this poem's end:

Of all my friends and figures

I prefer the woman who walks   in the loosest way

down the conveyor belt, along the metronomes and mechanical dolls,

like one who prefers to not be there—   had nothing to do with it—

does not want to   command or suggest, only to go on one's own way

through the   discordant collective sweep [314]

But even this figure must "pixelate" or live as "blooms

and ducts   of a repatterning [316].

Although this book often celebrates the "pleasure/ in becoming another one/of the unlocated" [72]," and Conoley very rarely traffics in the "post-card face" of domesticity, it would be a mistake to call these transfers otherworldy or anti-social:

I fall into the lace of your gutter,
                              pretty nice there
          and we have to wire prose into talk to get to the poem. (318)

KRYSIA JOPEK
HOURGLASS STUDIES
(CRISIS CHRONICLES, 2017)

I tried to write "about" this book, but the writing turned into:

"those story facts, dust of the empirical, collage spun into pastiche by emphatic critics stripping the coda. Everything reified; go home." (2)

Hourglass Studies moves in short sections lined as if prose whose almost aphoristic quality sometimes renders them lines. This form has similarities with other books I've recently read (Suzanne Stein's *New Sutras*, Alli Warren's *Little Hill* and Chris Nealon's *The Shore*, all published in 2020), in each to radically different effect. Perhaps I could do *Hourglass Studies* better service by just quoting some of these short sections that especially grabbed my attention, and calmed it down in the middle of a meltdown:

"Someone convinces we were needed in that house where sorrow slips in on a Saturday, accordions the stairs." (9)

"Wrists ache for a paintbrush to supersede the photograph. Neck falls to confound interval, whispers to the knees to straighten and heal, forget the long winter up ahead." (12)

"Names can be changed, change can be given, wind can push light objects through the street." (13)

"Push me! The boy orders   the swing   tangling verdant
[lush] decrescendo[s] [of] the marshland   arching   from the
definitive."

Or, sometimes a single-word can do it, if there is such
a thing. I could think of Dickinson's:

"internal difference –
Where the Meanings, are –

when Jopek writes *"[melanc]/*holy." (20)

4 years after reading the book, this figure—it doesn't
seem fair to call it a word—returns to me often as a kind
of healer. This use of brackets that push the envelope
of language's ability to harbor multiple meanings,
perspectives and moods which tend to get more complex
as the book progresses:

…..the hand[le] slips out of focus, displaces the current…(7)

…the last day of vacation around the [is]land, different each
time…(7)

…Torrential downpour and thunder [deco]rate sleep to tell
of the [s]hip, the [t]rain, the waiting to be carried [a book]
under someone's arm" (14)

"pass out pain[t] for everyone"

"Furiously night after night [p]urging emotions."

"The goodbye proven with [photo]graphs, waiting for the roof to heal, undo the laces, finish the prop[hecy], so there could be surprise again without the ego's shallow pit[fall]." (19)

"The notebook [of winter] fell from the wind[ow]. Everything heavy when days are X-rayed by night, the chest falls back [in c]loud." (20)

"The feet sting upon landing: memory [g]losses ambit[ion]. (20)

By the time we reach the final poem (section XII, as in clocks have 12 hours, years have 12 months, etc), the eponymous word "Hourglass" finally appears for the first time, even though there had been many clocks:

"The hourglass flipped the conversation over. How to end when one doesn't recognize the beginning?"

*"I wake and remember I am [a] stranger."…..Being what they seem,…..*time again has meaning"

The director's arms rock the camera and eucalyptus
Drunkenly
And [time] becomes a [char]acter" (30)

KO KO THETT
THE BURDEN OF BEING BURMESE
(ZEPHYR PRESS, 2015)

As news of another military coup and mass murder of citizens in Myanmar goes viral in the (selective attention of) the American media, many are expressing outrage, sympathy, empathy, thoughts and prayers,[73] yet fewer, apparently, are speaking of England and America's fingerprints in the misery of modern militarized Myanmar. In *The Burden of Being Burmese* (Zephyr Press, 2015), ko ko thett, a Burmese living in exile in England, provides that education, speaking truth to power in solidarity with the oppressed and his fellow poets who are being slaughtered by the government, many of whom he has translated. Since this book is his first translation into English, however, thett understands the burden of being read as represenative, declawed into commodity exchange: ("Buy me, get my country free," 61). In other poems, he turns the gaze on his first-world reader with subtle nuance.

Although this book is dazzling poetically and hilariously brilliant, it's not what one would call a comfortable book. As he provides the English-speaking world with educational portraits of many home-grown atrocities "where boys my age get routinely dehumanized"

---

73 See, for instance, "In Burma, They Have Come For The Poets." https://www.dallasnews.com/opinion/commentary/2021/03/21/in-burma-they-have-come-for-the-poets/

(19), "spent mortar shells are reborn as vases for/ Buddhist shrines and pagodas." (20) and "everyone suffers adjustment disorder" (20), he's a master of social and political ironies that, beyond nationalism, show the burdens of the various imperialisms that are sometimes more benignly called globalism.

We see a country being "colonized by bottled water," (4) "where street vendors who used to sell falafel for rice noodles/have found bootlegging dvds more profitable" (15). Nor is food colonization a new phenomenon, but part of a noble tradition, like chemical warfare, going back at least as far as the 19th century. Monosodium Glutamate, for instance, is: "the buddha's poop that has colonized our cuisines since 1908....from the shrimp cocktail of Nasa astronauts in space to/ the food aid package in east Africa." (86). Neither are Big Pharma and the opioid addiction immune from thett's satirical wit, nor is the English language: ("a language that never makes you feel good about sex," 14).

At times, one may detect a nostalgia-by-default for a prelapsarian pre-colonized time, though at other times, he has a great deal of mordantly recursive pleasure satirizing this tendency, whether seen in himself, or in others; for instance "my generation is best," which also manages to satirize "my country is best" nationalism in the process. Or check out the movement of this stanza from "chaos clock:"

cockfights used to be popular here

the blood sport is barbaric
people now have other options
scorecasting is not a zero-sum game
investment is pouring in, reeking draws fruit flies
ricky draws angles. (17)

Sometimes he speaks in the voice of, the "Caucasian engineers," (20), the imperial self, and the masters of manipulation, whether they take more visible form (tanks), or more invisible forms (banks). The speaker and situation of "urban renewal," may be an urban planner speaking to a city, and nature, in the voice of a psychologist, preacher or big brother offering tough-love advice to a friend. Lines that at first might not seem like such a bad thing tend to have a double-edged sword when considered as trickle-down policies. In "the public transit in your brain"(28), this speaker warns, there should be (and, dammit, shall be!):

dog parks for dogs,
amusement parks for amusements, child-friendly facilities
for the parents of children who may never grow up,
bingo halls for all ages and sexual preferences. (28)

Yet, on closer observations, one may ask questions: What about those who don't enjoy amusement parks? What about the playgrounds you defunded? Why are dogs being segregated into the dog parks (what he elsewhere calls "the hammer of animalism" 16). Do all ages and sexual preferences really want to be forced to play bingo? No! this is Blake's "charter'd city" on steroids, brain candy, happiness pie! Though thett may be talking about Burma in "urban renewal," he is so adept at making the atrocities of the martial law panopticon visible, his wry observational eye in these persona poems in the voice of worldly power, stripped of specific context, could be easily translated to many of America's and England's social crises (which makes sense, since we've exported them), in however etiolated a first-world form.

And, yes, even the soul is gentrified. Not only shall graffiti "be encouraged/ on the inner walls of your empty chest," but:

all administrative quarters of your soul shall be made/
soundproof to prevent the intrusion of street noises
malling, walling, enthralling, and everything else...
(29)

This sense of spiritual or psychic martial law reminds me of Jello Biafra's "Stay In Your Homes" ("the luxuries you demanded have now become mandatory.") Though this poem is presented as a future dystopia, perhaps America's future can be seen in Burma's present. We could also, however, see the past of Anglo-Americans in this portrayal of the durian-skinned soul. After all, it's not too different from the dominant Anglo-American philosophies during the time when England first colonized

Burma, and the one-way subject-object relationships they were used to justify—as in another poem spoken in the voice of worldly power:

> happiness is best served at room temperature
> [my room temperature, not yours]
> it goes down really well with *dukkha*
> [your *dukkha*, not mine]   (79)

Thett's implication is that soundproofing your soul may lead to making you an absolute tyrant. Lacking *mettā* (a Buddhist word for loving-kindness, compassion, or disinterested love), such a soundproof, bullet-proof soul radiates *dukkha* (the Buddhist concept of suffering, angst, anguish, frustration, pain, affliction, anxiety—the general burdens of life) and needs to be "cut" (53-54) with "fresh gags below the waistline" (16). He also directly addresses this imperial self beneath the well-intentioned American. Take, for instance, the first stanza of "fuck me untied:"

> are you one of those who will import
> our rice so you can bomb our village
> you believe in the charity of your moneyed class
> now that my body is stuck in your bottleneck, there is
> no spillover effect, save for your sperm.   (39)

In personalizing this global relationship between the first world consumer (and writer with "sweet monologues," 39) and the 'out of sight, out of mind' dehumanized producers (or human resources) as rape, in a world without *mettā*, thett expresses the trauma, depression and numbness personally. One effect of this is an absolute feeling of alienation:

> i no longer trust the public ride
> faced with the leviathan, i will be playing possum
> lying low like a benthic fish, if not committing
> another suicide   (39)

Looking for a sliver of hope in this loveless disconnection, a reader may detect a defense of the inward turn of poetic solitude as a survival strategy that, if nothing else, can practice obstacles, and prevent him from turning the violence and threats directed at him from others into an act of self-sabotage. Such faith, however, that this can lead to a kind of rebirth, or resistance to the aggressive hunger of the colonizer (or a lover who may act imperialist) on a strictly personal level, is at best temporary. Near the end of another poem, "the rain maker," thett presents, in a more detached third person tone, an "after picture" to the dark night of the soul in "fuck me, untied:"

> look how the dormant underdog,
> taken for granted rotten-dead,
> has sprung back to life on *dukkha* media! (71)

By referring to *dukkha* as a form of media, I feel a

skepticism towards the "resurrection" enabled by the path of possum-like dormancy. Perhaps we could read this as self-satire, but, in the context of the poem, this image is really a mirage onto which we, the reader, will inevitably project meanings, feelings, connotations or past experiences (as he sardonically invites us to "turn the projector on" in the first line). This "dormant underdog" is a type, an "it."

> sickened with divided attention disorder
> it jumps over the crown, chokes and
> strangles the aristocratic order   (72)

The divided attention disorder could be his own project of combining the personal with the political, the domestic with the global, the multi-tasking and hybridism. It could be those who try to combine poetry with social status in other poems. It could also a transcendental spirit or a revolutionary, which seems to have positive connotations, were it not for the fact that many who present themselves socially as transcendental (my kingdom is not of this world), or revolutionary become future dictators. After all, capitalism, too, "strangles the aristocratic order." Perhaps it refers to Aung San Suu, who had been elected not long before (and who, in 2021, was overthrown by military coup). Having seen this movie so many times, starring one who may even genuinely be trying to make things better only to make things worse, the next stanza suggests an alternative:

the kingdom now needs a flea leap forward
the newly elected leader may be comely
just don't expect her to change the clime   (72)

In my projections of thett's meanings, I take the "flea leap forward" as the possibility of lyric poetry, the inward turn, the need for dormancy against the "move-fast, break things" Zuckerbergian world that's fueled by and preys on the insatiable addictive hunger of consumerism. Thett's cynicism towards just about any strictly political solution is rooted in what in 21st century American poetics may be called slow poetry and/or eco-poetry in a way that appeals to wit-crackers like myself who may not be moved as much by an earnest plea to truly humble ourselves before the power of nature as if that could maybe stop global climate change:

isn't it fascinating?
how each and every cowry trapped in a hallowed-out bamboo
houses an entire symphony orchestra
(72)

The defense of flea-like smallness in this poem's final "mirage" could recall Emily Dickinson's "The spreading wide my narrow Hands/ To gather Paradise—." (466), yet even here, such a statement is not unqualified, for it must also be mentioned that the cowry was, in Burma, used for money. Unlike many poets who believe they can fight a spiritual war against capitalism by banishing economic terms from their poetry, I dare say that thett's reverence for nature comes through, like *mettā,* in between the lines of capital and its *dukkha.*

In digging deep into the conscience of readers who may feel they have no moral blind-spots, and poets whose conscience has "been ideologically castrated" (56), at one point he writes, "there's no municipal services to collect your moral trash" (16), and "your karma is you." (77) A question of morality arises: what is morality in a social media world of virtue signaling, where the private is more fishbowled, where "sale items, dressed in poverty and virgin virtue/ vie for the highest bidder" (15)? Do we need the feeling or concept of immortality to live a kinder, more moral life on earth? Thett is certainly skeptical of how the promise of an afterlife is employed by people in power who want you dead (at one point he calls them the "afterlife insurance salespeople" 79):

people are welcome, problems are not
living is expensive, but dying doesn't cost a dime
where else in the world can you enjoy a free funeral".
(17)

And:

to age is to get less serious
about life, to die is to be incinerated to be reincarnated,

a multi-purpose stadium for metal concerts and the
vispassana for the masses (29)

When I first read "Anxiety Attack" (73), with lines
like, "every detail of your life will be laid bare," it seemed
like a poem about judgement day, but as the poem
continues, it becomes clearer that the "immortality"
this poem is talking about is your reputation on earth
("future generations will be overwhelmed....researchers
will no doubt nose into your diaries" and, closer to home,
a literary person with "a penchant for post-modern flip-
flops," an emblem for moral relativism and what thett, as
"flip flop thief" (79), calls ideological castration.

I read this poem as a conscience scouring cautionary
tale, to at least question what the desire for any kind
of fame, however modest, is, and whether or not you're
implicated in it more than you think, and whether it has
maybe robbed your soul. This facing of the darkness of
dukkha (whether in others or himself) is not an attempt
to outsmart death as much as it's a reminder that we don't
have to wait for death.

In "the rain maker," he offers (faux) advice to his
readers, "you don't want to be another down comforter."
Perhaps *The Burden of Being Burmese*, working in the
trenches of arrogant contemporary corruption, suggests
it's better to be an *up afflicter* than a down comforter. But
though thett's book doesn't offer any specific solutions for
these systemic atrocities and human meanness, it engages
in a cathartic, detoxifying karmic payback to anyone with

ears; its meta-poetic aspects may even clear the way for more *mettā*.

Wit is highlighted even more in poems that explore the madness of discourse of a dissembling culture that may enable "divided attention disorder." For instance, "after 'the lie of art'"(41), transcends the page-v-stage distinction with its playful, but at times maddening, binaries that remind of Lydia Tomkiw and Algebra Suicide's "Proverbial Explanation for Why No Action is Taken," or "faith supper" which may recall The Buzzcock's "A Different Type of Tension."

In "no football color" (57), we see the 3-dimensional wit in a single-line, when he asks:

"shouldn't the referee always trust her lineman?" Saying referees rather than the more conventional quarterback implies what many suspect: the game is rigged, fixed, government spies, Astroturf people's movements, and what of the gender change to her? "Lineman" could also refer to poets.

Finally, I should not neglect the sad laments that appeal more to pathos than logos such as "the 5000th." Many times, in reference to the contagion of the oppressor's psychological aggressions, it's been said, oppression makes a wise man mad. In ko ko thett's poetry, "brahmin the economist" says "the mean reversion may or may not be inevitable," (46), yet *The Burden of Being Burmese* suggests that that economic jargon, perhaps, can yet be translated poetically into an ethics of post-capitalist *mettā*.

SANDRA SIMONDS
FURTHER PROBLEMS WITH PLEASURE
(UNIV. OF AKRON PRESS, 2017)

In a recent review of Sandra Simonds' *Further Problems with Pleasure, Publisher's Weekly* emphasizes the book's Gothic elements which "report the damage amid the ruins," but I find a transformative power beyond the damage in these poems' unfurling futurity that goes far beyond "profane observations competing for attention with declarative assertions on the absurdities of love and literature and 21st-century living."

I feel wisdom (for instance, "the absence of sadness/ may create bitterness" 61). Other words that first come to my mind are: experienced, brilliant, warm, vibrant, alive, present, intimate, generative, generous, passionate, anti-puritanical, gender-bending, fun, chastising, resilient, workaholic, righteous, conversational, self-mocking, romantic, theatrical and sublime equipment for living. And I'm sure I'm missing better ones, both denotatively and connotatively. And when PW claims the "speakers self-govern even when the world grows murky or difficult," they make it sound like Romper Room or Mr. Rogers— not spousal abuse!

While many books of poetry begin slowly with shorter poems, and tend to time-release some heavy central themes that don't become clearer, on first reading, until enough details accrue maybe around page 30, *Further Problems with Pleasure* jumps right in, with a 5-page poem to establish the ethos, logos, and pathos of a speaker trying to extricate herself from an abusive relationship (without revealing too many details):

> The one trick I've always fallen back on
> is to make a man think/
> he's the one rejecting me
> But it was so quiet in your room
> even if you had long books
> written by evil men...(1))

Despite, or even because, of titles like "Poetry Is Stupid And I Want To Die" or "This stuff is poison and It's Gonna Fuck Up My Shit," the poetry may yet have the power to get her out of this destructive relationship, even if she has to identify with Keats' urn, the bride *and* the mother, to do it. Imagination becomes a weapon and a survival tool. To escape a situation, or to transform it? Does poetry have the ability to make an abusive "partner" disappear? If inspiration can't come, can you force a sustained poetic trance-state with hard work? This is a faith tested relentlessly throughout.

We are also introduced to her sinuous, capacious, long-lines, which afford her an ability to navigate a wide range of moods and modes about as close to prose as you can be and still be poetry. On a technical level, her muscular lines use run-ons to condense & allow multiple meanings: "I know how to wash her mellow hair glides like a swan." Despite the conversational elegance of Simonds styles and/or voices, she writes in "Poem For Joe," that "They said my poems/ were a mess" (31), and, indeed, many strict formalists, minimalists or puritanical abstractionists may feel threatened by these poems, but on repeated readings, it becomes clearer that even the most seemingly meandering and flowing poems have a well-crafted structure in which words and themes that may have gotten lost in the fierce devotion to the present circle back with a charming vengeance to shape the poem (trace, for instance, the "career" of the word "mall" in "Fun Clothes: A Gothic"), as she digs her way out of the strictures of her detractors while finding joy in "the plasma of subjectivity revolving like a ballerina." (12)

+++

The title "Fun Clothes: A Gothic" (another maximalist long poem) suggests the cosmic and emotional balance Simonds' collection achieves. On one level, it could be usefully compared to Anne Boyer's recent *Garment Against Women* (or Cydney Chadwick's earlier *Enemy Clothing*) in its elastic feminist performativity that positions itself in relation to the omnipresent hetero male gaze, but this theme is also about embodiment in general, as the poem begins rather abstractly, with no body but the (sublime, and/or repressed) physicality of language:

Schizophrenia like suds in the afternoon, bubbles and bubbles of the glorious

prism, molds of forensic happenings, and you speak
softly in a delectable armory,
                    in feathers,
bursts, bras not afraid of being impoverished, afraid,
alas, that this disguise will
                    morph
to human flesh, the underneath in chains that vibrate
the invisible soundscape
of deposits, a debt the color of frog skin, how can he
hold back the incredible lush
                    device that is
the body….(24)

The theme of embodiment also occurs in the title poem, in which she takes a Chris Nealon quote as a starting place ("Sometimes I wonder what the novel would have looked/ like if instead of plots its characters had bodies"); Simonds writes:

    Maybe some want
a grand narrative instead of this
            instantaneous flesh flash mob
bullshit but I can't help loving
            the way you want me
to suck your dick. (32)

Notice, she's not saying she wants it, or that she'll do it. The PW review claims there's a "frequent parallel between bodily want and a kind of spiritual crisis," yet their use of the word "parallel" too easily accepts the terms of mind/ body dualism that this poem deconstructs, or transcends, as tenor and vehicle switch places in her elaborate conceit that also considers (or constructs) the body's eroticized relationship to consumerism. On another, overlapping, level, it invites the reader to consider the relationship between reading and writing poetry to the trial and error of clothes. In Simonds, as in Ovid's *Metamorphosis,* it is not necessarily the "self" that is changing costumes either, especially against the backdrop of a patriarchal Euro-poetry tradition in which women are more mused than allowed to muse.

***

If there's any possibility juice left in the muse tradition, Simonds milks it for all its worth. The muse tradition becomes especially reinvented in the polyvocal, gender bending "Baudelaire Variations" that spatially occupy the book's "center." The "Baudelaire Variations" show that Simonds excels in the shorter, tighter, lyric as much as the longer expansive poems that frame it. One could say that intimately engaging the 19th Century French "decadent" symbolist affords her access to the seediest sides of the canonical male (art) psyche that has so often colonized women: how does a 21st century woman respond to, appropriate, and reinvent that (alien) male tradition? In this, these poems could be great fodder for college comparison-*contrast literary analysis papers (like*

Tyehimba Jess' recent critical appropriations of Berryman's *Dream Songs* in *Olio*).

In "The Sick Muse," for instance, it might seem we could assume the speaker is Simonds herself, invoking (and talking back to) Baudelaire as her muse:

I can't succumb to you so quickly, but all my verse
               pours so easily into the rose love of your urns.
        I could try to hide it, but the depth is despotic
and all I really care to do is float on your rhythmic waves
(56)

Simonds is not merely criticizing Baudelaire's intoxicated emotional extravagances, but identifying with them in a way that would be difficult to do as a seemingly transparent authentic "I." Who, or what, is saying "I have hurt myself so I become dangerous" and "I wrote you the most brutal love poem love knows" (64)?

In Edith Wharton's *The Muse's Tragedy*, the heroine had been a victim of being made a muse by a man who didn't love her: "It was soul to soul, never hand to hand." In "Fountains of Blood," we certainly can't say the same for Simonds & her muse, clearing space for a more mutual musing.

When I first read "Fountain of Blood" I was especially struck by the longing in the final line: "I want you to open/ your eyes, every fucking night, to this new century." It was something I very much needed to hear at the time, as

I'd been obsessed with trying to devote a year to reading everything John Ashbery, who had just died, wrote, and I could feel Sandra Simonds slowly waking me to an alternative to all these ghosts inhabiting my psyche, a forward-looking beacon amid this "terrible century" (66). But, wait, Charles & Sandra would be laughing at me were they not too busy fucking. I mean, go back over the danger & brutality earlier in the very same poem:

Sometimes I want you to bite my neck hard
       and let the blood flow down in a fountain, the liquid, rhythmic
            and murmuring and eventually I want that blood to hit the little rocks
           of your testicles below my wet mouth." (53)

Frack the puritan/critic, or critic/puritan, Chris. Even sweet dear old Emily Dickinson ends, Again—his voice is at the door—" with the Gothic:

I'd give—to live that hour—*again*—
The *purple—in my Vein*—
But *He* **must** *count the drops—himself*—
My price **for** *every stain*!

A great comparison could also be made by contrasting the sounds of Simonds' English language with the sounds of Baudelaire's French.

Tough "death is never far away" in this collection, neither is love, whether for poetry, language, life, her children, or her fiancé, as in "Poem for Alex" near the end of the book (as if, in a way, for the narratively inclined, the book indeed has the much coveted "happy ending"):

> You don't have to be mysterious
> Or buoyant like we were so young but
> Now accustomed to manipulating language
> The world becomes sweet, malleable and oh look
> ,,,,,there's the Minoan snake goddess now
> with her ancient explosive powers.

Perhaps she needed to pass through the violent conflagrations of the love expressed in "The Baudelaire Variations" to achieve the beautiful transformative simplicity of the later poems in this collection. Yet, throughout this book, it is not simply erotic love, nor even self-love (self-as-possibility, possibility-as-self), but a general love for humanity and experience, for instance in "Elysian Fields" she writes, "I'm…not the type to give up/ on other people or the eventual occasions/ for new disasters" (78).

Not that she doesn't have ample reason to want to give up, especially on the male ideologues and utopian activists that make cameos in this book:

> It's free love until
> you have to wipe

a baby's ass," my friend says
             at dinner talking about
the possibilities
             of a free
love commune." (22)

Or:

You learned how to spell me in school terrible
       You need to mark every place Faulkner was racist
       And rewrite the novel as erasure." (27)

It's not that she doesn't agree that Faulkner was a racist, and hasn't herself fought on the front-lines of the anti-racist struggle, but, for Simonds, the obsession with "honor" (in "Spring Dirge" 2) and political self-righteousness can get in the way of, and tyrannize, the transformative powers of poetry. Sure, she explores some deeply political issues in this piece—for instance, how the technocracy can devalue poems, how Social Media is hostile to the more contemplative mode (76), and the personal can be called political here, but more importantly is the intimate possibility that can potentially speak beyond (or at least between) partisanships—for though Simonds is a poet's poet in the best sense of the word, it does not come at the expense of an ability to reach a more general reader (she's not so busy being a poet's poet that she forgets to be a poet).

Aware that "defending/ pleasure kills it" (90), despair

can be a pep-talk (96), throughout this collection Simonds' employs many imaginative avatars (from the comet in "A Lover's Discourse" to the nuns in "Our Lady Of Perpetual Help"), as well the *via negativa* (the negation of the negation, as well as "negative capability") to embrace those people and moods outcast by society, and find a new beginning in a world in which "wellness" often means "hellness" and reading too much of Blake's *Songs of Innocence* may have the power to give you pneumonia (pg. 75), suggesting that the only way to cure the physical illness is to speak with the "wry, disabused" voice of experience that cannot resign to a life of decay and decline, as Jolie Holland would put it, or use loss as an excuse to close off from the world. As Simonds puts it in "The Elysian Fields:"

> Which ancient philosopher thinks that life is
> a rehearsal for death?
> Or is that something from bullshit New Age
> mysticism I read at
> the hippie crystal shop I love? The
> suicides reverse it—
> They think that death is a rehearsal
> for flowers—specifically
> the night blooming ones. (81)

Further Problems with Pleasure, in giving ample room for both voices, and realizing you can't choose life without choosing death, suggests a more balanced approach that may yet help reground the world's "ailing infrastructure." It certainly has renewed my faith in the possibilities of poetry as few books have & gains deeper resonance on re-reading in ways that can seduce me off of Facebook, and make me want to respond in kind rather than in a review that waters down the book's intensities.

DELIA TRAMONTINA
CONSTRAINT
(DANCING GIRL PRESS, 2019)

Delia Tramontina's brilliantly constructed debut of warm, challenging, muscular maximalist statement poetry that appeals at least as much to the suggestive intelligence as the cognitive intelligence packs more logopieac intensity into 21 pages than many books of poetry do in 100, and gains even more resonance on repeated, slow, readings. Against a highly formal, sophisticated, urbane, backdrop with its penchant for dramatic intrigue, this polyvocal, gender-bending work of unpaginated discursive lyrical prose throws into question any easy assumptions about what exactly constraint is, and isn't (even though, aside from the title, the word never appears in the book).

If, for instance, people are constrained in professional or social gatherings, is poetry or writing, in a society of solitude, a way to liberate us, to put in writing what you could never safely communicate in polite or professional company without constraint? Or is writing valued for being more constrained than day to day social encounters, as a sublime form of impulse control?

At the risk of using the title as a can-opener, one of the dictionary definitions of constraint is "stiffness of manner and inhibitions in relations between people" and is associated (if not necessarily synonymous) with words like: formality, uneasiness, embarrassment, reserved, reticent, guarded, awkward, forced, self-conscious, and stilted. In Tramontina's hands, it's capacious enough to suggest an infinity of overlapping concepts and feelings and, more importantly, a comedy of manners that could also be "a treacherous accounting that encourages empathy" ("Urbanity").

So many themes are threaded, or threads are themed in this collection, which relentlessly samples, investigates and speaks to, a series of common pathologies & self-abuses in a society in which many "wear complicated ailments like chastity belts" and "skirmish with phobia until we are drunk on social dodgeball," with detachment from what could be termed pathos (though I wouldn't call this book anti-romantic in any pejorative sense). Encouraging empathy by emphasizing ethos & logos rather than affective appeals, *Constraint* asks can we talk about physiological holistic health in terms of sex (and vice versa) while also turning the tables on various traditional forms of patriarchal authority. A lot of fun can be had in the loophole of "judge not lest ye be judged" if it's okay to defensively judge those who have judged, or otherwise inscribed, you.

Tramontina's characters often become rigid points of view: the deputy editor and judge, the young melodramaticist, the complainer, the victim, etc. Not only does Tramontina's poetry shrink the traditional affect cross-dressing male erection muse, but also works to "castrate all editorials into morphemes, grunts & gestures." ("Beaten Path"), and emasculate the spurious superiority of the moralists who "tout erections as mission statements." These repressive, oppressive, and puritanical moralists are often found to be hypocritical as Angelo in Shakespeare's *Measure for Measure* (Do as I say not what I try to hide.), or as the "sightseer" and "stay at home saint" of "Transact" ("this dummy is less a randomized persona than a housebroken cadaver assaulting eroticism and reality in equal measure") who says, "Not to boast, but my top selling purity smells better than your pussy."

Or consider the voice that says, "buy me a hereditary advantage, I mean a cognitive predisposition to hyper-flexibility" ("Beaten Path"). I love the way she mordantly challenges the *first thought, best thought* dictum of post-beat poetry. The desire for Hyper-flexibility, adjusting to other people's demands and needs better, can sublimate the unrealistic urge for the privilege of hereditary advantage, but the speaker is still hoping someone else can buy this "cognitive predisposition" as if an armor against any chance encounter, which is another form of what Tramontina elsewhere calls "pre-frontal manipulation" or grandstanding often used to avoid intimacy, for instance.

Although the word "constraint" does not appear in this book, in the book's penultimate poem, "Urbanity," a voice advises: "Hold your urine, young one, and incite relief after you can gather anxious restraint." Given the fact that potty training is a core belief of civilization, some forms of restraint or constraint are better than others....or if one took this advice as poetics, or at least a characterization of what this book does, one might translate it to "poetry, at its best, is like learning to hold your urine for a long as possible to increase the pleasure of inciting relief" Or is that just an erection talking?

Yet, this book is not an essay, and there's always a dimension which resists this—or maybe any—interpretation; after all, even the voice of the sexual libertine indulged in many of these poems could also be a voice of constraint that "speaks better in preventive light" ("Modus Operandi"). Indulging constraint, ultimately, I find a deep permissiveness in this book that encourages empathy despite, or maybe because of, its lack of "emotional" language. *Constraint* is a major debut, from a writer who deserves to be more well-known.

DANIELLE PAFUNDA
BESHREW
(DUSIE BOOKS, 2019)

Whether one values poetic complexity on the level of single words and tropes, emotional range, physical metaphysics, transcendent relational immanence, lyric spots of time, a precise suggestiveness that allows for differing interpretations, or strong persona and theatrical intrigue, Danielle Pafunda's *Beshrew* does far more in less than 50 15-line sonnets than Shakespeare could in 145. Tense and hilarious enough to allow great gravitas with the power to conjure visceral responses beyond critical appreciation, *Beshrew* packs as much drama as Shakespeare's poetic tragic-comedies while rendering his sonnets stiff, and disembodied by comparison. In *Beshrew*, the groaning heart is no mere metaphor, pun on "hart" or abstract seat of emotion, but felt through the painscape of body, and the physicality of animals, more than the more 'comely'(17)—if alienating—forms of intellect Pafunda is conversant with enough to masterfully subvert, as if from within. Lust clashes with and embraces affection, in noir light, while the undetected fucks a detective to provide a report on "intelligence failure" (17) and leave patriarchal love conventions in a heap of "broken bodies/in gutter crud, failed refuse." (11)

I love the way this book resists paraphrase, or even summary. Every time I return to the poem of which I wrenched a line out of context, another word pops out of the poem to change the weight of the words. As Irene Cooper has remarked: "Through repeated readings of *Beshrew,* I feel like I'm approaching a new and irresistible mystery each time, whose outcome I cannot foresee." Or, as Pafunda herself puts it in a self-referential passage

> I will make sure you can't
> find this book. I will burn this book
>
> every time you pick it up. This book
> is catching fire imagining your hand
>
> on its bare spine. My spine is catching fire.
> I drop to the ground's deepest curvature.
>
> You cannot keep ahead of this.
> Each pulse does as much damage
>
> as the hard frequency of cells mismatched
> allows.   (13)

At the core of this book is an I- and-you dynamic. On an ethical/ affective level of character and plot, the "I" is introduced in the 4th poem:

> I'm a carbon slug swaddled in sour sheets
> What time of day is it? I don't go into work

anymore, I don't go get the children from school.
This blinking faucet of regret compounds me. (10)

This feeling of being bedridden, as if due to a immobilizing health condition, presumably analogous to the murdered body with which the book begins, leads her to seek for causes:

Who filled a bag of flies and burst it over
the heads of a thousand schoolgirls? (10)

The next poem implies that these insects may be words in a toxic book by a male author.. With the entrance of the disembodied/book/author/'you,' the plot heats up as Pafunda inverts the phrase, *I can read you like a book,* to read a book as if its author could be a lover, trying to suck the lover out of a book barren enough to be reduced to data points. Is the book to blame for murdering the body? In one sense, you could say *Beshrew* itself is a book review. Is talking back to (or beshrewing) this destructive book the only way she can heal herself from this lassitude?

As the speaker characterizes the act of reading and writing as a hostage exchange (13), Pafunda shows various aesthetic/ethical contrasts between the [author of] the book whose spurious morally superior disembodiment makes the speaker literally puke, and gag, and wretch, and her own more embodied relationship to writing:

Where you've tucked your pen in your notes,
I tuck my fingernail, burned and cursed and

shut my eyes tight (12)

Locating this other's logocentric book in the "afterdeath of perfection" (13) or a "past-dead pleasure camp" (16), she judges his book by what it *doesn't* say:

Through the page, I travel back to the page's

inception. I enter your hand hovering, your hot face
where something bolts in the dark and your dark

chest arcing with jumpstart. (16)

Throughout, Pafunda uses any means necessary—including playing *both* the S&B (sadist & bondage) role, as well as the M&D role (masochist & domination) to shake the interlocutor [reader, writer] out of the "pleasure proof male body" (32), as if feminism—insofar as it's trying to change men's toxicity—can be as much about heating the blood of the too cold as it is cooling the blood of the too hot:

Where, like a dream where the affect
suddenly balloons and warps, will I hinge
our two bodies? (17)

This may seem like a sexy come on early in her book, but 17 sonnets later, the speaker realizes the futility of such endeavour:

> What I cannot do is press
>
> my fingers into the equator that divides your body
> from flight and longing. I cannot press
>
> my skin well enough to yours to transfer. (34)

And when it comes to longing, is it possible words can yet be an adequate, if temporary, substitute, for that transfer? Is the speaker's body, too, divided from flight and longing? Early in the book, she writes:

> My wet, red, clairvoyant longing answers
>   all the equations with your DNA, your fingerprints—
> (20)

In context, this line comes after another ethical contrast between the speaker and interlocutor:

> It's your raw mouth raw
>
> against my bare-faced disaster every ticking
> hellscape deteriorating until the rich fucking
>
> wealth of hate, malice, government, law,

the sovereign citizen, dread, wretched power

recombines this particular fetish for your
scent. (20)

As the interpersonal and the more abstract political clash here, the speaker could be code-switching as it were, speaking the male-ist language of political violence & injustice ("my blood turns/ the color of a nuclear sunset.") because that's the only language he understands, even if he thinks he opposes it (see also the poems on 25 and 46).

Perhaps this is why Pafunda's speaker says, "don't think you know me" (27), "I prepare myself a place you enter/ and resign myself an exit." (14) and "This face is not/ mine, it's the face I wear when I go looking for you/and I want you to think I'm home, a good woman." (19). The author thus has plausible deniability when considering intentions and authenticity, but a healthy skepticism towards the word "good," with "Eyes igniting every stitch of reticence,/ every decent posture you are so inclined/are so good,..."(13). At least Shakespeare knew lust by daylight, not this interlocutor: "No scuzz, sentimental scrawl, betrayal/ of heart by hand. Not you." (13) She interrogates whether this 'good' person actually stirs good feelings: "When they put us on trial for/obstruction of good feeling, will you hold my/hand?" Then she finds herself answering this question about the future by judging his actions in the past: "Where were you the night I took my life,/stripped it from my skull like a face?" (13)

The other's book and its author are clearly not up for the task of loving. In the third & final section, the speaker gradually extricates herself from this destructive relationship in an act of self-assertion, judgment and a spell-breaking lament that the male "you" can probably only understand as revenge, but the speaker's persona is much more complex and varied than the Shakespearean heroines who *speak daggers* ("There's a stiletto in my throat/that no one's thought to frisk for." 41):

Perhaps this could be one of those stilettos:

There are many people dead on the inside
who'd like to cum on my face, my husband tells me."
(45)

Or if that doesn't work for you at this time and place, how about?

You can pull a soiled rag

from your pocket & shove it
deep in my throat & on it

I'll taste all the other women
You've gagged, the people

Of color, the Jews, the queers,

The itty-bitty babies." (51)

And by the end of this poem, the relationship between "you" as writer, and speaker as puking reader has reversed as she becomes the unmoved mover:

> against the bedpost of a narrative
> you're puking out in a very
>
> warm cavern, deep under
> the shipyard, deep under
>
> my stationary hull. (51)

But though there could be triumph in removing the gag and frisking stilettos, the catharsis only allows the speaker "to pivot, but I don't feel any better." (53)

If all this sounds too harsh on the poor male, certainly it's no worse than centuries of degrading love poems by men. And I wonder—is even writing the most positive review possible—especially if one is, say, a man writing about a book by a woman—, an act of erasure, of gagging, of rape? of arranging "for these rectangular suits to watch me?" (19) How to show how Pafunda's book is able to flip the script on suits of traditional patriarchy cultural authority, including the philosopher kings of the 21st Century technocracy, who fancy themselves more surveilling than surveilled and try to reduce the speaker to data points?

The prayer-book shaped, *Beshrew* ends with an evocation of Philomel, whose removal of the gag allowed her a power that goes beyond what traditional Euro-male 'rationalist' mindset reduces to the 'human.' And this doesn't really 'give away the ending'—the mystery of heart and body, or patience and page-turner, unsolved, but perhaps it is the elegant braggadocio of *Beshrew's* intimate painscape, "in the millisecond you create for the evacuation/ of reason" (53), that gives it its affective power beyond the critical intelligence.

Alissa Quart
Thoughts & Prayers
(Or Books, 2019)

Alissa Quart
Squeezed:
Why Out Families Can't Afford America
(Ecco Press, 2018)

"Everything goes/on the grill" (28) in Alissa Quart's capacious writing. Her recent prose (*Squeezed,* 2018) and poetry (*Thoughts & Prayers,* 2019) appeal to both my Creative Writing as well as my Critical Thinking sides. Taken together, these two books reframe the relationship between the public and private, commercial and non-commercial, seriousness and humor, work and care, as well as explode the stigma of the 'Jewish mother' stereotype.

In *Thoughts & Prayers,* the one poem that blatantly addresses specifically Jewish themes ("Pass") is also a profound meditation on language & symbols, words with no pretentions to adequately representing the physical world as portrayed in still lives, as she works dynamically in what gets referred to, often derogatorily, as abstractions—as if somehow that signifies a lack of grounding.

As she considers various connotations, and associations of the word "Passover"—and how previous Jewish writers have investigated the *aporia* between it and the phrase "pass over," she wonders whether "appropriation rotted out/ the original" (28). While considering the symbolic rituals in which "flatbread stands in/for slavery"(28), she invites a linguistic skepticism into the Seder, or you could say thoughts into her prayers:

> Because language and the physical
> world don't correspond
> words don't express
> full internal selves
> or space or time
>
> Pass over
>
> Life mostly symbols, analogies that tie
> us to each other, shadows
> on the cave, the flickering
> correspondences,
> truer as we age,
> an idea of the world in our head
> composed of paper and mâché
> Layers of different times
> or selves. No real world
> can resemble our inner
> mentality without huge gaps

Grammatically, we can read the phrase "shadows/ on the cave" as characterizing the symbols, or "each other." Is it the flickering that is "truer as we age" or the correspondences? Questioning the transparent correspondence theory of language may be a crisis for a reporter and cultural critic (for as she writes in another poem: "we name stuff, hope/that's proof. That's how/reporting works,"(7) but the poet is not necessarily lamenting the lack of a fixed correspondence, but embracing the fluid mysteries of a transactional sense of language. I get a sense that even if there are no correspondences between word and thing, there may yet be correspondences between beings or minds here.

By embracing the gaps, she's able to avoid seeing linguistic transactions in purely violent terms like Nietzsche's "mobile army of metaphors," or Balzac's characterization of the militarized mind on coffee. In one sense, this poem stands in defiance of Facebook founder Zuckerberg's idea(l) of "radical transparency," the crafting of a one-size fits all social media identity, and the alienation that causes. Rather, Quart moves beyond—or at least between—rigid ideas of symbolism, away from stiff dogma, maintaining an openness, a critical eye, a sense there's always more, if not yet to learn, at least experience—more people to *correspond* with, even if one has to use words as numbers more than words-as-things to do so...for instance, in "23andMe," a witty satire of the DNA-testing craze, with its parenthetical spirituality:

Another entity that finds almost everything
Yet never what we need (the unseen). No, really. (62)

Passover can be a form of blessing, and also ushering in spring, but it can also mean skip past or ignore; by repeating of the word(s) "pass over" at the end after her passionate celebration of the under-appreciated Jewish poet Armand Schwerner (presumably for not being 'experimental enough'), Quart also seems to reach out to the monocultural reader who might be tempted to "pass over" this poem as if its Jewish themes don't make room for him or her....and, if they do, it's their loss.

Her intimacy with the disturbing double meanings of other ostensibly individual stable referential words often is revealed with bitter warmth. For instance, in "Sakhalin"—the book's first poem, in which the struggle to break free from the "media prison" is clearly evident, she finds the terror of the sublime in the pun:

Loud and silent islands. *The Times*
website blares as another
agency—mine, yours—is
dismantled   (5)

She implies, or I infer, that the increasing privatization of government agencies that protect us against the unfettered free market also coincides with a loss of personal agency, what some psychologists refer to as an internal locus of control. Helplessness becomes a cultural epidemic against some mythical 1% ideal of the autonomous, self-made person in a world in which we've "been taught to seek only individual solutions for problems that are often systemic in nature." (*Squeezed,* 171)

The title poem of *Thoughts & Prayers* is a collage sampling of mass-media disseminated public language in response to the school shooting epidemic. Among these are "the words companies use in fabricating souvenirs that commodify mass killings" (35). On one level, it's a lampoon satire of doublespeak and the co-optation of phrases like "thoughts and prayers" by a clearly secular gun lobby and their media megaphones. It's also a genuine cry to take back the power of thinking and praying in a culture in which G-d is often equated with a gun "shooting our prayers." (35) I believe that Quart's work in the so-called abstract cultural superstructure is not opposed to, but rather, at the very least, a necessary complement, to physically trying to unarm a rabid white supremacist terrorist.

Structurally, *Thoughts and Prayers* tends to alternate between short-lined pathos-laden, private lyricism, and long-lined more public poems composed from aphoristic and often humorous one liners whose very form bespeaks the difficulties of trying to construct an attention economy against the ironies of 21st century maleist 'move fast, break things' attention-deficit inducing cultural zeitgeist. Lines like "Some students call their pain 'climate anxiety'," followed by "Bush II is now a Sunday painter, depicting the very soldiers whose mutilation he ordered," speak volumes ("Late Capitalism," 14).

Of the short-lined lyrics, "Coterie" is one of the most poignant grief poems I've ever read. Part elegy for an unnamed, but presumably semi-famous, friend, "Coterie" also explores the intertextuality of grief, as Quart negotiates many other mutual friends' or fans' various styles of grieving, from the most speechless and sincere to the most flippant paparazzi. This poem is also a lament for a social and cultural milieu, the dream of solidarity of a *fin-de-siecle* artistic coterie that has been destroyed, with the implication that this elegized subject was in a sense a casualty of the economic and cultural shifts she writes about in her prose, and, in *Thoughts and Prayers*, more comically, in "Apocalypse Anyway."

"Apocalypse Anyway" (25), a quasi-narrative aphoristic romp through her 20s in the 1990s, the so-called slacker era of the corporatization of hip-hop, punk and college radio—from Riot Grrrl to Spice Girl, happiness pie and Prozac nation before the internet had become a relentless cultural habit, *juxtaproses* the personal and the cultural with a healthy ambivalence. While in retrospect many fellow generation Xers may consider 90s to be a kind of prelapsarian time—"when the weather was literal, sometimes Modernist, but not yet political," Quart also remembers the ways in which it was worse: "When female writers made their names denying other women's suffering" (25)—not that such denying of suffering still doesn't happen, as in her satirical portrait of women of the ruling class in "Enclave." There's always the possibility that it's not the zeitgeist of that time we're nostalgic for, but merely the fact that we were in our twenties, for as she reminds us in *Squeezed:*

"By the time I entered the recessionary job market of the 1990s (a time when young people assumed the identity 'slacker' partly in preemptive self-protection from the rejection of increasingly fractured careers), a lifelong job at a single company was already becoming quaint." (171)

I detect regret and/or helplessness—if not necessarily guilt—in lines such as: "When elections went tabloid but we hadn't realized yet what that would mean."(27) And perhaps I'm projecting my own feelings onto this poem when thinking about those times, and wondering *why couldn't we see the signs of encroaching negative cultural change and do something to stop it!* Ultimately, "Apocalypse Anyway" seems to end on a personal-crisis, or an attitude she now may consider immature:

> when other people became my religion
> when I didn't think of anyone else
> when all I thought about was other people (27)

This attitude could also be an occupational hazard in her present life as a member of the working class precariat care-force (whether as freelance journalist or mother), and this may help contextualize her appropriation of the John Ashbery quote: "But the past is already here, and you are nursing some private project." For despite these temptations of helpless nostalgia, the private project

Quart nurses as an alternative turns out to be not so private after all.

As she reminds us in the prose of *Squeezed*, nursing is one of the "traditional caring professions,"(5) as are domestic workers—housekeepers, nannies, day care cooperative coordinators, teachers—whether college humanities teachers, or K-12—, and the domestic labor of birthing and motherhood:

"Today mothers still do most of our unpaid work. A 2015 McKinsey report calculates this as about $10 Trillion of output per year, 13 percent of the global GDP....
yet informal labor doesn't advance workers the way manufacturing jobs did during the last century" (and if men go into these professions—"where most of the employment growth is these days—they may receive the 'traditional' female lower pay"—5, 128, 285).

Much of the reason for this devalue and disdain of care workers, Quart argues, is the maleist ideology that "women 'naturally' serve others gratis." (128). And as *Squeezed* shows through meticulous research and personal accounts, this perennial ideology "for centuries and around the world," has been getting worse in the 21st century economy, which Jeremy Rifkin terms 'hypercapitalism.' "As the market economy expands still further," she asks, "What is left for relationships of a non-commercial nature?" (76)

Take, for instance, the human toll on patients—or health-care consumers—in the trend to replace hospital nurses and other health care workers—with robots. In *Squeezed,* robot-fearing nurses like Bonnie Castillo of the California Nurses Association tells Quart: "patients require a human touch. She meant that quote literally. As a nurse, she said, she would typically assess the texture of patients' skin determining, for instance, whether their skin was clammy or sweaty." (234)

Nursing also means breastfeeding, and in a world in which:

> women are always
> breasts and forced
> yet clever surrealists…
> covered in hot ejaculate
> of sonogram… (51)

the speaker of the poem "Mammo" intersects with the health-care industry from a consumer's viewpoint while also doubling as a reporter interviewing her "smiling blonde/ technician, a Chernobyl/ escapee," to end on a note of the kind of pithy irony adept at drawing connections between the personal and the systemic. "Mammo" ends:

> Her current job in
> radiation is ironic,
> the technician knows,

she says, "Distrust
leaders everywhere
still, it's better here. For
example, the rain." (52)

One could compare this to perhaps even crueler forms of capitalist irony in *Squeezed*, like the fact that "24% of housekeepers and 82% of live-in nannies leave kids behind." This separation of families, of which the Ice Detention Centers are only the tip of a systemic iceberg, leaves these working mothers with choices at least as difficult as, and more widespread than, the traditional maleist tragic hero, for instance Blanca from Paraguay's choice between "paying the price to get her son back by replacing his middle-class life in Paraguay with becoming part of the working poor in America." (*Squeezed*, 112)

Another poem that harmonizes her lyric and journalistic skills is "Clinic," a five-page lyric suite in 6 sections, which she characterizes as a "meta-text" around her journalistic account of abortion clinics. In this gut-wrenching portrayal of: "women afraid of dying while/ they are trying to find their life" (18), Quart steps away from her journalistic detachment to advocate for the difficult choices women, ranging from 19 to 41, who work at K-Mart, Home Depot, at daycares, at hospitals at night," must make:

one boss wouldn't let
the woman sell car parts

if she was pregnant…
the soldier who
"Said she was
doing this
so I can fight
for this country" (19)

Like the photographer Peter Hujar celebrated in "Against Amnesia," Quart looks "into the sitters/eyes then out of them, all at once." (41). In an era where "being a pregnant woman in America, no matter how many reality shows and greeting cards say the opposite, is a stigmatized identity," (*Squeezed*, 28) and women and doctors are murdered at abortion clinics by zealous hypocrites who are pro-life until birth while cutting any vestige of social safety nets that would allow many of these working-class mothers to actually care for the children, Quart's poem is what she elsewhere calls "civic poetry" at its best (and, yes, it's a rare poem that can make me cry).

Throughout, both books strive to embody the "ethical ideals of interdependence, flexibility, relatedness, receptivity…preservative love, discipline, flexible thinking" (257) which some feminists term "maternal thinking." Quart herself resisted becoming a mother until her late thirties because she "had to deal with my own suspicion that caring and mothering were somehow not intellectually or critically headed enough" and the "fear having a baby would annihilate [her] own identity," (*Squeezed*, 259). But despite the fear of "permanent marks" she mentions in the poem "Pre-Natal," "I found the opposite to be true." Indeed, in several of the poems her daughter becomes a muse-like figure whose "face illuminates mine" (14) even better than "noise-cancelling head/phones" (5). Against the contracts and financial instruments,

> Her questions remain free.
> Why do boys
> Have beards? Why
> Do women give birth? (In Ballard, 5)

By contrast, in *Squeezed* her daughter's questions turn more difficultly to economic class.

At this juncture, I can imagine a reader criticizing this review for mixing up her poetry and prose, but, for me, the question of whether *Thoughts and Prayers* "stands on its own" (by the still lingering 'New Critical" standards of lyric poetry) is as moot as the question of whether a great song lyric can stand up on the page, when you've already heard the music. And just as reading Shakespeare's plays, or Baraka's prose, helped me appreciate their poems better, Quart's argument in *Squeezed* about the value of a feminist ethics of care can be useful in considering the private project she nurses in *Thoughts & Prayers*.

In seeking antidotes, or at least proactive alternatives, to the blame epidemic—whether directed to self or to others—that has arisen in the wake of the disappearing middle-class, Quart argues that we need to *reframe care:*

"Why do we identify care with weakness? Can't we push back when people make remarks indicating that they find caring labor of all kinds, including birthing, intrinsically less important and intellectual than other kinds of labor? Why don't we ask why many people think of care as boring, soft, and submissive, not up to the standards and pace of our hard-edged time? And why do we so often prefer the opposite of care? (260).

"If we thought of care as a form of knowledge, we might recognize, as Daniela Nanau did....that parenthood, rather than being the negative image of traditional work, actually prepares and even sharpens us for the workplace; (262) affection would be not just a *sentiment* but an ethical practice and also a form of accepted work: it would be legitimate that we could be paid to love." (244).

"If automation forces us eventually to uncouple income from work—to recognize that robots have truly replaced us and as a result we need to pay people for not working— we will have to cease making moral arguments, from both left and right, about the value of work. But even more, we'll need to think differently. We'll need to learn to value various kinds of nonwork behavior that we do not honor now—and also to protect and honor the kind of labor that incorporate these nonwork behaviors. What happens to love after work becomes obsolete?" (246) "The warmth and feeling of human beings must be honored, at the very least." (248)

These prose passages could also be read a defense of (her) poetry, for those who care. Or, as she puts it in the poem, "Cancel This," "women's minds are wild. Protect their honor. It is yours as well." (63) And even if she can't convince a patriarchal CEO or Techie of her argument (though one could pray) to—essentially recalibrate the economy—maybe she can at least convince enough of the precariat guys, whether in the care-industry or truckers replaced by bots, that such feminism would actually help us too.

Judy Juanita
De Facto Feminism
(EquiDistance, 2016)

"Terminology makes for binary thinking dilemmas" (162)

"In protest movements, as in wars, the people on the bottom don't write history" (156)

Judy Juanita published her first book, the novel *Virgin Soul* (Viking) in 2013 at the age of 67, and she's certainly not resting on laurels. Since then she has published volumes of poetry, short stories, and plays on smaller presses. Her latest collection *De Facto Feminism: Essays Straight Outta Oakland (2016),* gives us a behind the scenes look into her journey in honing her writing craft while surviving as a proletariat single black mother, "an act of self-creation spanning 4 decades," (162). Eschewing the fictional mask of Geniece in her semi-autobiographical *Virgin Soul,* Juanita brings the political and the personal even closer in *De Facto Feminism.*

Much of the book adopts the first-person voice of memoir, arranged in a loose chronology, from her experience as the editor of the Black Panther Newspaper in 1967 to cleaning other people's houses to support herself and son in New Jersey in the 70s and 80s to the present and intimations of immortality beyond. In the title essay, however, she adopts the voice of cultural critic at the intersection of Women's studies and African-American Studies.

In this essay, Juanita, like Alissa Quart in *Squeezed* (discussed in the previous chapter), brings her poetic sensibilities to the struggle against economic injustice, sexism and racism with powerful reportage that appeals to pathos, logos and ethos. What Juanita calls *De Facto Feminism* overlaps in many ways with what Alissa Quart calls "Care Work." Their tones, the language they use, the imagined audiences and interlocutors they are primarily writing for, however, differ significantly. Juanita defines *De Facto Feminism* by way a binary thinking dilemma, contrasting it with what she calls *20th century feminism:*

20th Century feminism is "defensive, lean-in elite, scarce, historical, white-ish, precious, theoretical, lawful, contempt for men but not their $$$." De-facto feminism is "offensive, classless, proliferative, ahistorical, black and then some, inside/outside the law, do you with/without men" (146).

With the same assertive force of Ida B. Wells demanding a place in the front row of the march in celebration of women's winning the right to vote, Juanita understands the best defense needs a good offense, even if that means you'll offend something, or someone. Though she gets a jab at some white women of her generation who often defined feminism in ways that did not include black women, Juanita's emphasis is a celebration of the agency of the practical *de facto feminists* who "stand between peace and war everyday in Detroit, Oakland, Harlem, Miami,

Chicago, St. Louis, The White House, The View, Philly, Baltimore, LA—the Gaza Strips of the US" (147) For Juanita, *De Facto Feminism* is Black Feminism, regardless of whether its practitioners call themselves feminists.

The women Juanita celebrates "are far more feminist than the broadcast/weathercasters who've memorized feminist principles and theory from prep school through Ivy league." (153) By contrast, she offers an example:

"Shelley at nineteen had a brick shithouse figure, a five-octave voice and sweetness to spare. She also had a disinclination to sell her body for a recording contract. She languished in the bush leagues of jazz vocalists for yeas before the call came. She answered, left for Los Angeles, but not everyone has the stomach to sleep their way to the top." (152)

Reminding us that "in protest movements, as in wars, the people on the bottom don't write history," Juanita uses her literary skills throughout *De Facto Feminism* to speak of, to, and for, those women closer to the bottom, and asks "will it take 200 years for respect to come to those de facto feminists sitting on the bottom, squeezed into pink collar ghettos and brown security guard uniforms lined up at the minimum wage margins of this world?" (156)

Juanita traces her lineage back to Sojourner Truth, who freed herself from the slavery she was born into, "by escaping in 1829, going through excruciating hardships and court battles, some of which she won, and becoming a speaker and agitator for women's and black rights." (147).

Juanita never loses sight of the economic dimensions to white patriarchy, especially when coupled with "the stigma that black people carry as pigment" (151). Truth "sold pictures of herself, not in chains or with scars of enslavement on her back as other ex-slaves were doing, but in traditional portrait, fully clothed, strong. She wrote herstory." (156).

200 years after Truth escaped to freedom, Capitalism's economic colonization still forces black working-class women "to be what others would term illegal, immoral but not impractical." (151). Juanita's own great grandmother, an Okie from Muskogee, in the early 20th century, took books and magazines from the homes of rich white folks where she worked as a maid, and helped form her town's first free colored library! (160)

Like Truth and Juanita's great grandmother, today's *"de facto feminists* can't always operate openly." (147) One type of entrepreneur is the Candy Lady, a housing project entrepreneur who:

purchases packaged groceries, toiletries, candy, soda, and liquor in bulk. She goes back to the project and sells it to her neighbors. On the straight and narrow, she purchases goods at retail, pays taxes at the register. On the precipice, she operates minus a license, doesn't report profits on federal and state taxes. (148)

How different is the service these candy ladies provide than the more expensive corporate Instacart? Aren't these women providing a valuable service by cutting out the government mandated corporate middlemen?Other examples of black women in their day-to-day existence resisting economic colonization include:

A whole class of workers constitutes women who braid hair, part of the underground economy in the black community. Overwhelmingly black and youthful, they work from home, a cadre of postmodern kitchen beauticians who make a way out of no way, to raise children, make money, be stylish and *create community.*" (150—emphasis added).

Many of these women perform services that are often cheaper than going to an official hairstylist who has to pay an extra office rent. To me, they seem closer to the spirit of giving in a more community-oriented yet individualistic sense.

These examples contrast with the examples in Quart's "The Nanny's Struggle," in *Squeezed.* While Quart, in her extended portrait of the struggles of immigrant nanny Blanca separated from her son by the global care chain, does not really portray any characteristics that could be seen as "moral failings" by genteel white society, Juanita relishes the "blur of legality, morality, and practicality" (151) of the de-facto feminists she identifies with, with a defiant pride that itself interrogates not just the myth of the American Dream (which most of these women knew, as if from jump, was rigged against them), but also the foundations of the American economy and the spurious morality system used to justify it.

In Juanita's case studies, we see strong women over and over again building community by making a way out of no way:

Women with children and Section 8 act as quasi-landlords with their off-the-books tenants. In New Jersey, I lived in a six-unit building with several foxy single mothers who attracted and "housed" members of the New York Giants football tea during the season. Over the decade I live there, a rotating cast of ballers paid their ladies way and no small amount of said dentistry for said ladies and their offspring, clothes and food (and thrilled my song and his Pop Warner teammates). (150-151)

Considering that Alissa Quart suggests an economy in which being paid to love is a legitimate option, I would like to think she would include and celebrate these de facto feminists in her category care workers. In this sense Quart's *Squeezed* and & Juanita's *De Facto Feminism* complement each other. Indeed, as Juanita puts it, "a new wave of feminists instead might envision women of color setting policy and leading, being arbiters instead of being left behind" (153)

Finally, Juanita offers a powerful argument for why white people should care, not just for altruistic or paternalistic reasons, but for selfish reasons. According to Juanita, "Black people often serve as an early warning system for the American populace...For better and worse, the hardcore issues blacks face—guns, crime, poverty, failing schools—define the newest America." (261) As the mostly white middle class is being increasingly squeezed by the 21st century techno-capitalistic paradigm shift, Juanita reminds me of the black women at the Occupy Wall Street Rally holding a "blacks have always been the 99%" sign.

Juanita makes a strong, passionate, case for why we should listen respectfully to the wisdom of these black women. As she celebrates a hard-won wresting of agency against a power structure that does its damnedest to deny it, Juanita undoes the stigmas against black women, from the pejorative nanny stereotype to the pejorative welfare mother stereotype:

Ubiquitous de facto feminists are walking, talking political education classes who teach persistence when things don't work out, when no one comes to help or when facing death. They might even be goddesses or shamans, god forbid." (158)

The women Juanita celebrates transcend the false "binary thinking dilemmas" between artist and activist, and between individualist and collectivist to engage in an artistic activism, and an altruism that need not be self-abnegating to occupy a fertile, proliferative, place where selfishness and altruism, individualism and community activism can unite.

*****

As we celebrate the 50th anniversary of the Black Panther Party, the role of women is still not emphasized enough in biopics like the recent PBS *Vanguard of The Revolution* (2016). Yet even in *Seize the Time (1970)*, Bobby Seale wrote of the power of the first women in the Black Panthers to educate and recruit new members to the party. Juanita, ex-editor-in-chief of the *Black Panther* newspaper, gives her own account of the importance of these young women as bringing together rival factions to create and sustain a larger, more rooted, movement. Certainly, Juanita and the other women were no passive recipients of edicts from Bobby, Huey, and Eldridge, but de facto feminists in the making.

"Our gang of five affected policy and high-level decisions by virtue of our intense participation, outspokenness....we also formed liaisons and romantic relationships with brothers in the party. From the upper echelon to the lumpen proletariat, we lived, slept, ate and cooked with the BPP.... We were the initial link between the campus and the party. Three of us married 'brothers in the struggle' who also happened to be educated brothers. This is significant because our connections and intimacy (which some labeled promiscuity) connected brothers from the party with brothers from SF State. The BSU brothers like to talk about supplying the BPP with guns and money, but this bridge called my back supplied the people's army with equal and greater provision." (40)

De Facto Feminism also includes an essay Juanita wrote at the age of 20 for the *Black Panther Newspaper*, "Black Womanhood." In this essay, she wrote "the struggle requires her strength, not her will, her leadership, her domination, but her strength" (46). In 50 years hindsight, she calls this her phase of "naively determined black womanhood." (45) She includes the essay, however, precisely for the contrast in her coming of age journey.

Before she was a Black Panther, however, Juanita was very active in the San Francisco chapter of the Black Arts Movement (BAM) with other San Francisco State students. Juanita provides useful historical insights into the period of the SFSU student strike that created the nation's first Black Studies Program:

"As student activists at SF State, the Black Student Union fought to bring Jones (Amiri Baraka), Lee (Mudhubuti) and (Sonia) Sanchez onto Campus. We formed the Black Arts and Culture Troupe and toured community centers throughout the Bay Area with poetry, dance and agit-prop plays. We enacted ideas we were hearing on soap-boxes about black power, black consciousness, and black beauty. We staged mock conflagrations like ones that were taking place in urban cities. We were empowering ourselves, our communities and getting academic credit. A natural progression was community activism." (110)

When she joined the Black Panthers, she was drawn to the alliance between artists and activists, but witnessed, during an era of "shattering community," a growing split between the two groups: "to look at the BAM and its relation to the BPP renders a vision of the poets and the dramatists standing in counterpoint." (111)

In the essay *The Gun as Performance Poem,* Juanita writes about being caught in the cross fire between political activists and political artists during this time. Unfortunately, she became aware that "Activists, oft called anarchistic, despise artists who don't overtly join them." (108) Ultimately, "the activists upstaged the artist/intellectuals. I had immense sympathy for the second group, but pitied them (pitied their women more. How much subservience would soothe a wounded ego?)" (107)

Despite the chauvinism she found in the BAM more than in the BPP, and the factionalism and her torn allegiances, Juanita appreciated what the BPP and Black Arts Movement had in common, and celebrates this legacy:

"The BPP was appropriating the oppressors' language, and using it to shatter oppression. That new use of language, in the BPP and the BAM, was as powerful as any gun, and even more powerful because it aroused feeling and changed the terms of discourse between friends, enemies, lovers, generations and cultures. Being an agent of change meant I aroused deep feelings, affected discourse, found the powerful voices that I had heard in childhood, in church, in soul music, in the pulpit—in my own voice." (111)

Juanita's allegiance was both to art and to activism, and she didn't want to be forced to choose, and as we see her mind go back and forth between the BPP and the BAM, weighing the advantages of each and trying to develop a new synthesis, we see her ability to step back from the heated conflicts and tense divisiveness between the artists and activists to see the productive symbiosis: "Black music, musicians and dancers became ambassadors at large to the world. But the airwaves and new media amplified the beat, the dances, the Soul Train lines, the frizzy hair, the handshakes, the lingo (bro), none of which needed the Gun or its bullet because the BPP handled that task," (113) and part of the reason the BPP was able to handle the task is because of what women like Judy Juanita provided. As she digests the baptism by fire she experienced at age 20 in the Black Panthers as an agent of change, Juanita casts a wry retrospective glance from which to build a present and future, without debilitating nostalgia.

*****

A 4 Decade Journey Through Specializations to Hone Craft

I'm a woman. POW! Black. BAM! Outspoken. STOMP! Don't fit in. OUCH! The lesson? Sometimes when one takes a stand one becomes a lone wolf, a neighborhood of one, a community of one to declare sovereignty for art, sexuality, spirituality, and say-so, an individual." (7)

De Facto Feminism includes a much more varied range of writing than can be discussed in a short essay. Even if you have no interest in the Panthers, or community activism, or in feminism, there are many personally-inflected essays that focus on her life as a writer that are especially useful for beginning writers in their 40s, 50s and 60s struggling with the false clocks of an ageist society.

As we witness Juanita's account of her spiritual growth expressed in terms of honing her craft, we see her also exploring different social dynamics in which art circulates as she explores the social interactions in the theatre world, the stand-up comedy world, and the poetry world. In these essays, Juanita emerges as a working-class artist/intellectual who is highly skeptical of the ready-made categories, and the ridiculous gerrymandered specialized genres. The essay on poet Carolyn Rogers shows the fickle conditional love of readers and editors in the poetry world extends, sadly, even in the revolutionary Black Arts Movement. Rogers had been celebrated by the Black Arts Movement, but later forgotten as she eschewed the "militant" posture which made it easier to get published during this time.

Although she doesn't mention much about her role as teacher in this book, many of the essays can be useful in a multi-genre introductory creative writing class. In "A Playwright-In-Progress" she writes "I learn through making big, fat mistakes vs. reading/perfecting it in my mind." (73) Sometimes we publish precisely in order to make a mistake public, as if that is the only way to move beyond it. Part of why Juanita's such a great teacher is because she can relate to the student going through that, or the student who doesn't know which genre they should make their primary emphasis: poetry, fiction, or plays... for in this specialized society, you must choose one, and for one like Juanita, that is not always an easy choice. My students and I find this permission very helpful.

Many essays focus on how gradually the ingredients for her novel *Virgin Soul* came into being before she could integrate them into her a narrative voice. We learn in the introduction that she had "disliked contemporary fiction in the 70s and 80s, feeling it was narcissistic and a white out" (9) so she focused as her work as playwright, having 17 of her plays staged. It has never occurred to her to write about her youth in the Black Panthers until the 1990s when "A body of literature specifically about the BPP grew steadily." (9) Juanita found this literature, along with "the black chick lit phenomenon, heralded by Terry McMillan's waiting to Exhale *in 1992,*...underplayed the complexity of black life." (9)

"Putting the Funny In The Novel," begins with a discussion with her agent looking at a draft of her novel. He asks, "how come the humor in your conversation isn't here on the page." (81) In her patient, long term commitment to her art, Juanita decides to go beyond seeking out writers' groups to work the comedy circuit, not because she has any illusions about becoming a famous stand-up comic, but because it can help her writing.

Formally this piece juxtaposes prose accounts of the trial and errors and big fat mistakes she made in her years devoted to being a stand-up comic with some of the jokes she told. Here's two examples:

When my son's girlfriend had her baby shower, I found out I wasn't a grandma. I was the babydaddymomma. Even so, I was proud. Then I went to buy a stroller and got sticker shock. It cost more than I paid for my first car. (82)

The babbydaddy, my son, and the babymomma told me they had decided not to use the n-word around my grandson. The Next time I had him, he said dammit, everytime he got frustrated. When they picked him up, I said, "Which one of you African-Americans uses dammit in front of him?" (84—italics Juanita's)

By the end, she comes to the realization "I'm not a comic; I'm an ironist, an observational ironist. I venture closer to my novel's subject matter, being a young black militant in the 1960s. (86). I see a writer relentlessly measuring the inner world by the outer world, and vice versa.

In the end, by taking the long way, and challenging the social nexus that too often determines the circulation of literary texts in our society, Juanita celebrates her years of struggle, as if the reason she didn't fit in to one social scene is the same reason she can get along with more people from a wider variety of social scenes, and her findings can be useful for current generations of artists, activists and everyday people. One doesn't have to have read *Virgin Soul* to appreciate *De Facto Feminism*, but they certainly complement each other.

In another writer's hand, such reflections may seem self-indulgent, but Juanita never loses sight of the light she's shining for those unspoken which her younger self may have been tempted to judge. She never loses sight of the collective struggle, and of the fact that some things must be kept secret, in offering brilliant advice for organizers: "Caucus as an intransitive verb meant your group agenda had to be strengthened privately and exhaustively to have maximum impact." (111) Indeed, this is a book a 20, or 30, or even 50 year-old, could not have written.

5

Intersections of Style and Intentionality: Retconning the *Harsh Realm* of the 1990s with Daniel Nester

C S: Reading *Harsh Realm,* your first book of poetry in 15 years, I get a sense of the uncanny. In one poem you mention you lived at 16th and Spruce in Philly. I did too (probably a few years before you), but in deeper ways too, and I suspect my reading of the book is very different than readers who didn't have somewhat overlapping interests and experiences of the time, like people born after 2001 or in other places? Did you imagine particular readers as you wrote this book?

DN: I am wondering—I have always wondered—who would want to read my writing, especially these days, at my age. I suspect there are shared sensibilities between us regarding how it fits into the Philly and NYC scenes— and I keep forgetting you got your degrees up here in Albany, where I've been since 2005. Of those three, it's New York that was the most transformative and drenched in things that inform the present book. I get serious pre-1999 flashbacks of Philly in Albany: the smallness of the scenes, the territorial nature of staking claims to running little fiefdoms. And that's *outside* of academia! It's almost as if college towns beget parallel systems that both criticize and imitate the industries that dominate the area. Anyway. I don't have loads of students interested in my work—I make a point not to talk about my own writing in class. I teach undergraduates who would much rather talk about their own writing, really.

CS: I admire your written "eye" skill for vivid sensory detail grounded in the lived experience of psyche and body of the speaker throughout *Harsh Realm*, and how you have a better memory, more visceral detail of the 90s than I have: To take just one early synesthetic example:

> "...pogoing in the mud,
> in Piscataway, hearing Michael Stipe
> sing for the first time, I wore white jeans
> and a Corona poncho. I cut off the jeans.
> chucked the poncho, and wore a Murmur
shirt" (pg. 17)

It is almost as if this sound demanded a style, a look, for instance. Virginia Konchan speaks of these as "remixed" poems. and I wonder if many of these poems in this book are rewrites (or say, samples) of poems, or notes, you wrote back then, but now seen from the point of view of a present speaker in a very different emotional state of being?

DN: That particular run of lines is expanded on in a chapter from a memoir I wrote called *Shader*. I do remember that concert pretty vividly, since at the time I was a new and rabid R.E.M. fan, listening to the first two full-length LPs, *Murmur* and *Reckoning,* nonstop. I suppose as a result of writing that, I did more online research I might have done if it was a poem. I confirmed that the R.E.M. gig, which was free and outdoors at Rutgers New Brunswick, was in fact in Piscataway, which just sounds great, and I also confirmed in the Old Farmer's Almanac that it was rainy around that time.

I've always been self-conscious of the presentation of the self in everyday life. I've always suspected I didn't fit in or obsessed over what others think or have thought about me. That R.E.M. gig was liberating in that I discovered people who didn't care what others thought how they looked or acted, and felt I fit in. Now of course, that is another pose, and other persona one adopts. But it was a genuine liberation, as I recall it.

CS: R.E.M's first two albums were crucial for me too. I like the way you counter the dominant myths of fashionable lifestyle music of the 1990s, in such early (space-clearing?) poems as "I can't say punk was important..." (8) Not only does this poem, to me, perfectly capture the sense of belatedness our generation felt, but also that it was the glamourous "punk rock girl(s)" (as the Dead Milkmen put it) that drew many to become partisans of particular scenes; like for me there's a sense that if these had been "goth girls," you would have gotten more into goth?

DN: I like this idea of space-clearing, or maybe claiming. "I can't say punk was important" is a bit of an answer-poem to some Diane Seuss poems I was reading in *Frank: Sonnets*, which as I write this has just won the Pulitzer. I love those poems, and there were a couple that seemed to embrace punk ethos in a way that just escaped me then, and from today's vantage point feels very class-specific.

Goth, as a concept and in practice, eluded me at the time, and maybe still. At least by the late 80s, Goth and punk were pretty much one and the same in many social spaces and clubs I encountered, so the difference really wasn't there to make. I understand what you're getting at, that goth was a kind of "third way" to go, as much as maybe New Wave might be as well. Punk, or being "real punk," was a genuine obsession in the late 80s and early 90s where I lived, in South Jersey and Philadelphia. I suppose it's still something people obsess over. And "punk" is such an elastic term that it's lost its meaning. But back then, to be punk cost money. It required access to money or you to be born into the kind of caste where money wasn't a factor, so you could engage in that scene. If you were lucky enough to find yourself as a punk in a punk scene, then you were someone who had access to people who were wealthy or kids of the wealthy. It felt absurd to be inside some punk club where you just knew the kids were acting out a rebellions that didn't register to me genuine as a working class kid. It seemed like rebellion karaoke. The worst part: I really loved the music, and couldn't understand why you had to take some sort of aesthetic loyalty oath to be considered a true lover or punk.

CS: I hear you; I knew some of these rich kids too. In a way I felt they envied us poorer kids, it's like when expensive boutique stores started selling pre-made ripped jeans. Anyway, reading this poem, alongside "Heavy Metal did not die in '91" (14), a "we poem" that also, not without self-deprecating humor, becomes a working class anthem, given the sociological, class contrasts in these poems. In these poems, as well as the poetryland poems, I can't help but identify with the frustrations of the speaker against what I call the OUGHTISTS. Against the backdrop of, say, that Thurston Moore documentary, "the year punk broke," in which "broke" can be taken two ways, in these, as well, as "The Death of College Rock," (17) I also find your interventions on behalf of the iconoclasts that these movements were ostensibly touted to free away from the trickle-down corporate demographic targetters to be appealing and refreshing. Is there anything you'd want to respond to here?

DN: I like that term, OUGHTIST.

CS: I borrowed it from Brett Evans.

DN: Interesting. The way I look at it, in my mind then and in the poems, is that all of this culture we're talking about is mediated in some way, be it MTV or some Simon Frith book you pick up at a used bookstore or some group of middle-class kids in line for Cure tickets. There is no pure way to experience these things, and definitely not writing about these things. At the same time, there is no way moments listening to hair metal that can be just as genuine and heartfelt and sublime-approaching as any other cultural experiences. The issue I've always had, in music as well as poetry, is how the critical discourses that surround reception foregrounds middle and upper class reception, and not only discounts working class reception, but the art that working class people love. Remember

Heavy Metal Parking Lot, the 1986 documentary of the Judas Priest/Dokken concert in Maryland? I remember watching it in the 90s and celebrating it as well as giggling at the metalhead fandom as well. I think it's a powerful thing to be at once self-conscious and sublime-seeking when it comes to, say, listening to Dokken at the height of their powers. On top of that, there is this idea, in the "Nirvana killed hair metal" narrative, of some sort of good triumphing over evil. It's maybe score-settling on my part in the form of a poem-as-barstool rant. But I see it in other pop music writing today. I am skeptical of the poptimism of the recent generations of music critics, but I guess that's another topic.

CS: It's interesting though! Of the pop-culture poems, "Nostalgia Ain't What It Used to Be" reminds me both thematically and tonally to Burmese writer ko ko thett's "my generation is best." In contrast to these poems that read the self in terms of pop culture (and pop culture in self), "The Plan Shifted With a Ferocious Snap" portrays a speaker in the act of reckoning about his youthful recklessness. But this meditative "I used to" themed prose-poem is interrupted on several occasions by forces' in the speaker's present environment: the first is the noise pollution of a rant. When the meditation on the past resumes in the second stanza, the act of othering takes on more urgency, as it's clear the older, more contemplative speaker, still must confront darker temptations to be reckless:

"One night, driving/out in the pines, I shut off the

lights in my car, and took on the highway in the dark,/ quiet, unmediated by light or sound or direction. I held a cold coffee in my hand,/waiting or wanting to hit some tree. I waited some more. Then the glow from my/phone lit up the interior." The "intrusion" of the phone turns out to be so much more. Was this a very difficult book to write?

DN: I can't really say that the book as a whole was difficult to write, but I will say "The Plan Shifted With a Ferocious Snap" was a specifically difficult poem to write, primarily because it deals with reckoning with a death wish. Driving in the middle of South Jersey and turning your lights off and thinking or perhaps hoping to hit a tree or a wall, that's not exactly what I would call healthy behavior. The memory has all kinds of moments around it—triggers, I guess I'd call them—most to do with going back home where all these memories lurk in the woods. And so as I think of the poem now, the cell phone call might have caused me to look away from the road and lead to an accident, but instead it snapped me out of it. If any poem in the collection should come with some sort of content or trigger warning, I think it's that one.

CS: Did *Harsh Realm* germinate in you a long time? When did you first conceive of this book? Did you go back to scenes where these memories took place as research? You mention that you had written a memoir called *Shader* before the poems? Did you come to feel that there were things you wanted to say in the memoir that could only be said in poetry?

DN: Some of these poems have been knocking around a while, for years, while others came out in the past five years, after I wrote the *Shader* memoir. The poems cover the period after I write about in the memoir, for the most part. Why I decided to write about that period of my life in prose, and the next in poetry is something I still think about. One pet theory I have is there is something about writing about the 90s and the dawn of digital technologies that necessitates a fractured and even granular poetics. A single-paragraph prose poem seems to say on the page HERE IS A MOMENT. It says to the reader, *that's all there is.* When of course there are connections to be made, perhaps with other single-paragraph prose poems in the book, but also with the white space on the page and whatever is happening in the reader's head. Another pet theory I have is I don't want to make those connections. There is a certain kind of false nihilism that comes out of the 90s, a product of prosperity and stupidity, borne out of a desire to seek out discomfort. That particular poem also has some echoes of Robert Lowell's "Skunk Hour"— but for all the wrong or worst reasons. That idea of the speaker-as-voyeur moving around this othered space.

CS: At the Zoom Book release party I "attended," you only read one of your "Poetryland" poems, as if you were purposely trying to spare the audience of mostly non-poets. While some of these poems, such as "From My Desk, c. 1997" and "This is Not a List Poem," emphasize a critique of some prevalent aesthetics (I, for instance, certainly wrote my share of, in retrospect, cringe-worthy "list poems" during that time); in others, aesthetic & ethical arguments and ethics blur—for instance, in "Debate Outside The Four Faced Liar, 1999," we see an oughtist bugging the speaker about the need for "a sense of play," in a very unplayful, and annoying way, highlighting the (hypocritical) discrepant hubris in a hilarious (meta-playful) way.

DN: I do resist reading those "Poetryland" poems in mixed company. My assumption has always been that non-poet civilians just wouldn't get those poems. But when you describe the nexus of ethical and personal and aesthetic concerns in those poems, it makes me think that maybe I could read more of them.

I published an essay years ago about leaving the New York City poetry scene called "Goodbye to All Them," which laid out a couple aspects of how cruel and careerist poets in NYC can be. It kind of went viral, getting mentions in all these different mainstream places, and I started hearing from people all over about how it resonated with them. Like, someone from Kansas saying how it sounded like their scene, or some artist from Ireland and their experiences with, like, other landscape painters. The takeaway for me was that it's not just poets who are subjected to a clannish ethical wasteland. I found that oddly reassuring?

In *Harsh Realm*, I think what I am writing about is slightly different. It's more along the lines of retcon attempts or correcting the historical record. The one I did read that Zoom reading, "Two 90s Poetry Readings," went over just fine, and that poem was about as inside baseball as you could get. Using initials instead of real names make the poems perhaps more universal or like 19th Century novels.

I will always lay claim to being a grump or snob about certain poems. It's just impossible to love every poem and every poet's work. Poetry is so vast in its approaches, I do think it always has fed on itself, in the best and worst ways.

In the middle of a reading I attended recently, a poet friend asked me, "Do you think it's possible to hate poetry and love it at the same time?" And I totally got what they were asking. My answer to that is yes, yes, yes. I think it's essential to hold onto the idea of anti-poetry and poetry in one's head at the same time. And I bring this up because I think when I write about another poet badgering me about aesthetics—using a very 90s-type argument about elliptical poetics as a way of discounting personal experiences and "exposing" narrative as some bourgeois tendency, as I remember that debate now—I think about it with a kind of nostalgia. People really thought this was a life-or-death discussion, right outside a bridge-and-tunnel Irish bar in the Village! It seems quaint to think about it.

As a true product of the 90s, my main coping mechanism when faced with conflict is humor and ironic distance. The world of poets and forging alliances and networking and readings and editing small journals and promoting other people's poems, back then, seemed like a full-contact interpersonal sport to me. It goes without saying that writing poems wasn't enough.

CS: I find your portrayal of the toxic ethos and traumatizing dynamics of the mostly male-dominated scenes of that time to be compelling in ways that go beyond mere "score settling" and self-pity. Many of these character portrayals, and ethical critiques of other (unnamed) poetry scene types, such as "To The Heckler At My First Poetry Reading, 1994," bring me back to that time with a lot of "uncanny feelings and unsettled bellyaches of energy" (8).

DN: That experience reading poems in a real venue as a 25-year-old and having this drunken poet heckle me the whole time was nothing short of traumatic. I didn't want to write about it because I still feel embarrassed about it, all these years later. But I knew that if I was going to write about becoming a poet in the 90s, I would have to write about that awful night. I never looked this dude up, but I found out this person was not some chimera who appeared at the back of the Tin Angel folk club, but was in fact a member of the Philadelphia poetry scene. And maybe that's why no one told him to stop? I'm still not sure. If anything, it made me happy to just leave Philly and start all over. If there is one thing I have learned about writing nonfiction, particularly memoir, it's that if you're going to write about someone who did something wrong to you, you need to at least examine your own motivations for writing about it. That poem about my heckler was something I could have written about for more than 30 years but didn't. And that's because I couldn't. The guy still exists out there, and writes poems, and never thought to apologize. I've had drunken nights myself where I misbehaved, but I did that whole thing where I called the next morning and apologized. After writing the poem, I think I realized that this wasn't one of those one-off things. I think this is just what happens in poetry and the one very valid coping mechanism is to write a poem about it.

CS: Yes, I think it's very valid, and you handle it with grace and flare. When I read a sentence (from "More Poets") like "whether this is a failure of the city, or merely/ of the poet, is an open question," I remember how many of us younger poets (including myself), in poetry scenes at that time, in our attempts to dig ourselves out of the divisive pettiness we felt in elders, ended up falling into such cruel dynamics ourselves—in a way that just makes me want to escape from the whole "poetry scene" dynamic that tends to bring out the worst in people at least as much as today's social media, with the temptation to speak before thinking, without any awareness of how we might come off to others.

DN: That's completely true. I would like to think that, because now I am older and have other interests and am no longer so monomaniacally focused on poetry and poem-making, I am not as susceptible to the divisive pettiness you're talking about. To be honest, I'm torn between trying to assert myself in some ways—writing poetry reviews, putting readings together, publishing journals—and think of that as a way to just be involved, as opposed to taking up space others could, and should, otherwise inhabit. It's a relief, to be honest. I have been cruel in many of the same ways I write about, and some other ways I haven't written about. I was really inspired by David Trinidad's 2016 collection *Notes on a Past Life*—that poem "More Poets" is sort of an homage to one of the poems in that collection. The way Trinidad wrote in narrative and artful ways about a poet's life felt both breezy and transgressive at the same time. Breezy because the poems are just eminently readable, filled with New York references from about a decade before my time, as well as all this yummy gossip that reads as sincere. It made me realize I could write narrative poems again in ways I've tried to avoid, for fear of being uncool or "mainstream" or some other nonsense. It also made me realize that I don't mind writing for a coterie of other poets.

CS: I like breezy and transgressive; I feel that in your book too. Did you feel a sense of purgation digging through these "retcon" memories? By emphasizing the negative, were you responding to a feeling of 90s nostalgia that many are tempted to have these days?

DN: I feel a little purge-y when I read these poems. If I put in my self-promotional marketing hat on, I do think there is something in the air about the 90s now. Not only people who lived through the 90s but also people who are interested in it.

CS: Do you feel that, perhaps, these days, poetry scenes are more supportive of each other than they were then?

DN: I really don't know. It's kind of obvious, but scenes are as much more digital and virtual now as opposed to proximal and geographical. I do think that, in the last 30 years, poets who have professionalized themselves and have gotten really, really good at institutionalizing things that weren't institutionalized before. We're in a world where Submittable makes it possible to submit to hundreds of journals all over the country and the world, all without reading them, and charge fees. We're in a world where submitting 10 times to the same journal in a single year is not only normal, but encouraged. Where poets are now getting PhDs but also not going into academia because tenure-track jobs have disappeared. People still want to be poets and make their mark, but the definition of how a mark is made has shifted. There is still nothing and everything at stake. At the same time, and more importantly, I love how there are not just white dudes and tokens anymore—the field feels more diverse, and it has improved the poems I read.

CS: Yes, I love how it's more diverse now too and am very excited by many poets who began publishing in the 21st century. You mentioned you might do a reading where you emphasize reading these "poetryland poems." Have you? I feel this could be useful to younger writers who are trying to form more supportive communities, as well as those who are sick of worrying where they belong or fit. Even if you don't share your own writing with your students, I imagine that when a student expresses a desire to be published or do readings, your experience in this school of hard knocks provides excellent, caring, advice. Is there anything you want to say about these?

DN: Now that you have asked, and reminded me about that, I should definitely schedule a Poetryland Only Reading. So when this thing is published, I will have a link!

Most of the students I teach aren't writers, and that, to me, is refreshing. It feels gratifying to know I am the first teacher to show them what some aspects of creative writing is, how it can improve their lives, no matter what they go on to do after college. I have some experience helping students get published or doing readings or making their way in the literary world. Not as much as I gather from other professor-types who teach at, say, MFA programs. When students do ask or express interest, I totally help and encourage them and offer them a realistic outlook on how things will be. I have always edited literary journals, and for the past 10 years or so, the one I edit, <u>Pine Hills Review</u>, is loosely affiliated with my college, and students help edit it as interns or as part of a class. That sort of hands-on experience feels interdisciplinary and organic to the student profile I have at my current job.

For many of my students, I know I am not the ideal mentor—I'm just a working class white guy from South Jersey. So a lot of my help comes from helping my students find their communities, whether it's Cave Canem or Kundiman or VIDA or other places. Most of my students don't even know there are these institutions out there, waiting for them to feel like they can be part of supportive communities. I do feel like that is real mentorship and good advice. I have former students who have gone on and done MFA programs or have gotten published, and have made their way into the world in ways I never did. That's mind-blowing at this point.

CS: It makes me happy to hear you so gratified by being the introductory teacher (me too). You mention the digital technologies that emerged in the 90s may necessitate a "fractured and even granular poetics," and how Trinidad's *Notes on a Past Life* helped you write narrative poems again without the fear of being uncool or "mainstream" or "bourgeois." One of the reasons I'm drawn to the narratives of *Harsh Realm* is that, in an age where the fragmentation of the digital realm is so culturally omnipresent, the attention and the discipline required to actually construct a more meditative sustained narrative becomes more and more attractive. Yet, beyond any argument of "what the age demanded" (perhaps a kind of *deacceleration* of its grimace), I feel your narratives do make room for what you call "the granular." Would you like to elaborate on any of these formal concerns of your poetics, or your revision process?

DN: I would like to think that the process a poem that I write takes—from reading poems of other people, thinking about language in my head, listening to music, scratching notebooks and poem drafts—has gotten more genuine or true to what kinds of poems I can best write. I am not sure I was consciously thinking I was kicking it old school or whatever in the poetic modes department, but I do think that, after returning to writing poems on a more consistent basis after a bunch of prose projects, I didn't feel the weight of technique anymore, at least not as much as in the past.

CS: Is reading poems by others the usual way you begin the process of writing a poem? Are there any poems in Harsh Realm that came about without reading poems by other people?

DN: Reading other writers definitely would be one of several ways a poem might begin. I mentioned Diane Seuss and David Trinidad. Lucille Clifton and Fernando Pessoa are always on my desk. I'm a huge fan of Matthew Lippman, who wrote about this book, and he indirectly led me back to reading Gerald Stern. I wrote an essay about being a student of Philip Levine for a collection a few years back, and that led to a poem in the collection that imitates his 1992 poem, "On the Meeting of Garcia Lorca and Hart Crane." It's called "On the Meeting of Frank O'Hara and David Lee Roth." At the same time, there are things I read and listen to and enjoy immensely that just don't find their way into my poems. I'm cool with it, but I don't think anyone who reads my poems would guess I am a huge sound poetry freak. Slam poems, too, although that might peek through. But sound poets and Language and post-Language poets, love them all, but they don't show up in my poems. It's like when CC Deville of Poison jokes about about all his influences—Hendrix, Jimmy Page—and he ends up playing Poison songs. That's me.

I don't think I am alone when I talk about the interferences and distortions that come along. There's the anxieties of influences and the social, coterie aspects in poetry scenes—again, I would like to think—has been put in a less pronounced place. I'm being super-general here, I know. But what I am trying to say is that I worry less about what I think people think, what other poets think. I trust my instincts for when a poem is going to happen.

For example: I feel like I've always had a feel for the line, or a particular line that I can identify with as having some sort of meaning or feel to them. It wasn't always that way. For example, even though I got a lot of pleasure out of it, I was worried I was somehow retrograde in thinking or hoping each of my lines would have its own world of meaning, independent of the poem. It's sort of an "every frame a painting," fetishy habit I picked up in workshops over the years, and it directly influenced how I break the line. Breaking before syntactical units so that each line seemed like some complete thought, that seemed to me to be a given when breaking lines. But over the years, I have tried to disrupt that practice and let lines hang and even lose track.

These thoughts really come to the fore when I think of some of the more narrative poems in the collection, like "The Death of College Rock: September 5, 1995," which recounts an episode of wandering around New York and catching an awards show on a TV. The lines get shorter for me, to give some tension to the grammar and syntax, and I also think it reflects the jumpiness of the time, of being in your late twenties and not knowing what the fuck is happening. What also comes to mind is returning to older styles I used when I was younger, like when I had the influence of certain William Carlos Williams poems hard-coded in my drafting process.

CS: Revisiting this poem in light of your comments, I am struck by how my earlier question totally ignored the importance of the final line, in which the cultural opinions yield to the character of the speaker (figure becomes ground?); but thinking about lines, perhaps an excerpt could illustrate:

> "If you were to establish
> which songs were objectively awful,
> this song would be the index case
> against which all other objectively
> awful songs were compared."

I like the way this seems like a straightforward discursive statement, but in these medium length lines "objectively awful," in the second line becomes "objectively/awful" as if to highlight the emotion of disgust the speaker feels in a hyperbolic self-mocking statement. I can hear your voice in this performative rhetorical utterance. I imagine gestures. I wonder if you prefer to read this slower at readings to emphasize the line breaks and the tension that creates?

DN: Right, I am delighted you picked that up. The

enjambment right there to me would be an example of me doing work to avoid the directly prosaic when a reader encounters the poem. At least with my own performer's tool box, I might even speak in the iambic lockstep "poet voice" to play up that enjambment, so listeners would get that I am disrupting the syntax there. It's also a good example of my breaking my earlier habits of having lines work as independent units of meaning, because when you're writing a poem that has narrative or expository surface, another way to compress language and give it energy, it seems to me, is to introduce enjambment.

CS: I also like the way the social milieu you describe/ invoke in "poetryland" differs from that of "players in horrible rock bands, or those who care to remember true failure—wordless, naked-ass failure." ("Hot Blooded," 33). The meanness, and the sharp wit of the contentious ego-based poetry scene seems muted in the more collaborative art of music making. Arguments happen, but more in form of lighter banter, as in the 3rd paragraph/stanza of "Hot Blooded."

"After the gig, the singer's girlfriend complains in her thick Danish accent that she cannot hear ze words. It makes sense that she wants to hear her man sing about her ass. Taking a page from literary theory, I explain that sometimes words aren't important, that the simple sound of her husband's easel-aided utterances would suffice. She rolls her eyes and carries her old man's antediluvian teleprompter out to the cab."

And while there may be arguments about arrangements

and aesthetics, but in "The Drummer in Our Band Tells Us He's a Virgin," they fade into moments of brotherly vulnerability and even, if compared to the poetryland poems, a kind of tenderness. Woven through this relatively straightforward narrative we see references to Othello. I admire the way you handle this "digression device." For me, it could suggest what the speaker is thinking while this situation is happening, and this breathes mystery into the poem that can come in form of questions: How does this band practice scene connect to a Kabuki production of Othello, with an overblown "honest Iago?" I'm not asking you to talk about your "intention" on a meaning-level here, but if you'd like to add, or correct me on, anything here, I'd love to hear…

DN: I've been saying to people I feel more comfortable in music-related spaces—stores, clubs, gigs, practice spaces—than I ever was in literary spaces. Maybe it's because in a music store it's a once-removed situation, or there was no pressure to not suck, because I knew I sucked, or didn't care that I sucked.

That poem about one of playing in my bands goes back a ways, but I do remember thinking the memory of watching a kabuki Othello production was related to this moment in the rehearsal space in the East Village. I wish I could make these digression device-type leaps more consciously or artfully, which is how I am taking your characterization, perhaps hopefully. I was having fun and pleasure with the assonance of that long o-sound. Bubbling underneath is the beta machismo of how some bands passive-aggressively argue with each other, in a small room but with microphones, and what I remember about Othello the most is how Iago orchestrates a whole sequence of events.

CS: Do you still make music?

DN: I do still play guitar, albeit really badly. I love the gear, the amps and pedals. I yearn to be in a band again, to play with other people. It's probably unlikely to happen, although my daughter plays drums now, and someday I may go downstairs and plug in. Just to jam and get loud.

CS: A family band would be great! On a more micro level, as I reread this book, I look back over the many lines, or short passages, I've underlined, and quite a few of them are about language and metaphysics, in a rather casual offhand, and funny, way:

"Someone may write, 'What is feeling?' Someone answers: 'It's kind of like consciousness, dear, except you give it some goddamn value.'" (8—The Art of Prose (with Digressions)

Sometimes the word "God", makes an appearance, in unexpected ways. One poem ends with "Let God's love ruin it. And God's love always ruins it" (31). And another writes: "Hint: it appears very likely our faith in God interrupts whatever truly tries to speak to us, which is a version of us, of course." (56). Both of these lines are from poems addressed to a "You" uttered with an authority and a tone of wisdom, but do not belabor their points. I don't feel atheism as much as a sense of letting go from reified words that get in the way of feeling, or should I say consciousness?

DN: You're talking about a strand of poems of mine I feel less sure-footed talking about, poems where I am letting go of meaning as much as I can. I am forever hoping a poem will come through me in ways that are less conscious. I think that it's in poetry where half-knowledge, or half-understanding things, can somehow become something else. And I suppose there's where metaphysics and attempts at a variety of aphoristic experience comes into the mix. In my best moments looking at poems, I notice shades of meaning pop up that I did not intend but still add to the poem. That, to me, is the attraction to writing a certain kind poem; it's a field of answers looking for questions. When that distills even further, I find mentions of God and faith popping up. That's not just twelve years of Catholic school rearing its head, although it's a part of it. It's post-faith me trying to come up with a referent to all of those things I can't figure out or don't want to figure out. God's the best name for it, at least in some poems.

CS: I recently quoted your attraction to a poem as "a field of answers looking for questions," to a friend, and love what you say about the process of letting go of meaning. The book's final poem, for instance, I read at first as making an important point about "sad cowboy songs," but the more I reread it, the weirder it gets, and meaning "becomes something else." Regardless of what some idea of "the reader" thinks, do you find sometimes that, when reading your own poems in this collection that they step outside of their utterance and can inspire you to feel different questions than you were aware of when writing them, like the old adage of poems knowing more than the poet does?

DN: I don't know if other poets feel this, but it takes a lot of work to let go and trust the language. Sometimes when I do that, the language ends up as a load of goo. I have notebooks upon notebooks of that kind of stuff: failed experiments and starts.

And then a poem comes along like "On Realizing Poison's 'Every Rose Has Its Thorn' Has the Same Chords as the Replacements' 'Here Comes a Regular,'" the poem you're referring to, and it feels like the language and negative capability falls into place. That long title does the expository heavy lifting, and lets readers know exactly what the poem that follows addresses, but it's not just addressing something I suspect you know, as a real musician: there's only so many chord progressions, only so many ways to put together a song, so of course there are going to be overlaps and, to me at least, versions of pastoral, a green world where different aesthetic impulses co-exist. It's a possibility that I am always looking for, intersections of style and intentionality, the fields that I am talking about would be both in the mind and on the page, where we can at once acknowledge differences and clashes as well as find poetry.

CS: Scattered throughout *Harsh Realm* are a few poems

that bring your 21st century more domestic life into the picture, for instance "Future Days"(42-3). After navigating a page and half of memories, both dark and light, from the 90s framed in a more recent present, the poem swerves into a more stammering cadence as the memories get closer:

Alone with my headphones and coffee straws,
        passwords written in chalk on bricks gather
light from a window,
        and I remember the day in the hospital just
down the street
        from here in Albany, in the second-string coffee
shop
        with high windows, when my daughter's legs
turned blue
        last summer, and I couldn't drive straight or
walk straight,
        and I ran into the room where she was in bed
and she was
        OK but scared to have her face with tubes in it.
My chest
        froze there in the hallway, and I touched her
small ears
        and sang her name a little bit—it was all I could
do to stand there
        too appear fatherly, to breathe in and out,
helpless and still." (43—Future Days)

"Eavesfall" (40) and "Gethsemane" (62) are 'lighter,' poems also set in a domestic present. I find "Gethsemane" especially refreshing and charming, after these darker poems from the 1990s. The exchange between father and daughter, for me, has a kind of Frank O'Hara insouciance of "deep gossip," in ways the poetry coteries (of the 90s at least) could've used more of. I wonder if you've written more poems like this; it makes me happy to see this speaker in the present. Have you shown any of these to your daughter?

DN: It's funny you put "Future Days" and "Gethsemane" in the same question, along with "Eavesfalls," but I guess it makes sense. Each mentions my daughters, or a daughter, and maybe their presence grounds some of the more highfalutin pantheistic feelings in the poems we just talked about. "Future Days" was a bear of a poem to stick with—I felt it had that "I do this, I do that" thing going for it, and the form of it felt open enough to throw in everything from the annoying dude who talked out loud every day in my local coffee shop and memories of poetry readings in Brooklyn where no one showed up.

CS: It's nice to see people respond to that poem on Facebook.

DN: To go back to another question, "Future Days" is a poem where I was trying out new ways of thinking about the line, and where words could break and still mean something but also disrupt an easy, comfortable reading experience. I also think "Future Days" is important for the collection, since it brings together memories of Poetryland's absurd focus on who is doing what and why things don't happen, with what happens every day: people drink crappy coffee, students in graduate school struggle with their papers, the kids we have end up in emergency rooms. And the more I thought about this, the more I thought about how Can and Neu! and the motorik drum beat relates to how I was living my life, or trying to: it's a rhythm that's a "restrained exhilaration," is how it's described somewhere. It's how I try to actively listen to music while trying to write at the same time.

In the course of answering these questions you've asked, I do notice I am often setting up one tendency against another—narrative versus lyric maybe, darker poetryland poems versus lighter ones from the present. I don't necessarily think it's healthy to do this, but more and more I feel it's part of my process: I'll write one way in reaction or rebellion to another way, or write about one subject as a way of getting away from a topic I can't stand exploring anymore. When people read these poems, they may not realize these are moments that happened years ago, and that's intentional: I do want readers to think I am writing something that just happened yesterday and they're getting the immediate reaction. For me at least, it's those poems that are the most challenging to pull off, and not just because of writing in the present tense or anything like that. It's the challenge of keeping that immediacy and deep gossip in the poems as they move through drafts. I have to work really hard to make those poems seem easy, whereas other poems that draw from more definite timelines in the past may come more naturally. My oldest did read "Gethsemane" when it was published, and what was great is I had to explain where the title came from, all the temptations of Christ and the stations of the cross. She had no clue about any of it. So just to get her up to speed on the title, I had to give her a crash course on Jesus. Her reaction to that was as if I was telling her the story of some musical artist from the 80s that just went viral on TikTok—it had relevance but not really. It was refreshing, at least to me, that she wasn't burdened with religion. I've been writing poems about some of this. Maybe that's the next book.

Using Selections from
Ming Di's New Poetry from China
(Black Square, 2019)
in the Classroom

For M, & ZQ

In my Spring 2020 English 1B course (a required course introducing non-majors to 3 different genres of literature: short stories, plays, and poetry), I noticed a change in demographics for the first time in 12 years. While previously, most of the students were either Black or Latino/Latina, this was the first semester my class was mostly Chinese and Chinese-American. I realized I had to change my syllabus, and quick. After class, one student who I'll call M (for I fear the specter of persecution he faces in China for his outspoken interests and views, as well as by MAGA Americans who were ramping up violence against Chinese, and Asians in general, who they were blaming for the "Kung Flu" as well as for "taking our jobs"), met with me one and one and told me he reads a lot of contemporary Chinese poetry.

I told him I am extremely ignorant; I read a few Misty Poets in translation back in the 1980s/1990s and am aware of Xu Lizhi. He was impressed that I knew Xu Lizhi and mentioned that the Chinese authorities consider his work dangerous and don't encourage reading him. I decided to include Ming Di's recently published *New Poetry from China* anthology (Black Square Editions, 2018), and it became a vehicle to learn from my students about a subject I know almost nothing about. Not surprisingly, it was the contemporary poets, many much younger than I, who resonated most with the other students as well, especially political dissidents jailed or killed, and the importance of "worker poetry."

Ming Di's anthology was/is an eye-opener to me, as she engages in a clearly daunting task. How does one create an anthology of under 250 pages to introduce English speaking Americans to a diverse range of poets spanning a century (1917-2017) from a country with a population of over a billion, while also translating the majority of them? Though she keeps her commentary minimal, she frames the book with a discussion of the origins of the New Poetry in 1917.

Hu Shi (1891-1962) is generally acknowledged and acclaimed as "one of the most influential figures in the May Fourth New Cultural Movement, which demanded democracy and freedom," and for his seminal essay "On New Poetry" (1919), which argues for the use of the contemporary vernacular in poetry (similar perhaps to William Carlos Williams or Langston Hughes here). Di argues that Hu Shi's long-debate in verse from his diary dated July 22, 1916, "Reply To Old Mei—A Poem in Plain Speech," should be considered his first attempt at New Poetry," even though Hu Shi himself came to believe it failed (25):

"By today's standards, it may seem as hybrid writing with some poetry and some prose (as poetry can only be lyrical and/or narrative but not a debate or an argument, which belongs to the essays, according to the old definition). He even puts footnotes into the poem by using parenthesis, which looks exciting today." (236)

Di is considered controversial for this 21st reassessment of Hu Shi; Chen Ju, for instance, scoffed and referred to this poem as doggerel. Di also introduced me to the work of **Chen Hengzhe (1890-1962)**, the first woman scholar, professor and writer in modern Chinese history (238). Because her two translations of Chen are short, I will include them here:

Moon
Thru' a thin cloud a new moon climbs
then fades out, a cold falling leaf;
but its radiant face reflected in the creek
stays in the clear water and won't leave

Wind
At night I hear the rain on my window.
I get up and see the moonlight, a waterfall.
Leaves fly around, soaring, and batter
The pine trees. The young cones fall.

Hu Shi praised these poems, but although they are written in the 'new language,' unlike "Reply to Old Mei," they are still constrained by how many words should be in each line and how many lines in each stanza, the regulated 5-word quatrains of the High Tang Dynasty (618-907). Later poems such as "People Say I'm Crazy" (1918, not included in this anthology)," a dramatic monologue with irregular lines, no rhymes, about an elderly patient rambling in a hospital" could be considered New Poetry.

Regardless of whether Ming Di's anthology is considered "representative" (she herself writes, "omissions are not accidents,"), it has achieved a more profound goal which is giving Americans like me, hitherto mostly ignorant of Chinese contemporary poetry, an introductory sample for further investigation. Near the end of her anthology, Ming Di also includes two migrant worker poets who especially resonated with my students, **Xiaqiong Zheng (1980)** and **Xu Lizhi 1990-2014).**

***

In China today, according to a paper by M, there are over 250 million migrant workers and 80 million industrial workers, "yet (Chinese) society hardly hears the voices of the vast, marginalized industrial workers' voices." This process started in the 1980s, as the industrial workers in state-owned enterprises were phased out (resulting in a huge unemployment crisis), and replaced with migrant workers in sweatshops. One of these workers was **Xiaoqiong Zheng (1980)**, who became the pioneer of the New Chinese Worker Poetry. In her early poem, "Industrial Zone," she writes:

So many lamps are glaring, so many people passing by
Place yourself inside the bright factories, memories,
machines
The speechless moonlight, lamplights, like me
Are so tiny, fragments of spare parts, filaments
Using their vulnerable bodies to warm the factory's
hustle and noise
And all the tears, joy, pain we ever had
Those noble or humble ideas, spirits are
Illuminated, stored up by moonlight, and taken so far
To fade away as unnoticed rays of light

When she writes "Place yourself," I feel she's responding to my question, not just about what workers think, but also what they feel, as their very souls are "stored up" in the products of their labor, and "taken so far" to fade unnoticed in a market of conspicuous consumption and planned obsolescence; workers are treated like, and become, the "fragments of spare parts" they have to work with. J tells me I'm reading American guilt into it, and teaches me about its context on August 15th, the Mid-Autumn Festival.

In the context of Chinese poetry since 1917, M considers Zheng's poetry a breakthrough: "she had broken the worker-intellectual opposition existing in China for the past 100 years...for the first time, the poetry of workers begins to focus on individual experience instead of political slogans of imagined communities; workers are no longer just part of a broader community." In contrast to poems sanctioned by the upper level guidance of the Maoist era, "the 27 years of political poetry" from 1949-1976, these poems are written by the workers themselves, "independent individuals who have their own tears, joy, and pain."

M also points out how Zheng focuses on gender discrimination and how female migrant workers are the most vulnerable of this marginalized group. "China's patriarchal family severely restricts the life path of every woman, especially in education, family labor division, employment and marriage choices. Most are young unmarried women. After the age of 25, if they do not get married, they are generally considered worthless, and the golden period of their lives (18-25 years old) is requisitioned and plundered in sweatshops to promote the development of cities and industries."

After Zheng's success, M notes that "Working Poems" was officially supported in the early 21st century, "including being launched as a 'brand' in Guangdong." As a result, many working poets 'consciously or unconsciously assimilated to the official and folk organizations to become professional poets. However, Lizhi Xu was not one of them."

***

I first discovered **Xu Lizhi (1990-2014)** through activist, rather than poetry, channels. On October 5, 2011, at the height of the Occupy Wall Street Movement, Apple founder Steve Jobs died tragically young of pancreatic cancer. While many were expressing thoughts & prayers, I discovered (on my Apple laptop) the tragic conditions in the Foxconn factory that makes computer parts in Shenzen, China. At least 14 workers had committed suicide in 2010. As a result, Foxconn installed nets to prevent them from committing suicide. A few months later Xu Lizhi wrote a poem in tribute to the interior life of these human resources, the struggles and strength of these workers, forbidden even a dignified death, "The Last Graveyard." Here's the first 6th lines"

Even the machine is nodding off
Sealed workshops store deceased iron
Wages concealed behind curtains
Like the love that young workers bury at the bottom of
the their hearts
With no time for expression, emotion crumbles into dust
They have stomachs forged of iron...

The metaphorical relation of "buried love" to concealed wages gets to the heart(lessness) of global capitalism in a way that would take a contemporary cultural-Marxist theorist paragraphs of logos to evoke. This last line, if taken out of context could appear in a Maoist sloganist poem celebrating workers' as abstractions of super-human strength, the next 2 lines, however, flesh out the metaphor:

Full of thick acid, sulfuric and nitric
Industry captures their tears before they have a chance
to fall...

Tears, bodies. Personification of dehumanization: I can't go on about devices like personification. This is no mere metaphor. Does the first line make you want to vomit? Does the second line make you want to cry? How raw do we want our materials? Easily replaced parts. Tears, bodies, screws...

A screw fell to the ground
In this dark night of overtime
Plunging vertically, lightly clinking
It won't attract anyone's attention
Just like last time
When someone plunged to the ground
("A Screw Fell to the Ground" 1/9/14)

In a world of hostile external forces that infect body, mind and spirit, Xu tries to find a way to somehow release these toxins (which become their 'wages') to make some room for love or life force. He still has a sliver of contemplative consciousness left to be able to see "They've trained me to become docile," to "grind away my corners, grind away my words." In another poem, grabbing the pen becomes a desperate clutch to *breathe*:

Flowing through my veins, finally reaching the tip of my
pen
Taking root in paper
These words can only be read by the hearts of migrant
workers

He also brutally literalizes the metaphor of "poetry
workshop" in "Workshop, My Youth Was Stranded Here"
("Beside the assembly line, tens of thousands of workers
line up like words on a page/ 'Faster, hurry up!'). One
commentator refers to his work as "cold and pensive,
directly facing a life of misery," but if you want something
"lighter," something that promises the strength of filial,
ancestral lineage as if family values can flourish in, or
push back against, such working conditions, you might
appreciate "A Kind of Prophecy:"

Village elders say
I resemble my grandfather in my youth
I didn't recognize it
But listening to them time and again
Won me over
My grandfather and I share
Facial expressions
Temperaments, hobbies
Almost as if we came from the same womb
They nicknamed him "bamboo pole"
And me, "clothes hanger"
He often swallowed his feelings

I'm often obsequious
He liked guessing riddles
I like premonitions
In the autumn of 1943, the Japanese devils invaded
and burned my grandfather alive
at the age of 23.
This year i turn 23

We could talk about the "missing capitals" in the last 3 lines, the dramatic pacing, the way the device of parallelism becomes a premonition, the historical analysis: is what the Japanese did to him any worse than what Foxconn does to us?

Or perhaps we could find some solace in domestic life:

A space of ten square meters
Cramped and damp, no sunlight all year
Here I eat, sleep, shit, and think
Cough, get headaches, grow old, get sick but still fail to die
Under the dull yellow light again I stare blankly, chuckling like an idiot
I pace back and forth, singing softly, reading, writing poems.
Every time I open the window or the wicker gate
I seem like a dead man
Slowly pushing open the lid of a coffin.
("Rented Room," 2 December 2013)

It sounds like he lives in a bathroom, is forced to eat where he shits.. Death could seem liberation....[74]

***

One of the poems included in this selection was "I Swallowed a Moon Made of Iron." I was happy to see that Ming Di also included this poem, with a different translation. Here's the two English translations side by side:

I swallowed a moon made of iron
I'm swallowing an iron moon,
They refer to it as a nail
a screw they call it.
I swallowed this industrial sewage, these unemployment documents
I'm swallowing industrial wastewater, unemployment, orders.
Youth stooped at machines die before their time
People die young, who are shorter than the machines
I swallowed the hustle and the destitution
I'm swallowing migration, displacement
Swallowed pedestrian bridges, life covered in rust
skywalks and rusty life.

---

74 All translations, unless otherwise specified, are taken from: https://libcom.org/blog/xulizhi-foxconn-suicide-poetry

I can't swallow anymore

> *I can't swallow anymore.*

All that I've swallowed is now gushing out of my throat

> *All that I've swallowed rush out/ of my throat*

Unfurling on the land of my ancestors

> *spreading like a shameful poem*

Into a disgraceful poem

> *on my fatherland.*

(Nao project)   *(Ming Di)*

Since I don't know Chinese, but have so many students who do, I thought a comparison-contrast of the two translations would be a great paper topic prompt option, and, thankfully, one student took me up on the offer: ZQ writes that Xu "created a satire that even the moon, which is supposed to symbolize heartwarming reunions with family, becomes very cold and heavy and makes him more lonely." Of the many subtle differences in these translations, ZQ focuses on what he refers to as the "passive tense" (the Nao project one in bold above) past tense version and the "active tense" (present tense) Ming Di version.

ZQ generally believes the "passive tense" translation "does a better job in word choice and maintains the structure of the original poem." He believes that to translate the first line as "I'm swallowing an iron moon" makes it sound "like Xu Lizhi is willing to do it," while the passive tense version makes it sound like he's "being forced to." He also prefers the Nao Project's version for the 4th line: "'Youth stooped at machines die before their time' is indirect and contained mixed ideas… Xu Lizhi did not directly use the word "people." Youth can be defined as young people or a period of time at a young age…when he refers to "youth" as time, it tells that Xu Lizhi and his coworkers are scarifying their *youth* in exchange for low reward."

ZQ also believes the "active tense translation" of the final couplet is more "straightforward, but alters the structure of the original poem and does not express Xu Lizhi's message." To back his claim, he claims Xu Lizhi is clearly appealing to the ancient tradition in which it was an honor to be a poet, and making a contrast with how being a poet "becomes worthless. The word "fatherland" in the active translation did not deliver the satire behind this poem because it only tells its origin. On the other side, 'the land of my ancestors' delivers the satire of Xu Lizhi on this disgraceful cold and heartless society of China."

ZQ certainly deserves an A for making a very convincing case to why he prefers one translation to another, but others disagree. One student said "unemployment, orders" sounds stronger, more forceful, than the translation ZQ prefers which merely says "unemployment documents." My biggest take away from reading ZQ's brilliant paper is the clear reverence for both Xu Lizhi's craft as well as his passionate moral argument, and manifests much more ease and agility with the kind of 'close reading' attention poetry either demands or invites, leaving ample room for the play of aesthetic and political interpretations in class discussion

***

According to a biographic summary from The Nao project, Xu left his home in Jieyang, Guangdong (whose local economy was destroyed, and countryside polluted), a place so isolated he couldn't even order books (his main source of pleasure and meaning in life) on-line because they wouldn't deliver, to work at Foxconn in 2010. He also wrote essays, film reviews, and news commentaries (which I have not yet read). They also mention that, even though he was getting attention for his writing, he had applied for a position as librarian at Foxconn's internal library for employees," but had been turned down. They neglect to mention, however, something M taught me in his paper: the stand Xu Lizhi's took for the workers in his refusal to sell them out:

"When poet-critic Xiaoyu Qin contacted him and listed him as one of the ten poets in the documentary *Verse of US,* Xu refused. He basically broke off contact with poets. The experience of Lizhi Xu indicates the dilemma of many worker poets in China in some aspects. Writing poems welcomed by the authorities or the intellectuals is almost the only way for them to get rid of the exploitation in factories and plants. However, for some poets, that means giving up their identity and poetry life. Even after the poetry of the workers walked into the public eye with support of the intellectuals and authority, it only means that individuals in the working class were able to break away from their class. When the workers are no longer concerned about workers, they are no longer workers' poetry."[75] Xu, by contrast, "transforms his personal pain into eternal perseverance"

According to an acquaintance of Xu's called Zheng (pseudonym) in the *Shenzen Evening News*, Xu's suicide resulted from both "internal and external factors: not only the disappointments he had undergone, but even more so the solitary poetic spirit in his bones," a translator's note quarrels with the reliability of this acquaintance's explanation; it "neglects the profound hatred of life on the assembly line reflected so clearly in many of his poems...and why so many other workers—at Foxconn and elsewhere—have chosen to commit suicide—even those were not poets."

M ends his essay, with a sentence from Xu's "Quatrain" which shows the power of solidarity that his spirit has given his fellow workers: "Someone has to pick up the screws on the ground/ This abandoned life will not rust."

***

---

75 I asked M more about this (because I remembered liking Qin's poem in Ming Di's anthology), and he wrote: "Personally, I don't like Q's documentary nor his book; his attitude towards Xu and other worker poets is more like, "that's fascinating. I didn't know workers can write poems too.")

I asked him about why he thinks first person poems of individual experience have more galvanizing collective revolutionary force than the more abstract poetry of slogans. He wrote:

"In China, the reason we value individual experience is that for so many years, since the Mao era, people recite those slogans everyday. Personally, I feel, in an ideal situation, there should probably be a balance between slogans and individual experience. The overwhelming victory of either side may represent a severe problem with society. When slogan wins, it reminds me of the Cultural Revolution in China in which the fanaticism of people as a collective creates both tragedies and slogans. When individual experience wins, it reminds me of an extremely self-centered society in which most people become politically apathetic.[76] Some sensitive artists may feel the greater environment and choose to write different things; it reminds me of the Misty Poets after the time of slogans and the slogans in France during May 68."

I asked M if he had been a migrant worker himself, and had managed to escape, and he wrote that he had grown up isolated from, and had no interaction with, migrant workers, but when he got admitted to one of the top high-schools because he was ranked in the top 0.1%

_____

76   Perhaps *The Shenzen Eveing News'* emphasis of the solitary poetic spirit in Xu Lizhi's bones, rather than the external environmental factors, in his decision to commit suicide could be one example of such co-optations."

of the high-school entrance exams, he quickly despised the atmosphere of these elite high-schools and colleges "where only one kind of voice is allowed to exist." It was by being a photographer that he became concerned with migrant workers, and began doing work for the NGO aiming to protect the rights of industrial workers while doing a photography project to record the conflicts in the urbanization process of Chengdu.

He also sent me examples of rock songs (with translated lyrics), and makes a provocative argument that may have some American analogues when it comes to questions like: "Is hip hop poetry?"

"I think Misty Poets best represent the literary and artistic world in 1980s China; however, the musicians like Zhang Chu, Dou Wei, etc. can best represent the literary and artistic world in 1990s' China," and includes a few links, including a song about the reform in the 1980s which caused hundreds of thousands industrial workers to lose their jobs:

https://www.youtube.com/watch?v=uh0rqCMRPOs

:https://www.youtube.com/watch?v=iHalSivNp-c):

https://en.wikipedia.org/wiki/Zhang_Chu_(singer)

POETRY DETONATES DUALISMS
AN INTERVIEW WITH MARTINE BELLEN
(*AN ANATOMY OF CURIOSITY*
MAD HAT PRESS, 2023)

Martine Bellen has been a quiet force in poetry for over two decades. Her second book, *Tales of Murasaki* (Sun & Moon Press, 2000), was selected for the National Poetry Series by Rosmarie Waldrop, and acclaimed collections from Copper Canyon and other small presses have followed; in 2015 Spuyten Duyvil released *This Amazing Cage of Light: New and Selected Poems*. A contributing editor for Conjunctions, Bellen also has composed libretti for three operas, and her poetry has been included in numerous anthologies, most recently in the 2023 volume of *The Best American Poetry*.

Elizabeth Robinson writes that the poems in Bellen's latest collection, *An Anatomy of Curiosity* (MadHat Press, $21.95), "are capable of the most agile swerves, demonstrating that a serious inquiry can sail on music and play, through myth and dream: here are the malleable, chewy realms of metamorphosis." Fascinated by these agile swerves, I brought some of Bellen's poems into the creative writing class I teach, and I am grateful to my students for a spirited discussion—some of their insights and questions, in fact, are incorporated into the following interview.

Chris Stroffolino: I want to begin with a comment you made in a recent interview with Indran Amirthanayagam, that you "work more from the surreal than from myth." I feel the first poem in *An Anatomy of Curiosity*, "Bad Times at the El Royale," works *through* a Hollywood mythology, wending beyond that and crescendoing to a dream sphere:

You and I are in the body bag, sleeping beside
a volcano that vibrates and reaches up us
like a fist through a throat, signaling
to a lifeguard to swim across ages
and currents, through celestial meridians,
toward our swirling sound bridge,
beautiful mind, plenary weave, a coat of every note. (5)

While the sinuous flowing music is transporting, I am also struck by the peril, and I wonder if the prayer to the lifeguard is answered. Do you want to say anything more about myth and surrealism in this poem, or elsewhere in your work?

Martine Bellen: A number of things drew me to the movie *Bad Times at the El Royale.* In it, nothing is what it seems and no one is who they say they are, so some of the poem is about washing away who we pretend to be or think we are. Because of this, detergents and washing machines play a part, though as you suggest, the last section of the poem turns menacing and violent—the soundtrack switches. This happens to me often in dreams; suddenly, the scene pivots and I'm alone and have lost my ability to speak. So in *An Anatomy of Curiosity,* the loss of voice that can happen when you›re in danger and can›t call out for help is a strand woven into the design. One can have the experience of being unable to reach the bridge between self and others.

What I meant in the conversation with Indran is that myths, being ancient, shared belief systems, have bridges and gates, and my poems roam the mythic landscape while quilting (in the surrealist sense of juxtaposition) "our swirling sound bridge, / beautiful mind, plenary weave, a coat of every note." (5)

CS: As I reread the poem in light of your response, I notice "bridges" can be a noun (common and proper, since Jeff Bridges is in the film) and a verb, and I feel the gated community of Bill Gates as well—your imagining's sudsy synesthesia indeed washes the language. I also love that you bring your Zen Buddhist practice into this capacious trans-denominational quilting while you roam; the rhythmic alliterative flow of variations on the word "prayer" in "Deafening Prayer" is an especially joyful example. How did this come about?

MB: I started "Deafening Prayer" around Election Day, when a radio announcer said that voting is praying. I hadn't thought of voting that way before, but it's so true: We send out a petition for who we wish will win the race in the same way we pray for anything we want. Then I asked myself, What isn't praying? and I realized that everything is a prayer. From there, a fragmented inverted list poem commenced.

Also, since you mention both Bill Gates and Buddhism: While working on this book, I was sitting with koans, those riddles/questions in Zen practice that a meditator focuses on (a popular koan is "What is the sound of one hand clapping?"). Koans are used to free one from dualistic thinking, the idea being that the experiential is unimpeded by the limits of language, but when we attempt to describe experience in language, we crash onto dualistic Earth.

Poetry is, I think, a type of language that can detonate dualism. And Zen priests and practitioners have a long history of writing poetry. In fact, anthologies of koans are structured with the koan, a short commentary, and finally a capping poem, which is the experiential insight. Most of the koans I was sitting with when working on *An Anatomy of Curiosity* are from *The Gateless Gate*, a collection of forty-eight koans compiled in the 13th century; when meditating, "gates" or barriers are passed through and the meditator moves on to the next one. So throughout *An Anatomy of Curiosity*, I have included various "gates" (though not Bill)—for instance, in "Myth of the Bluebeard-ed Bluebird" I write, "'Going up,' elevator operator chimes as he closes one gate" (74) (remember old-school elevator gates?) and in "Monkey and Spirit Bird Triptych," "It's all about where you drop the garden gate"(77) (that's Miles Davis's music space). So yes—bridges and gates are the infrastructure of some of the poems, connecting our island delusion.

CS: I do remember those elevators, and I definitely see your gates and bridges working in many ways to pass through barriers of dualistic thinking and create connections. In this light, I'd like to look at "Myth of the Bluebeard-ed Bluebird" with you in more depth:

> "Going up," elevator operator chimes as he closes
> one gate.
> "Going down," is chanted at the far end of the elevator
> bank,
> > the river bank,
> > > banks of earth sloping
> from land to sea, from water wake
> to streams of sleep
> > from limbs to fins. (74)

This short stanza brings so much into play: in the first line we sense the confinement of the elevator (symbol of progress, the ego at the wheel?), though the second line feels like a yin to its yang, and taken together with the first can possibly do "koan work"; its passive voice and its contrast of chant with chime suggests to me that "what goes up must come down" but also implies an echoing. Then the next five lines dance away from the confinement of the "banks," taking on a chthonic (rather than economic) connotation. The language also suggests multi-directional transport, both "up" and "down" stream, as if a "gateless gate," or at least a wider sense of subjectivity, emerges. The poem continues:

In this myth, you want nothing more
than to land in a fully stocked big-box stationary store
                    but the mall is poorly lit, and portals lead
to floors
of canopied woods before deforestation and paper mills.
(74)

At first, this desiring "you" (inside the elevator that's become a portal) seems disappointed or anxious, implying perhaps the death of our civilization, but also the loss of time-space coordinates—there's no stationary place to land—but, in the next stanza, there's an opening as myths mingle:

Nymphs flaunt their good fortune on escalators to faux fountains
satyrs squeeze into try-on rooms,
whispering oaks, in maquillage, with roots of skulls and spines (74)

You cap it off with a shorter-lined lyric that, among other things, has me thinking about "countenance":

The structure's columns
mirrored

sartorial
wear
your countenance
bear
the ceiling
conceal the celestial, the cerulean.(74-5)

To sum up: I wonder if this poem is structured like the koan anthologies you mentioned: koan, commentary, and then the capping "experiential insight."

MB: Let me backtrack a bit to your reading of the lines

the riverbank,

                                        banks of earth sloping
from land to sea, from water wake
to streams of sleep

                        from limbs to fins.

as multi-directional transport—I love your sense of how the words interconnect and sound. I was also attempting to wake up the positive devolution we can experience as we fall back on our full selves, shelves of selves (folded in The Gap) in which there is nothing lacking and nothing superfluous—from limbs to fins, it's all there.

Additionally, I'm very fond of your reading of the elevator as portal or time transport to our department store, a shared, common, ridiculous, fairy tale space in which it's so easy to get lost (and is indeed never stationary). I believe those who design department stores intend for us to lose ourselves—personally, I have a hard time breathing when I'm in one. The poem "Mother Hubbard" also wends its way through a department store. And again, one gets lost.

CS: It's interesting that both the poems you mentioned that include gates appear in the final section of the book: "Dream-Mares, Glue Traps, and Other Dark Matter." When reading that title, it's hard not to think of horses being made into glue as well as bridges becoming walls. What can you tell us about this section of *An Anatomy of Curiosity*?

MB: The book's third section includes hauntings and threats. Readers might know a '60s TV show called *Lost in Space* in which the family robot, when confronted with potential peril, would call out "Danger, Will Robinson!" The poems in "Dream-Mares, Glue Traps, and Other Dark Matter" don't all have present dangers, but there is always something lurking—and yes, in these poems, horse glue might mucilage the broken lines. For example, in "Monkey and Spirit Bird Triptych," spry spirit birds turn rogue and "suck out Monkey's lifesaver hole"(77); in "Confession," poetry itself devolves into protolanguage, and in the absence of language, transforms into a kiss— though the kiss is the one that revives Psyche.

CS: What you call "positive devolution" abounds in "Confession," a virtuoso seven-page meta-poem in which I find, to borrow another of your phrases, "nothing lacking and nothing superfluous." I'm especially amazed by its shape and narrative structure as it wends its way from crisis to quest to crisis to prayer to an encounter with the goddess Nyx before that "prodigal / kiss." (91) Can you say anything more about the structure?

MB: Thanks, I'm so pleased you experienced that poem as tight and full also, as the tone is more conversational than most of my poetry. I tend not to write narrative poems, and not to write short-lined poems that proceed straight down a page, so I was allowing myself to explore a new field when writing this. Although the protagonist of the poem, Poem, is said to be losing it—and maybe in these dark days we're living through, poetry is thought to have lost it—its breath is sustained, and even after the kiss, the breath doesn't end with a period (nor does the poem). The short enjambed lines are an homage to sustained breath.

CS: I love the way you harmonize narrative and lyric impulses. On one hand, the reader gets empathetically involved with the drama of the inadequate, lost poem—searching for subject matter to give it direction so it can become a sacrificial victim in Nyx's ritual—it's a fructifying meta-myth with suspense and foreshadowing. On the other hand, the sustained breath of the short lines from the beginning (even in polysyllabic phrases like, "a born zigzagger, / topographically agnostic") belies the narrative, or presages it dying into the lyric now.

MB: The lyric impulse, which is the final skeletal thread, definitely outlives the narrative one. Close to the end of the poem, as you note, everything devolves. To signal the loss of the narrative, there's a quick sketch of the Canova sculpture *Psyche Revived by Cupid's Kiss*—which my husband, James Graham, kindly drew—that's referenced in the poem.

CS: This is a brilliant and beautiful collaboration with your husband. In his sketch of the sculpture, Cupid's face and body do not seem to be as defined as Psyche's, which seems more muscular and active in the moment of embrace, but his wings evoke pillars of rope. Earlier in the poem, you had introduced the sculpture as a "winged marble man / revealed before a beauty / spiked into deathlike sleep." (86) At first, I had no idea this "beauty" was meant to be Psyche. Is the sketch meant to enhance the verbal description of the sculpture?

MB: I refer to Psyche as "beauty" since Psyche's troubles arise because of her beauty. It's great you see Psyche as active, as she is a journeyer in all her states; nevertheless, at this very moment Canova captures, Psyche is frozen because her curiosity, her inability to resist temptation, has "gotten the best of her, yet again." The word "spiked" suspends the action as the last line of the stanza—that word is especially nuanced, waiting for viewers, listeners, readers to awaken and endow animation on Psyche, for Poem is nothing without its audience.

CS: Yes, there's so much in these three lines, even the connotations of "spiked" from drunkenness to drug needles to violence—it's as if, in order to revive Psyche, James's sketch is killing the personified poem (or at least its narrative).

MB: Killing or freeing. When we're freed from our stories, Psyche is finally immortal.

Once the poem lets loose its narrative, it begins to wind down, the wind and breath set free:

in the poem
in the palace
with its storehouse
of candelabras
and crystal vases (91)

is where all our pictures and sounds are stockpiled, from our lifetimes and perhaps also the karma of our ancestors and relatives, and even miscellanea from the gothic castle/landscape of Coleridge's "Christabel."

CS: Gothic, yes, as Nyx provides the necessary atmosphere, amniotic fluid for this poem in which miscellanea can become:

> giant tigresses
> romping through
> narrow atriums
> into a ventricle of the heart! (91)

Although Psyche and Cupid are not as foregrounded in "Confession" as Nyx is, but more in the wings (as it were), they take center stage in the following poem, "An Anatomy of Curiosity."

MB: The story of Cupid and Psyche is one I have been drawn to from a young age, and with "Confession" and "An Anatomy of Curiosity," I wanted to get inside the pleasure of that story. I loved the intimacy of Robert Duncan's writing on Cupid and Psyche in *The H.D. Book* and, like him, I wanted to extend my experience with it. I've always thought of it as a hybrid fairytale/myth, but I'm not sure where or how I first heard the story; it was first written down by Apuleius in *The Golden Ass*, but I surely didn't read that rendition until college. What caught me is how Psyche is reminded to repress her curiosity, and when she doesn't, the story gets especially exciting: she spills wax on her beautiful lover, flies too close to the sun.

CS: I love the way you introduce the myth in Chapter One of "An Anatomy of Curiosity," while Chapter Two brings into play a more modern myth, as Psyche becomes an object of the sublimated curiosity of "scientific analysis." The contrast between narrative and sustained breath you noted in "Confession" is similar to that of the figures of the Detective and Psychic here, as you move beyond antithesis to a syncretic joining of the discourse of Freudian "drives" with mythopoesis: "Hemispheres of land beneath a surface of chaos, Chronos."(93)

MB: The dualities we discussed earlier are echoed in "An Anatomy of Curiosity." In Chapter Two, the deducing Detective (and don't forget *Oedipus Rex*, which inspired Freud, is maybe our first detective story, or at least an early one) and Psyche/Psychic/Soul are dichotomous spirits in that mysterious "black box of the brain," and we know Psyche and Pandora couldn't resist boxes.

CS: And in Chapter Seven, as "questions arise from the stem of the body" (95) and Psyche lights the candle that scares Desire away, language becomes as musical as the unheard music it's ostensibly about:

Think of a dream seamstress, a songster, a siren,
  A shore breeze with wavy tresses
 Bowling out the beaks of pipers,
  The hollow low notes that dip on the concave
clavicle,
        Wending viola strings.
Think of a pattern cutter, a dreamstress,
    Tree witness and earlobe globes

Nothing permitted, permanent
The writhen octopus
Or octave written in wind."(96)

Meanwhile, I wonder about the connotations, the tone, of "Nothing permitted, permanent." At first, I feel sadness and despair here, but then I sense a double meaning of "nothing" as a presence, as if the voice is not merely lamenting but also signaling and singing the immortality of Psyche, or at least celebrating music freed from the page, even if it's transient and unpermitted—the sublime gospel of the blues. It also recalls the first line of the book: "I left my permission slip in a past." Forever changes, permission slips (as if it's revealed to be merely administrative). Was this Da Capo movement intentional when considering the structure of the book? Can the book's last line, *"off an eyeblink   in a flame wink..."(99)* be a koan?

MB: Those words *"off an eyeblink   in a flame wink..."* appear at the end of the book's final poem, which is printed in German (I wrote the poem in English and Hans Jürgen Balmes translated it into German). So if one were dreaming through this life and this book, and this dream is in a language which one sometimes understands and sometimes doesn't, and one hears/reads *Flamme winkt der Luft* and then *in a flame wink*, one might find oneself suspended between language, in the marvelous still, in the pause of poetry.

Acknowledgements

An earlier version of the essay about Sandra Simonds first appeared in *Jacket 2*.

An earlier version of the essay about Anselm Berrigan first appeared in *Boog City*.

Earlier versions of the essays about Judy Juanita and Tureeda Mikell first appeared in *Konch*.

An earlier excerpt of the piece about David Berman appeared in *The Believer*.

An earlier version of the essay about Mary J. Dacorro appeared in *Halo Halo*.

Earlier versions of the essays about Danez Smith & Anne Boyer first appeared in the *Rumpus*.

Versions of the essays about Joanna Fuhrman, Brenda Hillman, Gillian Conoley, Alli Warren, Delia Tramontina, Danielle Pafunda, and Alissa Quart first appeared in *Entropy*.

The piece on Gil Scott-Heron was written for *The Langston Hughes Review*.

The conversation with Adeena Karasick was published in *The Brooklyn Rail*

The conversation with Daniel Nester was published in *Matter*.

The conversation with Martine Bellen was published in *Rain Taxi*

Thank you to Hannah Tawater, Ishmael and Tennessee Reed, Niela Orr, Eileen Tabios, David Kirschenbaum, Anselm Berrigan, Virginia Konchan, Eric Lorberer, and Tony Bolden.

Thank you to Brenda Hillman who suggested in 2014 that I write reviews again.

Thank you to Alissa Quart who suggested I collect them into a book, and include some writing about music to break it up.

Thank you to Jodi Monahan who suggested including the Dickinson & Wheatley essays,

Thank you to Karlyn Clarence for her proofreading and useful insights.

Thank you to Tod Thilleman and Spuyten Duyvil Press for their faith in this project.

&, most of all, thank you to all the writers who tolerated my attempts to write "about" them.

CHRIS STROFFOLINO has published 6 books of poetry, most of which are out of print, including *Speculative Primitive* (2005), *Stealer's Wheel* (1999), and *Light as A Fetter* (1997). Most recently, *Drinking from What I Once Wore* (2018). A book of prose reminiscences at the intersection of the personal and cultural, *Death of a Selfish Altruist*, was published by Iniquity Press in 2017. Radio Survivor.org published his history of the corporate takeover of radio, *Radio Orphan*, in sequential form, in 2012. He co-authored a study of Shakespeare's *12th Night* with David Rosenthal (IDG Books, 2001). Spuyten Duyvil has also published an earlier collection of essays on mostly contemporary poetry, *Spin Cycle* (2001), a prequel to this book.

He has released 4 albums of songs under his own name, including *Single-Sided Doubles* (2009), *Predator Drone* (2011), *The Griffith Park Sessions* (2014), and *12 Songs of Goodbye, and 1 Song of Hello.* (2019). Recent poetry has appeared in *New American Writing, 14 Hills, Bennington Review, Volt, Konch, Chiron Review, Big Hammer,* and *The Town: An Anthology of Oakland Poets* (Nomadic Press, 2023). He is currently seeking a publisher for *Medi(t)ations*, his first full length book of new poetry in 20 years. He has taught Critical Thinking, and, sometimes, Creative Writing, at Laney College in Oakland since 2008, where he lives in a closet with no heat but a piano in a hallway.

Made in the USA
Columbia, SC
11 September 2024

41602810R00250